This book was donated by:

Friends of the
Oakland Public
School Libraries

Fopsl.org

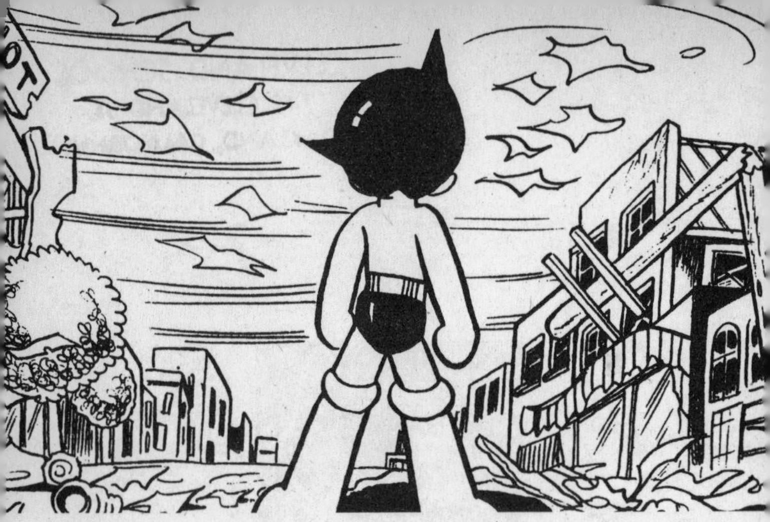

OT

Table of Contents

by
Osamu Tezuka

translation
Frederik L. Schodt

lettering and retouch
Digital Chameleon

Dark Horse Comics®

publisher
mike richardson

editor
chris warner

consulting editor
toren smith for **studio proteus**

collection designers
david nestelle and **lani schreibstein**

English-language version produced by **dark horse comics** and **studio proteus**

astro boy® volume 11

TETSUWAN ATOM by Osamu Tezuka © 2003 by Tezuka Productions. All rights reserved. English translation rights arranged with Tezuka Productions. ASTRO BOY is a registered trademark of Tezuka Productions Co., Ltd., Tokyo, Japan. Unedited translation © 2003 by Frederik L. Schodt. All other material © 2003 by Dark Horse Comics, Inc. All rights reserved. No portion of this publication may be reproduced, in any form or by any means, without the express written permission of the copyright holders. Names, characters, places, and incidents featured in this publication either are the product of the author's imagination or are used fictitiously. Any resemblance to actual persons (living or dead), events, institutions, or locales, without satiric intent, is coincidental. Dark Horse Comics® and the Dark Horse logo are trademarks of Dark Horse Comics, Inc., registered in various categories and countries. All rights reserved.

The artwork of this volume has been produced as a mirror-image of the original Japanese edition to conform to English-language standards.

Published by
Dark Horse Comics, Inc.
10956 SE Main Street
Milwaukie, OR 97222

www.darkhorse.com

To find a comics shop in your area, call the Comic Shop Locator Service toll-free at 1-888-266-4226.

First edition: January 2003
ISBN: 1-56971-812-1

10 9 8 7 6 5 4 3 2 1
Printed in Canada

A NOTE TO READERS

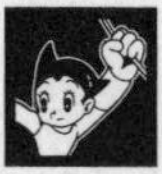

Many non-Japanese, including people from Africa and Southeast Asia, appear in Osamu Tezuka's works. Sometimes these people are depicted very differently from the way they actually are today, in a manner that exaggerates a time long past or shows them to be from extremely undeveloped lands. Some feel that such images contribute to racial discrimination, especially against people of African descent. This was never Osamu Tezuka's intent, but we believe that as long as there are people who feel insulted or demeaned by these depictions, we must not ignore their feelings.

We are against discrimination, in all its forms, and intend to continue to work for its elimination. Nonetheless, we do not believe it would be proper to revise these works. Tezuka is no longer with us, and we cannot erase what he has done, and to alter his work would only violate his rights as a creator. More importantly, stopping publication or changing the content of his work would do little to solve the problems of discrimination that exist in the world.

We are presenting Osamu Tezuka's work as it was originally created, without changes. We do this because we believe it is also important to promote the underlying themes in his work, such as love for mankind and the sanctity of life. We hope that when you, the reader, encounter this work, you will keep in mind the differences in attitudes, then and now, toward discrimination, and that this will contribute to an even greater awareness of such problems.

— Tezuka Productions and Dark Horse Comics

THE LAST DAY ON EARTH

First serialized from March to June 1964 in *Shonen* magazine.

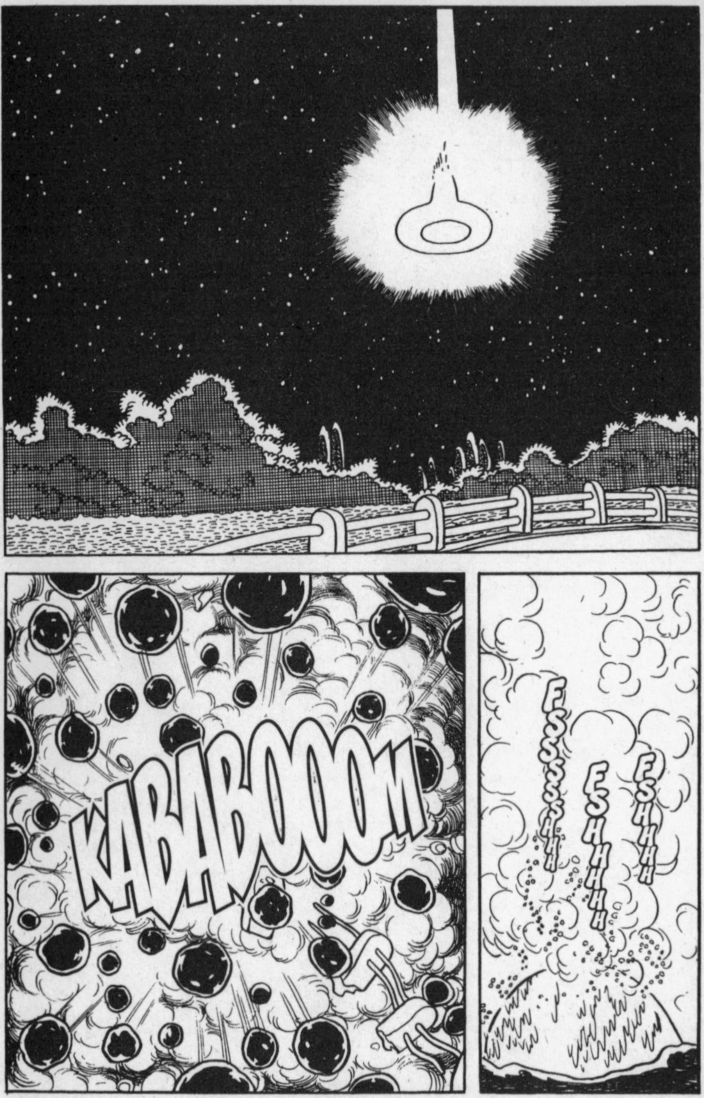
KABABOOOM
FSSSSSHHH
FSHHHHH
FSHHHH

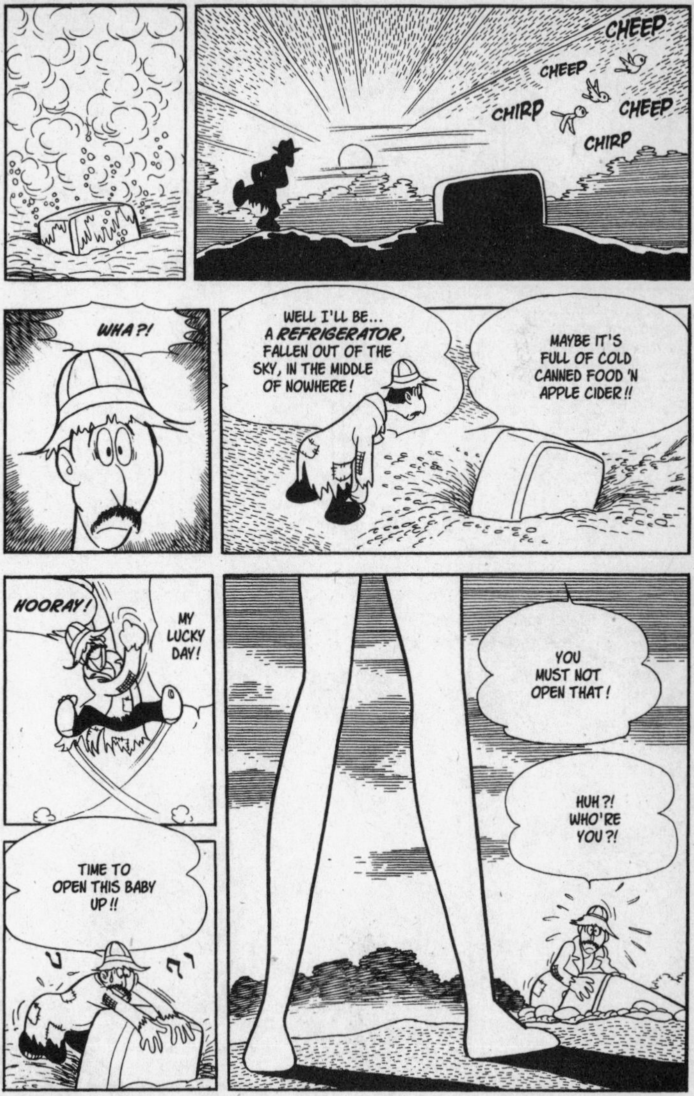
CHEEP
CHEEP
CHIRP
CHEEP
CHIRP
WHA?!
WELL I'LL BE... A *REFRIGERATOR*, FALLEN OUT OF THE SKY, IN THE MIDDLE OF NOWHERE!
MAYBE IT'S FULL OF COLD CANNED FOOD 'N APPLE CIDER!!
HOORAY!
MY LUCKY DAY!
TIME TO OPEN THIS BABY UP!!
YOU MUST NOT OPEN THAT!
HUH?! WHO'RE YOU?!

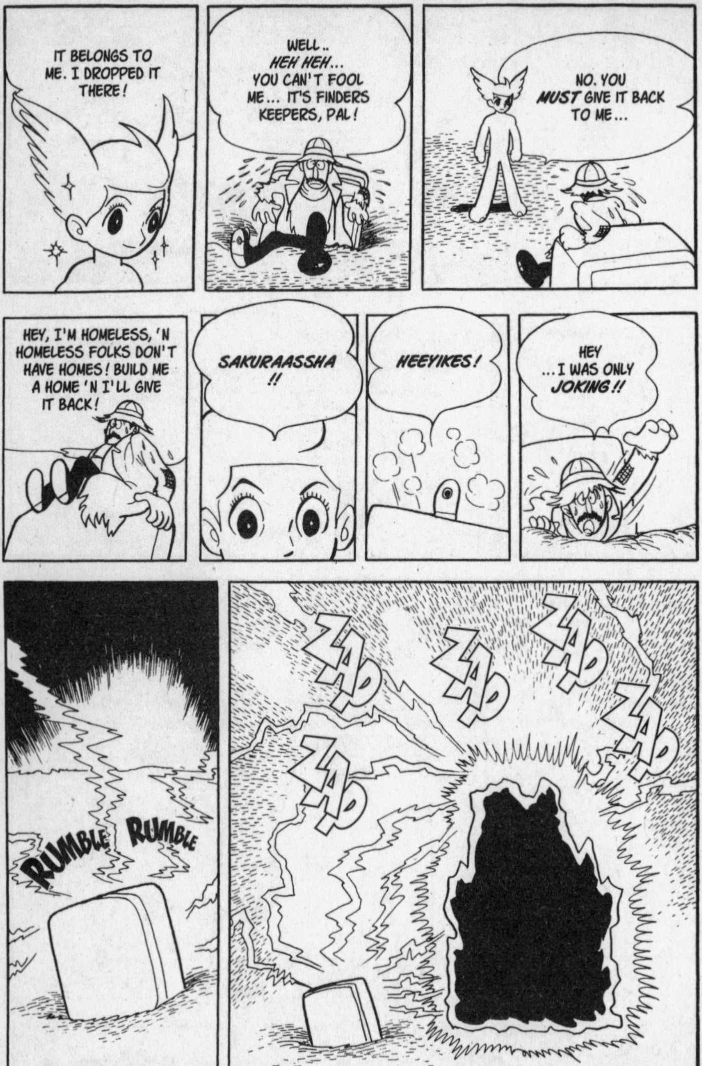
IT BELONGS TO ME. I DROPPED IT THERE!
WELL.. HEH HEH... YOU CAN'T FOOL ME... IT'S FINDERS KEEPERS, PAL!
NO. YOU MUST GIVE IT BACK TO ME...
HEY, I'M HOMELESS, 'N HOMELESS FOLKS DON'T HAVE HOMES! BUILD ME A HOME 'N I'LL GIVE IT BACK!
SAKURAASSHA !!
HEEYIKES!
HEY ...I WAS ONLY JOKING!!
RUMBLE RUMBLE
ZAP ZAP ZAP ZAP ZAP

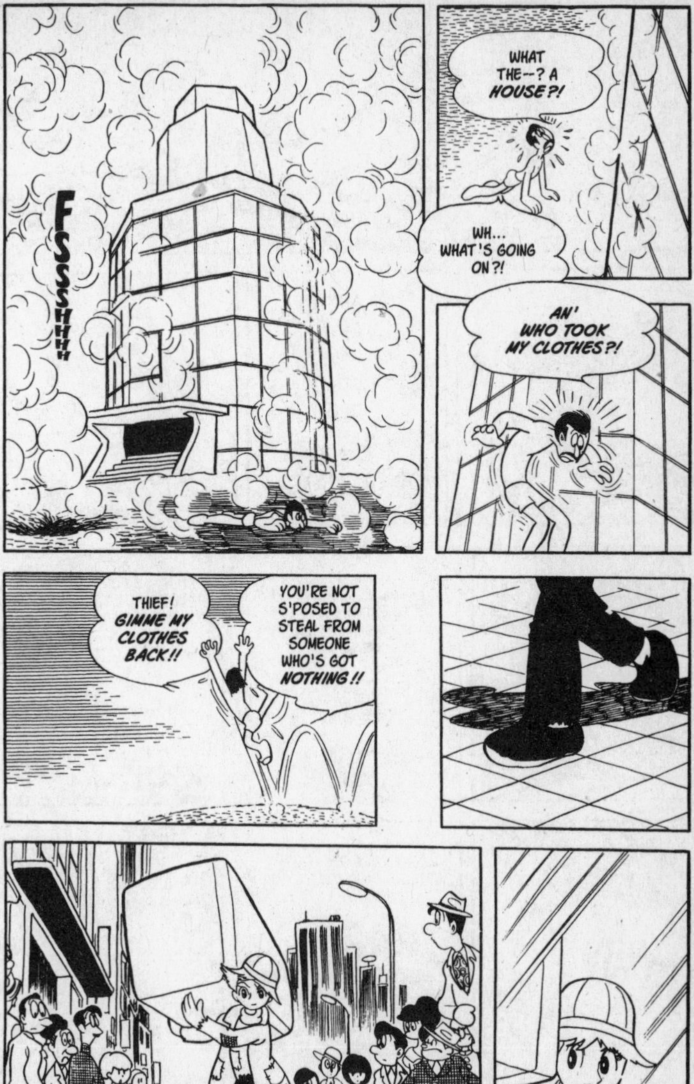
FSSSHHHH
WHAT THE--? A HOUSE?!
WH... WHAT'S GOING ON?!
AN' WHO TOOK MY CLOTHES?!
THIEF! GIMME MY CLOTHES BACK!!
YOU'RE NOT S'POSED TO STEAL FROM SOMEONE WHO'S GOT NOTHING!!

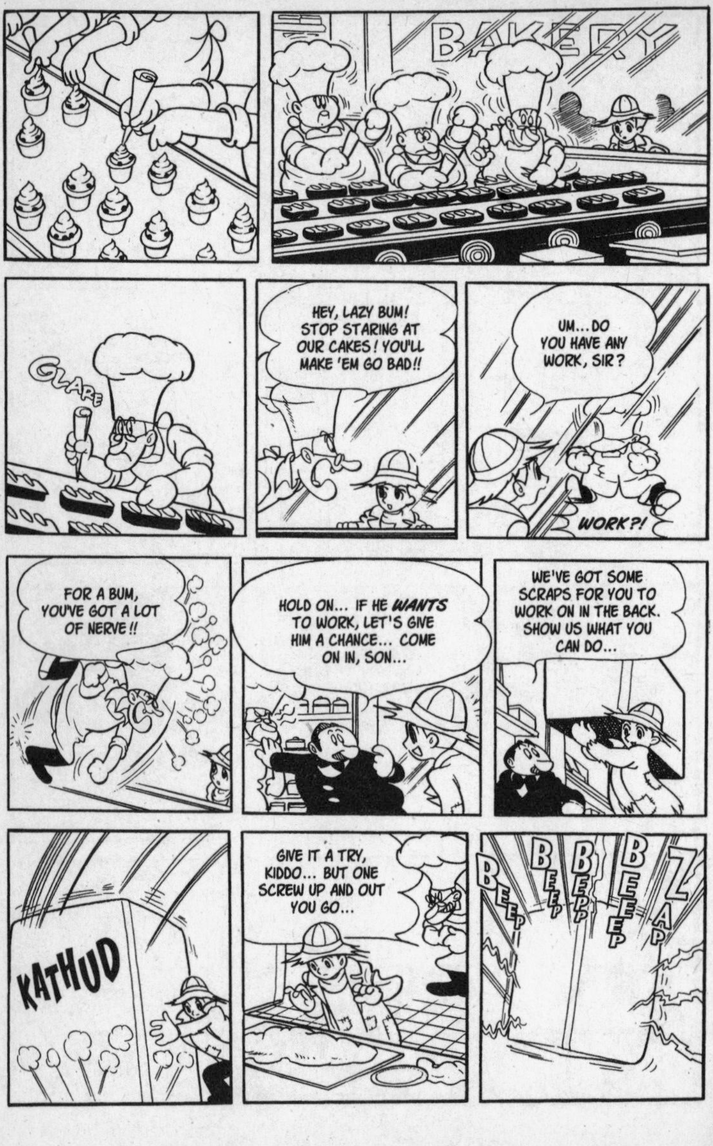
BAKERY
GLARE
HEY, LAZY BUM! STOP STARING AT OUR CAKES! YOU'LL MAKE 'EM GO BAD!!
UM... DO YOU HAVE ANY WORK, SIR?
WORK?!
FOR A BUM, YOU'VE GOT A LOT OF NERVE!!
HOLD ON... IF HE *WANTS* TO WORK, LET'S GIVE HIM A CHANCE... COME ON IN, SON...
WE'VE GOT SOME SCRAPS FOR YOU TO WORK ON IN THE BACK. SHOW US WHAT YOU CAN DO...
KATHUD
GIVE IT A TRY, KIDDO... BUT ONE SCREW UP AND OUT YOU GO...
BEEP
BEEP
BEEPP
BEEEP
ZAP

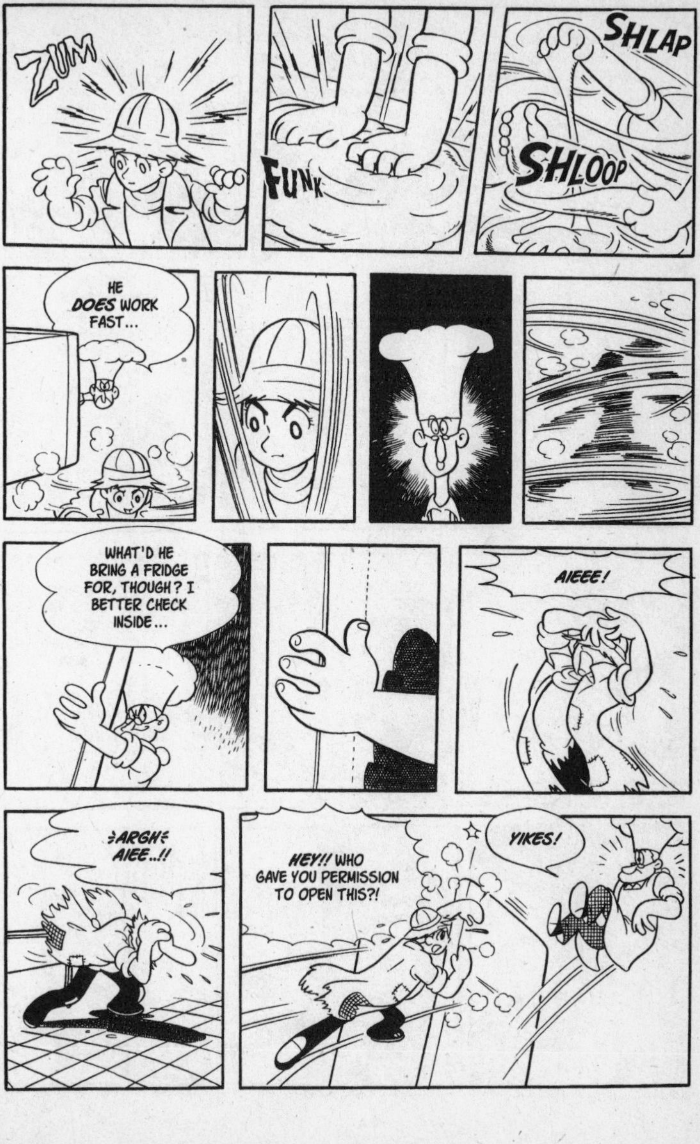

ZUM
FUNK
SHLAP
SHLOOP
HE DOES WORK FAST...
WHAT'D HE BRING A FRIDGE FOR, THOUGH? I BETTER CHECK INSIDE...
AIEEE!
ARGH AIEE..!!
HEY!! WHO GAVE YOU PERMISSION TO OPEN THIS?!
YIKES!

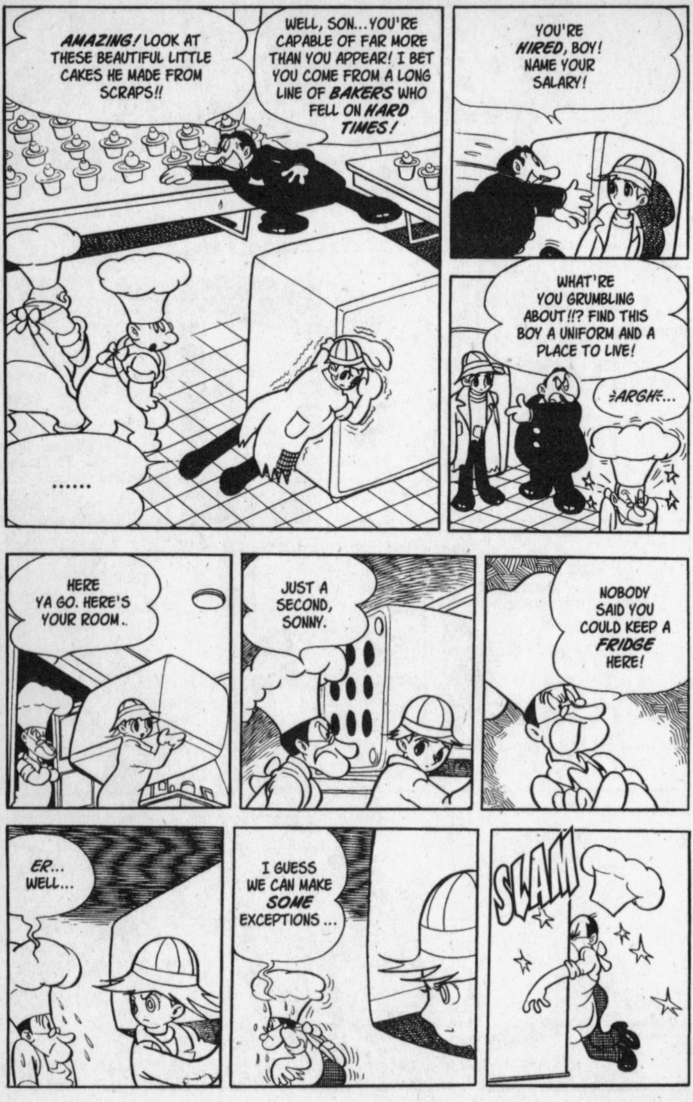
AMAZING! LOOK AT THESE BEAUTIFUL LITTLE CAKES HE MADE FROM SCRAPS!!
WELL, SON...YOU'RE CAPABLE OF FAR MORE THAN YOU APPEAR! I BET YOU COME FROM A LONG LINE OF BAKERS WHO FELL ON HARD TIMES!
......
YOU'RE HIRED, BOY! NAME YOUR SALARY!
WHAT'RE YOU GRUMBLING ABOUT!!? FIND THIS BOY A UNIFORM AND A PLACE TO LIVE!
ARGH...
HERE YA GO. HERE'S YOUR ROOM..
JUST A SECOND, SONNY.
NOBODY SAID YOU COULD KEEP A FRIDGE HERE!
ER... WELL...
I GUESS WE CAN MAKE SOME EXCEPTIONS...
SLAM

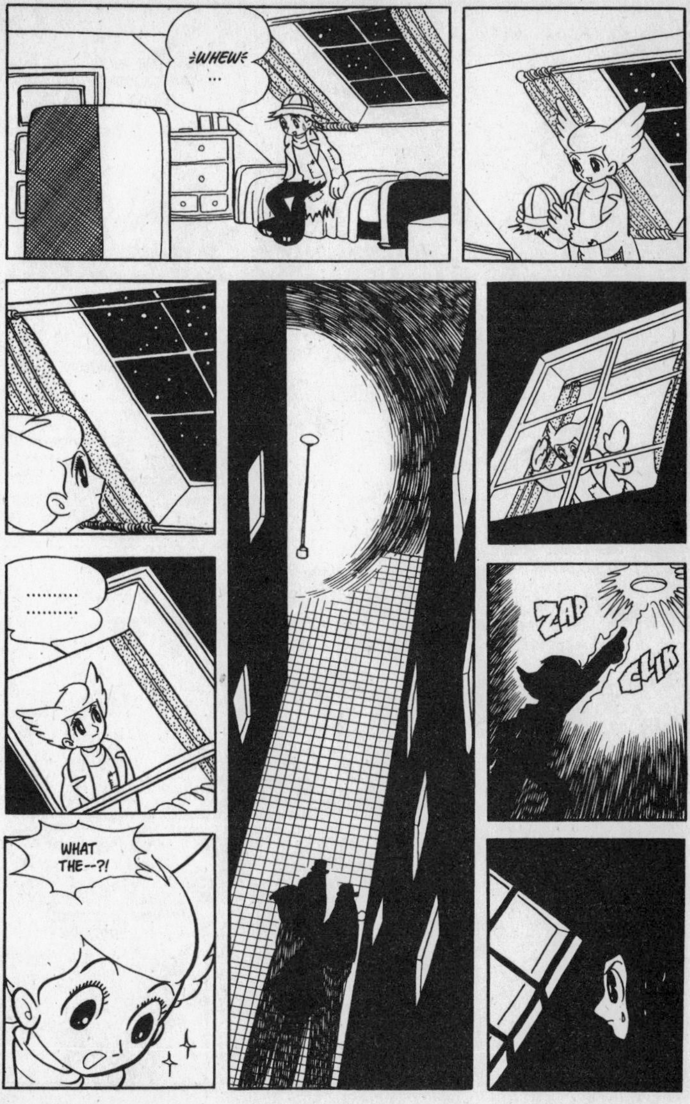
WHEW
...
....
....
WHAT THE--?!
ZAP
CLIK

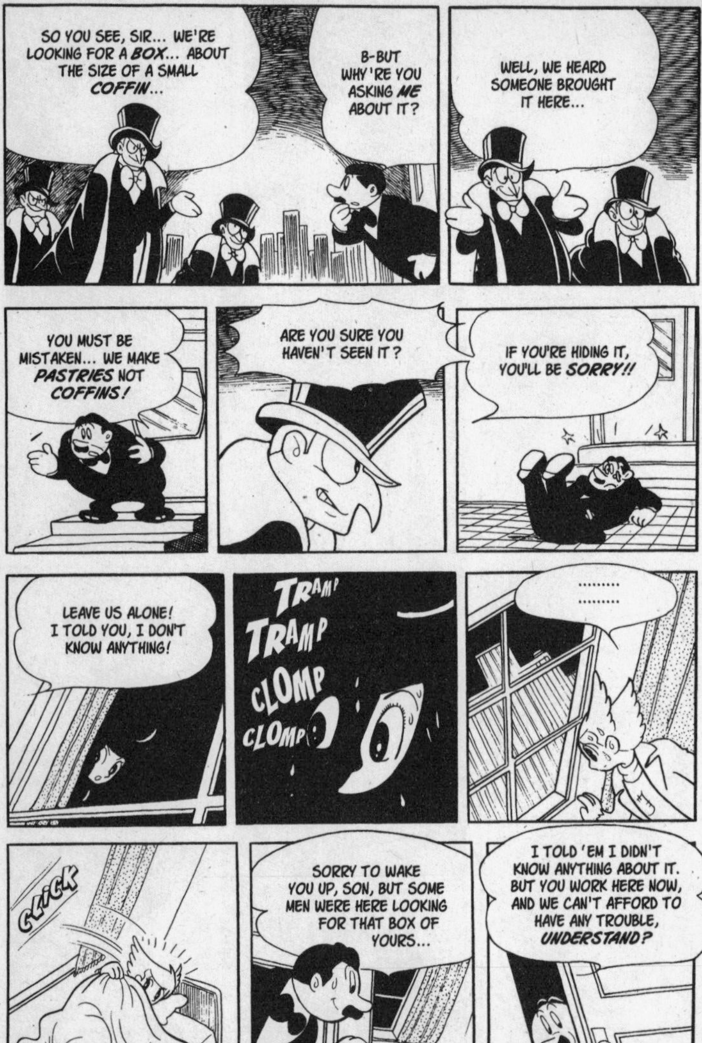
SO YOU SEE, SIR... WE'RE LOOKING FOR A *BOX*... ABOUT THE SIZE OF A SMALL *COFFIN*...
B-BUT WHY'RE YOU ASKING *ME* ABOUT IT?
WELL, WE HEARD SOMEONE BROUGHT IT HERE...
YOU MUST BE MISTAKEN... WE MAKE *PASTRIES* NOT *COFFINS!*
ARE YOU SURE YOU HAVEN'T SEEN IT?
IF YOU'RE HIDING IT, YOU'LL BE *SORRY!!*
LEAVE US ALONE! I TOLD YOU, I DON'T KNOW ANYTHING!
TRAMP TRAMP CLOMP CLOMP
....
....
CLICK
SORRY TO WAKE YOU UP, SON, BUT SOME MEN WERE HERE LOOKING FOR THAT BOX OF YOURS...
I TOLD 'EM I DIDN'T KNOW ANYTHING ABOUT IT. BUT YOU WORK HERE NOW, AND WE CAN'T AFFORD TO HAVE ANY TROUBLE, *UNDERSTAND?*

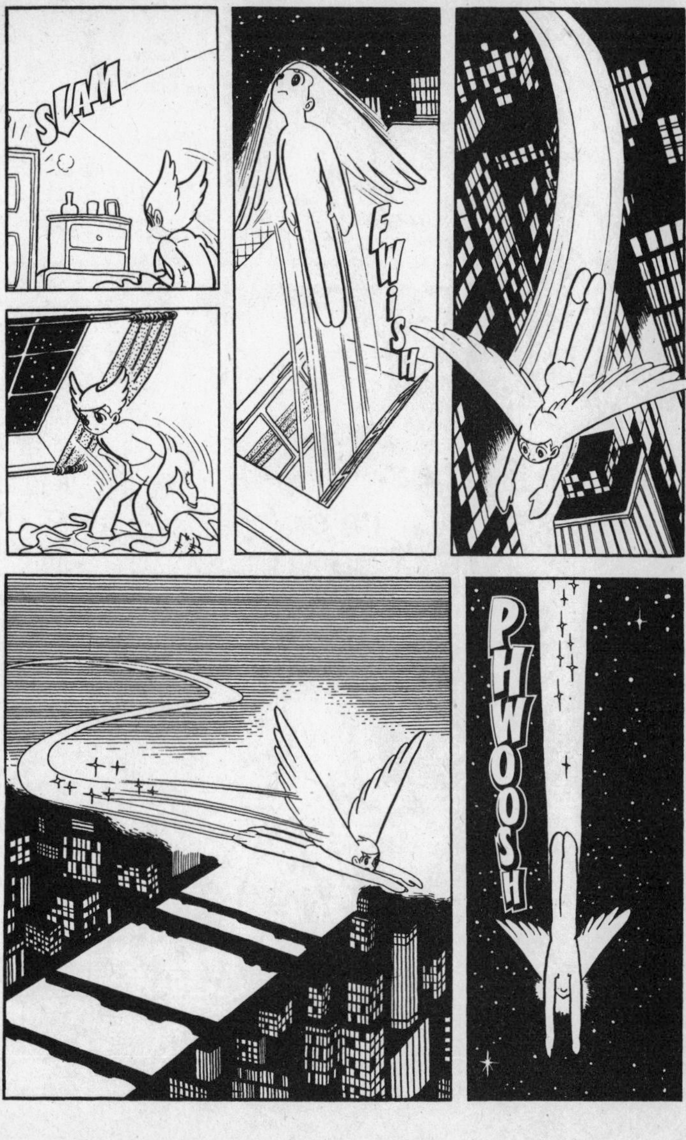
SLAM
FWISH
PHWOOSH

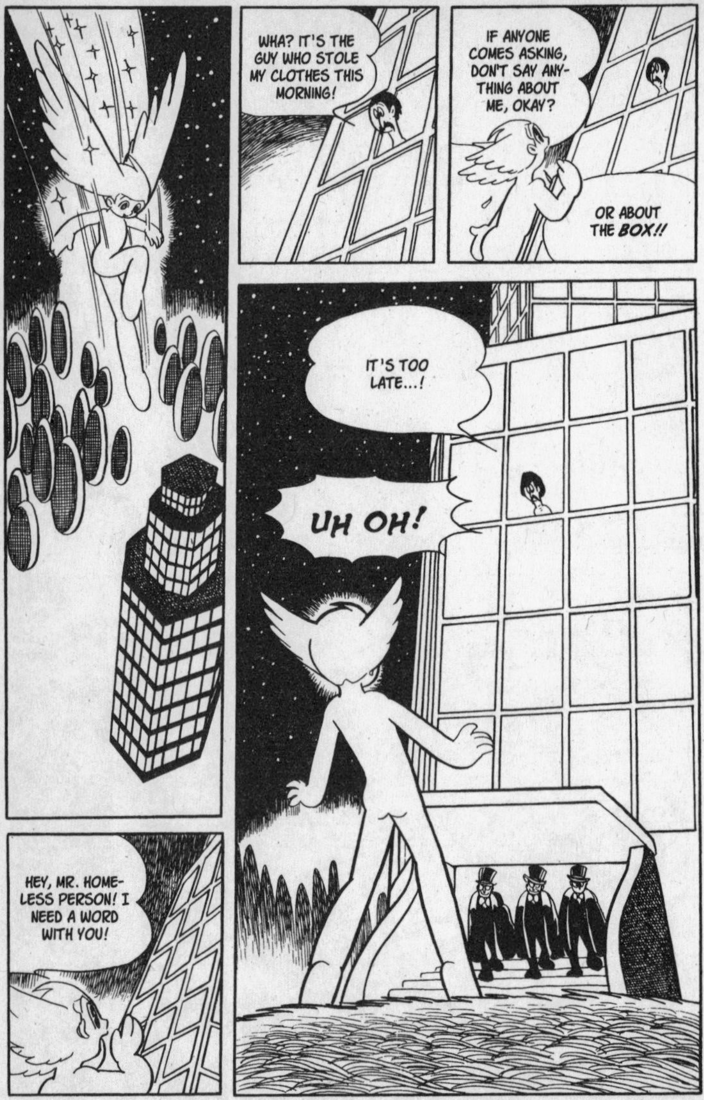
HEY, MR. HOME-LESS PERSON! I NEED A WORD WITH YOU!
WHA? IT'S THE GUY WHO STOLE MY CLOTHES THIS MORNING!
IF ANYONE COMES ASKING, DON'T SAY ANY-THING ABOUT ME, OKAY?
OR ABOUT THE *BOX!!*
IT'S TOO LATE...!
UH OH!

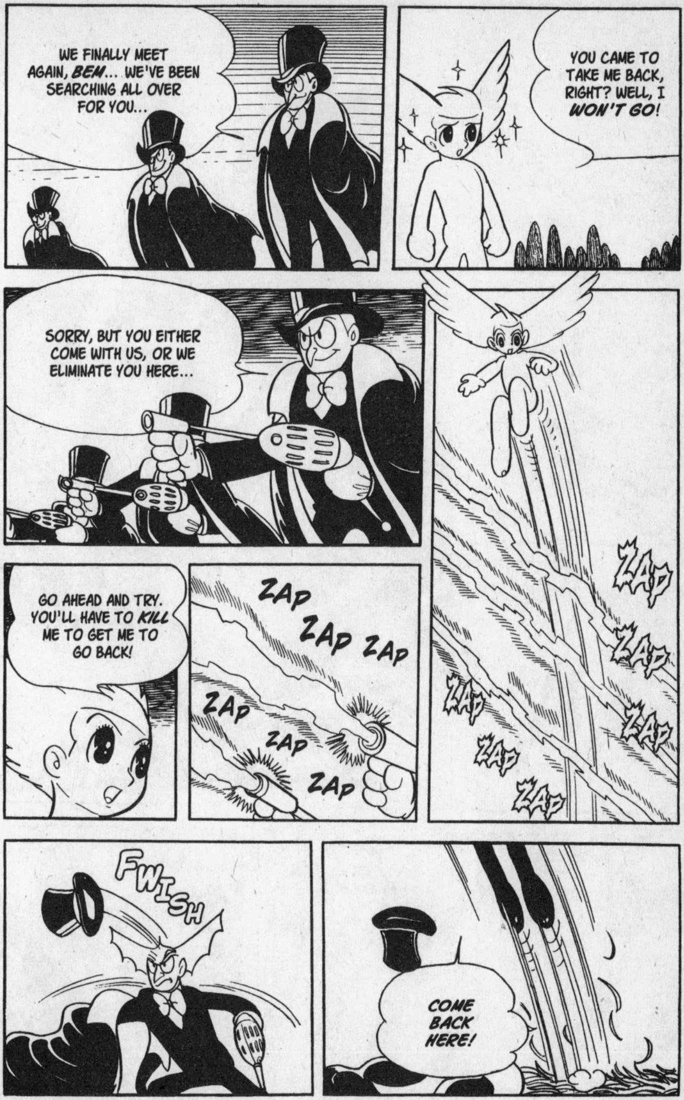
WE FINALLY MEET AGAIN, BEM... WE'VE BEEN SEARCHING ALL OVER FOR YOU...
YOU CAME TO TAKE ME BACK, RIGHT? WELL, I WON'T GO!
SORRY, BUT YOU EITHER COME WITH US, OR WE ELIMINATE YOU HERE...
GO AHEAD AND TRY. YOU'LL HAVE TO KILL ME TO GET ME TO GO BACK!
ZAP
ZAP ZAP
ZAP
ZAP
ZAP
ZAP
ZAP
ZAP
ZAP
ZAP
ZAP
ZAP
FWISH
COME BACK HERE!

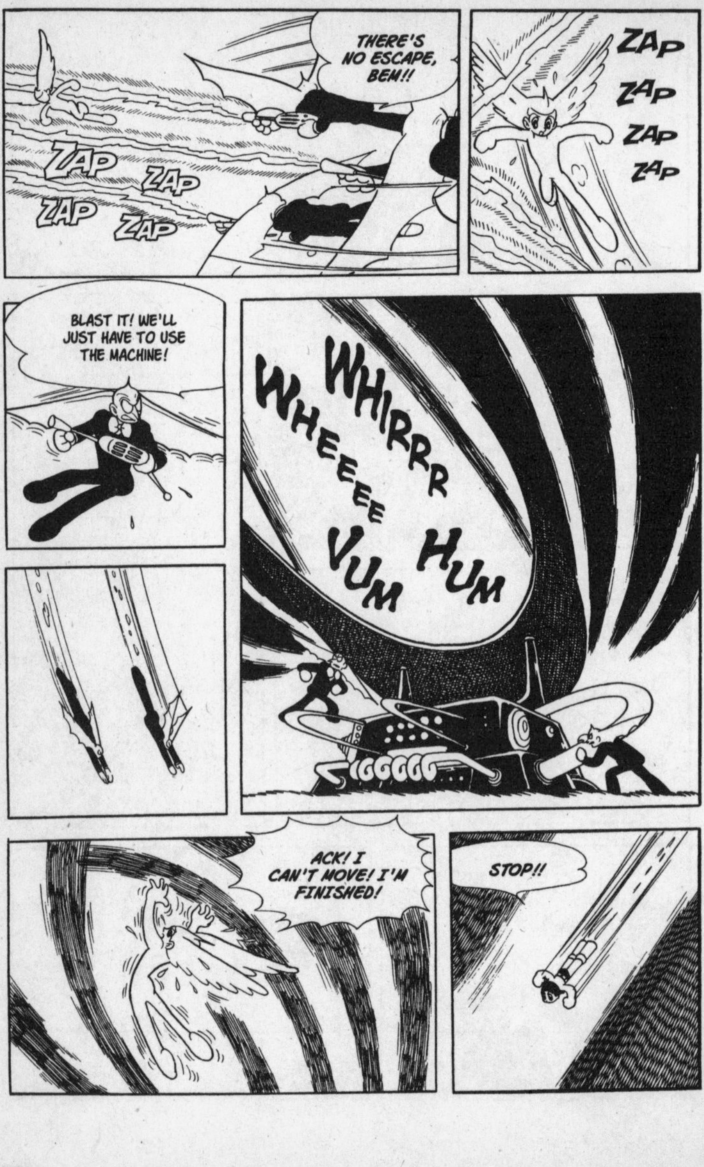
THERE'S NO ESCAPE, BEM!!
ZAP
ZAP
ZAP
ZAP
ZAP
ZAP
ZAP
ZAP
BLAST IT! WE'LL JUST HAVE TO USE THE MACHINE!
WHIRRRR
WHEEEEE
HUM
VUM
ACK! I CAN'T MOVE! I'M FINISHED!
STOP!!

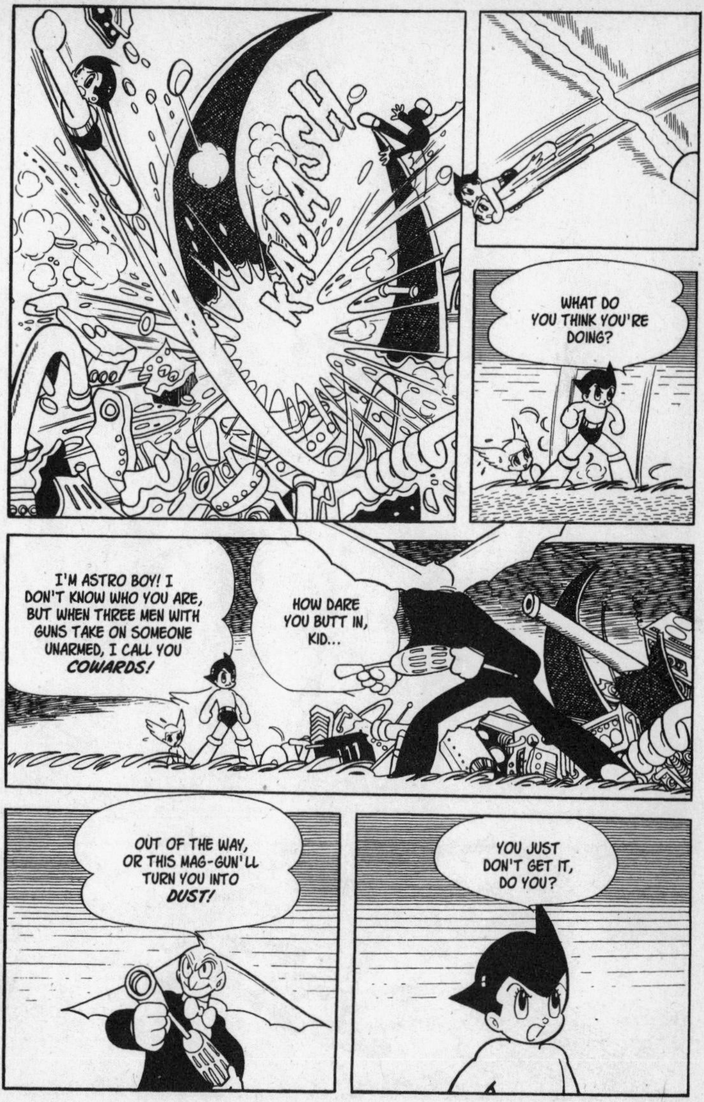
KABASH
WHAT DO YOU THINK YOU'RE DOING?
I'M ASTRO BOY! I DON'T KNOW WHO YOU ARE, BUT WHEN THREE MEN WITH GUNS TAKE ON SOMEONE UNARMED, I CALL YOU *COWARDS!*
HOW DARE YOU BUTT IN, KID...
OUT OF THE WAY, OR THIS MAG-GUN'LL TURN YOU INTO *DUST!*
YOU JUST DON'T GET IT, DO YOU?

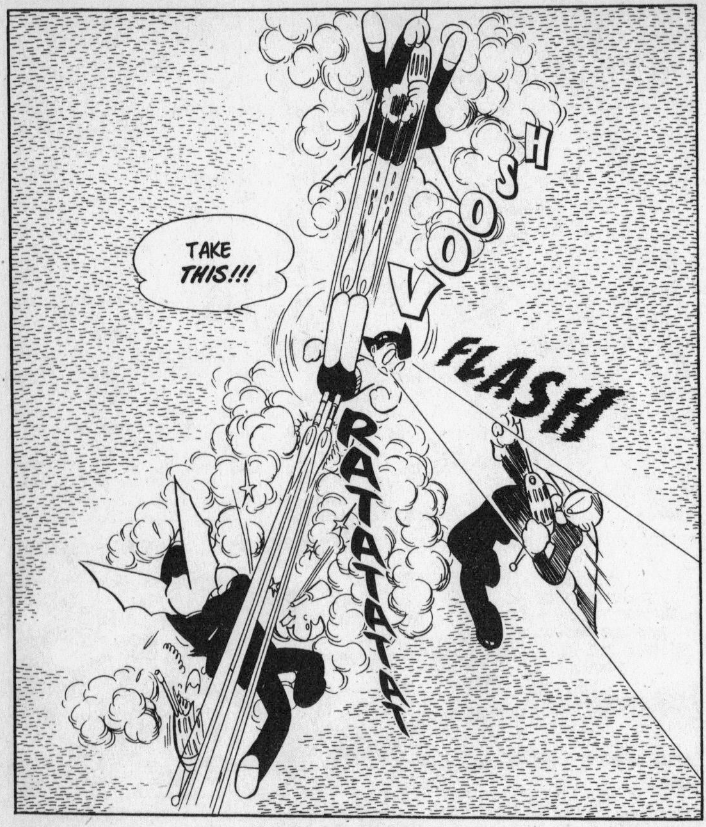
VOOSH
TAKE THIS!!!
FLASH
RATATATAT
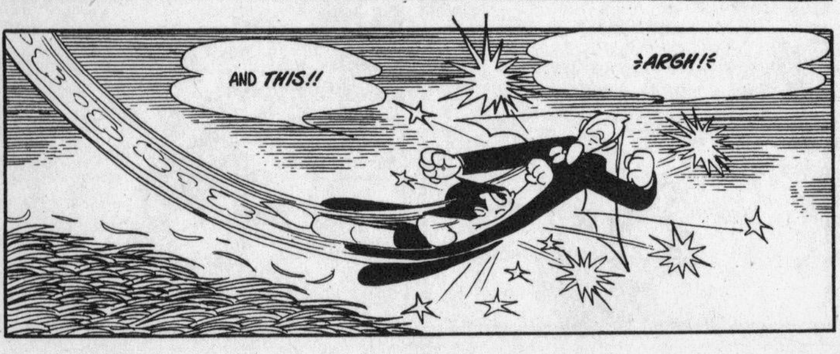
AND THIS!!
ARGH!

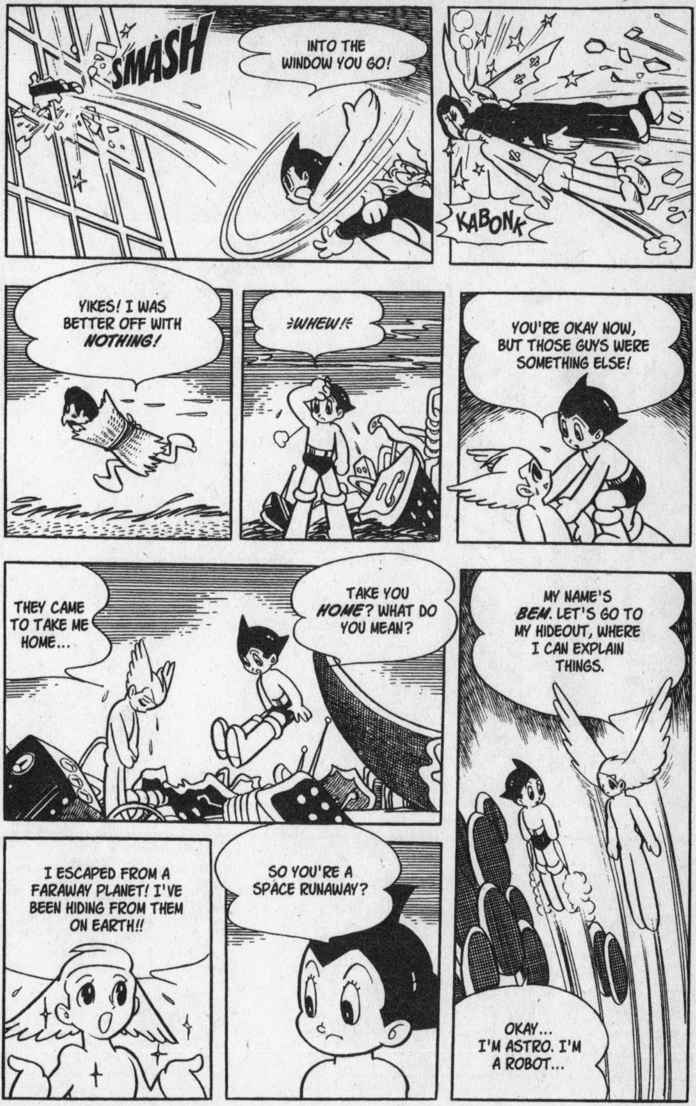
SMASH
INTO THE WINDOW YOU GO!
KABONK
YIKES! I WAS BETTER OFF WITH *NOTHING!*
WHEW!
YOU'RE OKAY NOW, BUT THOSE GUYS WERE SOMETHING ELSE!
THEY CAME TO TAKE ME HOME...
TAKE YOU *HOME*? WHAT DO YOU MEAN?
MY NAME'S *BEM*. LET'S GO TO MY HIDEOUT, WHERE I CAN EXPLAIN THINGS.
I ESCAPED FROM A FARAWAY PLANET! I'VE BEEN HIDING FROM THEM ON EARTH!!
SO YOU'RE A SPACE RUNAWAY?
OKAY... I'M ASTRO. I'M A ROBOT...

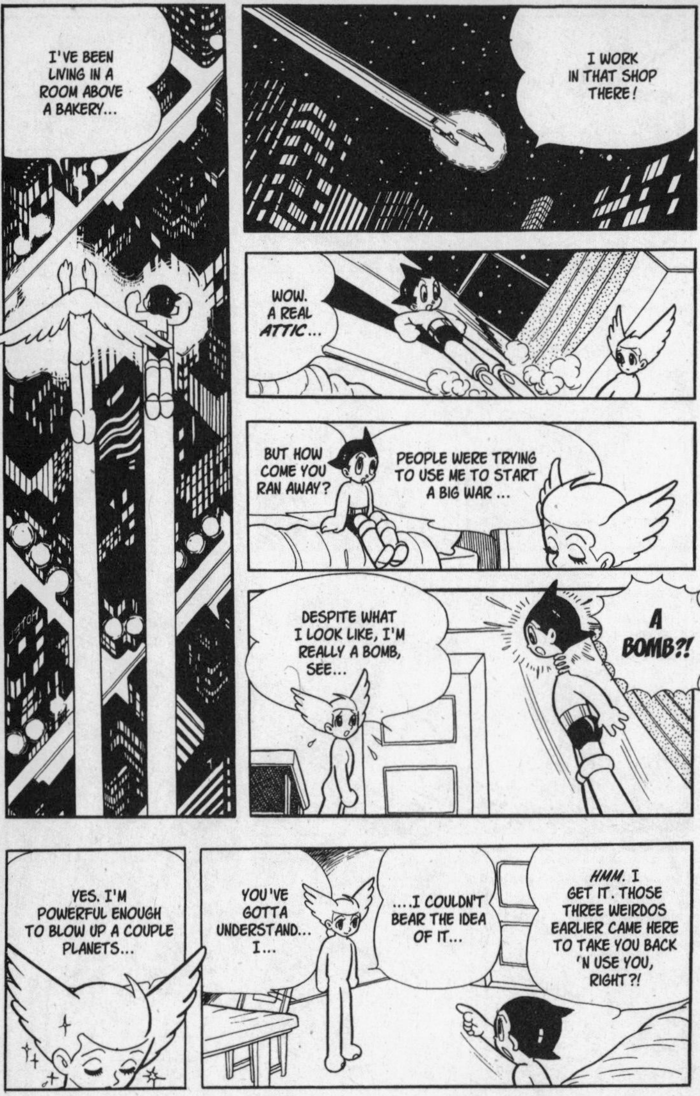
I'VE BEEN LIVING IN A ROOM ABOVE A BAKERY...
I WORK IN THAT SHOP THERE!
WOW. A REAL *ATTIC*...
BUT HOW COME YOU RAN AWAY?
PEOPLE WERE TRYING TO USE ME TO START A BIG WAR ...
DESPITE WHAT I LOOK LIKE, I'M REALLY A BOMB, SEE...
A BOMB?!
YES. I'M POWERFUL ENOUGH TO BLOW UP A COUPLE PLANETS...
YOU'VE GOTTA UNDERSTAND... I...
....I COULDN'T BEAR THE IDEA OF IT...
HMM. I GET IT. THOSE THREE WEIRDOS EARLIER CAME HERE TO TAKE YOU BACK 'N USE YOU, RIGHT?!

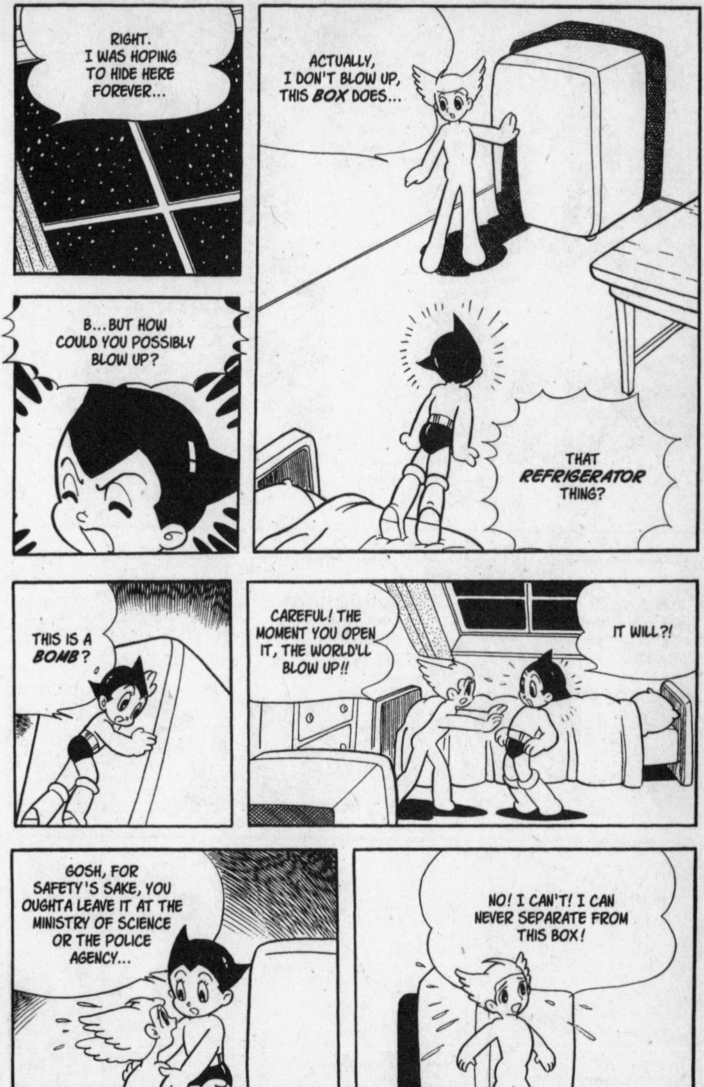
RIGHT.
I WAS HOPING TO HIDE HERE FOREVER...
ACTUALLY, I DON'T BLOW UP, THIS BOX DOES...
B...BUT HOW COULD YOU POSSIBLY BLOW UP?
THAT REFRIGERATOR THING?
THIS IS A BOMB?
CAREFUL! THE MOMENT YOU OPEN IT, THE WORLD'LL BLOW UP!!
IT WILL?!
GOSH, FOR SAFETY'S SAKE, YOU OUGHTA LEAVE IT AT THE MINISTRY OF SCIENCE OR THE POLICE AGENCY...
NO! I CAN'T! I CAN NEVER SEPARATE FROM THIS BOX!

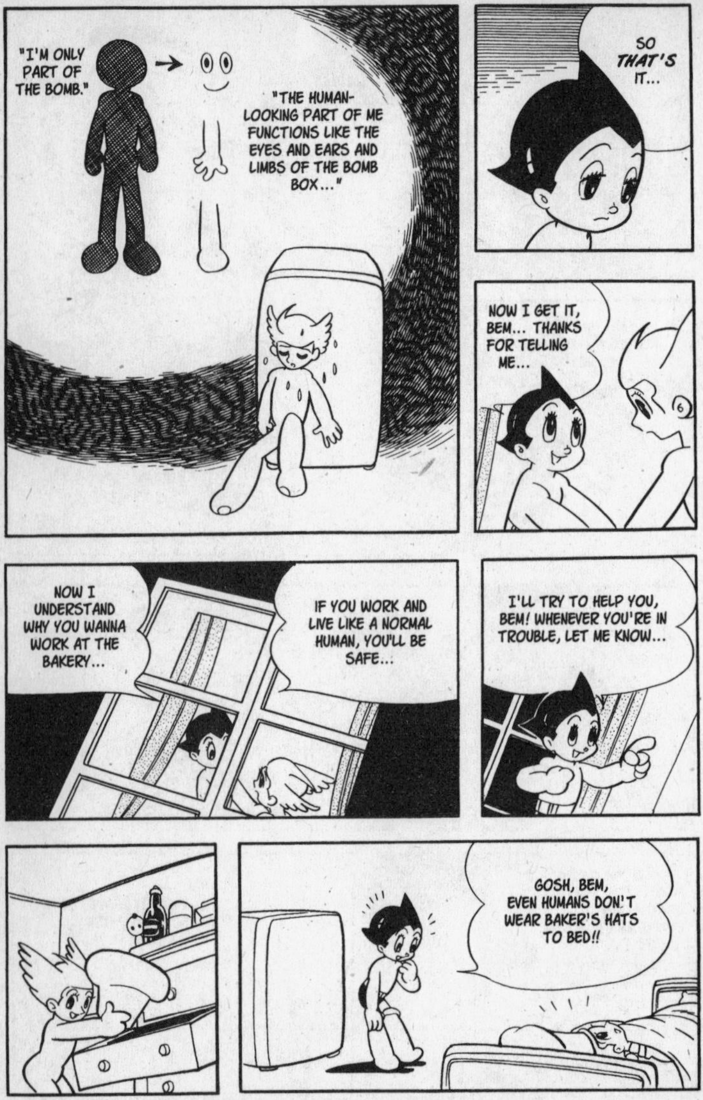
"I'M ONLY PART OF THE BOMB."
"THE HUMAN-LOOKING PART OF ME FUNCTIONS LIKE THE EYES AND EARS AND LIMBS OF THE BOMB BOX..."
SO *THAT'S* IT...
NOW I GET IT, BEM... THANKS FOR TELLING ME...
NOW I UNDERSTAND WHY YOU WANNA WORK AT THE BAKERY...
IF YOU WORK AND LIVE LIKE A NORMAL HUMAN, YOU'LL BE SAFE...
I'LL TRY TO HELP YOU, BEM! WHENEVER YOU'RE IN TROUBLE, LET ME KNOW...
GOSH, BEM, EVEN HUMANS DON'T WEAR BAKER'S HATS TO BED!!

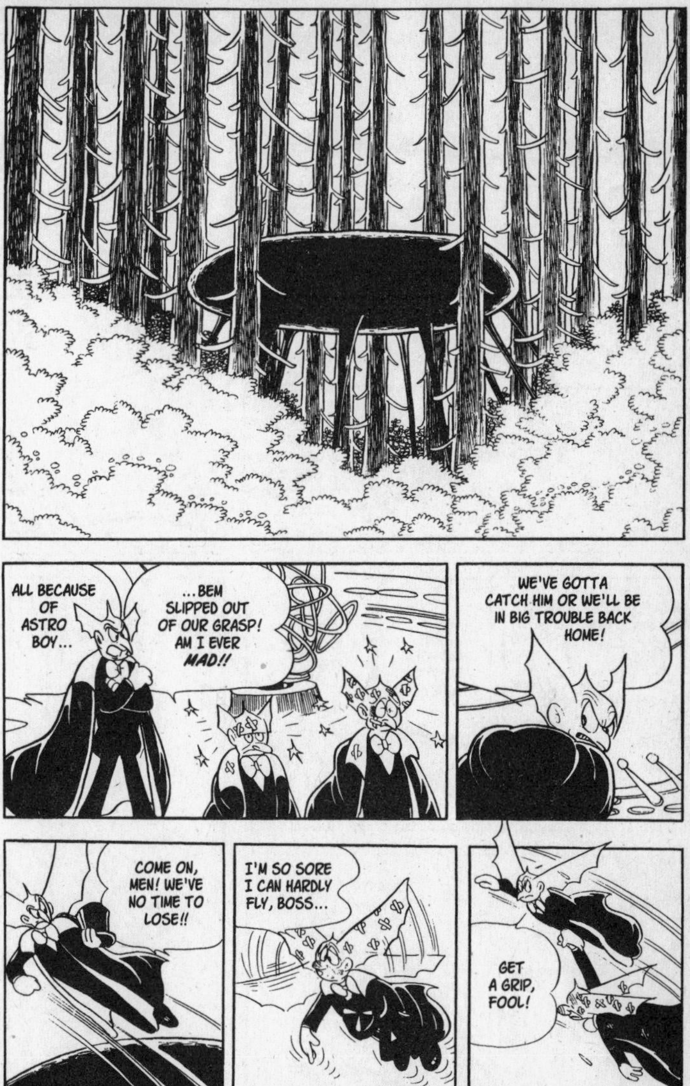
ALL BECAUSE OF ASTRO BOY...
...BEM SLIPPED OUT OF OUR GRASP! AM I EVER MAD!!
WE'VE GOTTA CATCH HIM OR WE'LL BE IN BIG TROUBLE BACK HOME!
COME ON, MEN! WE'VE NO TIME TO LOSE!!
I'M SO SORE I CAN HARDLY FLY, BOSS...
GET A GRIP, FOOL!

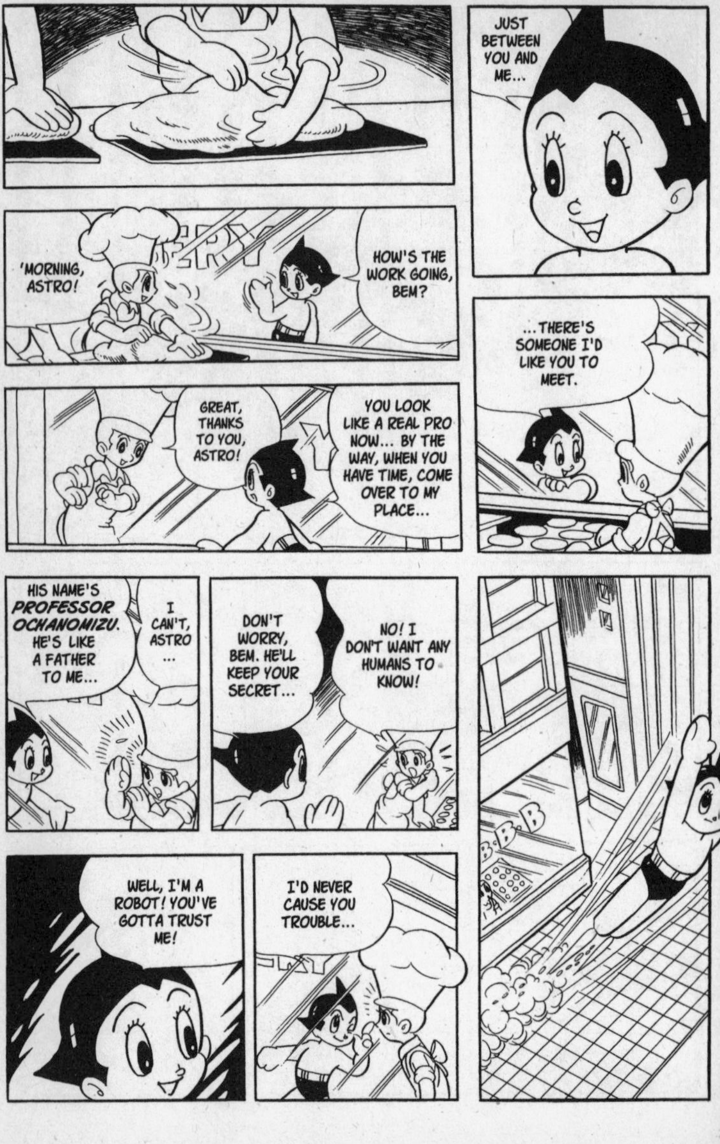

'MORNING, ASTRO!
HOW'S THE WORK GOING, BEM?
GREAT, THANKS TO YOU, ASTRO!
YOU LOOK LIKE A REAL PRO NOW... BY THE WAY, WHEN YOU HAVE TIME, COME OVER TO MY PLACE...
JUST BETWEEN YOU AND ME...
...THERE'S SOMEONE I'D LIKE YOU TO MEET.
HIS NAME'S *PROFESSOR OCHANOMIZU*. HE'S LIKE A FATHER TO ME...
I CAN'T, ASTRO...
DON'T WORRY, BEM. HE'LL KEEP YOUR SECRET...
NO! I DON'T WANT ANY HUMANS TO KNOW!
WELL, I'M A ROBOT! YOU'VE GOTTA TRUST ME!
I'D NEVER CAUSE YOU TROUBLE...
B B B

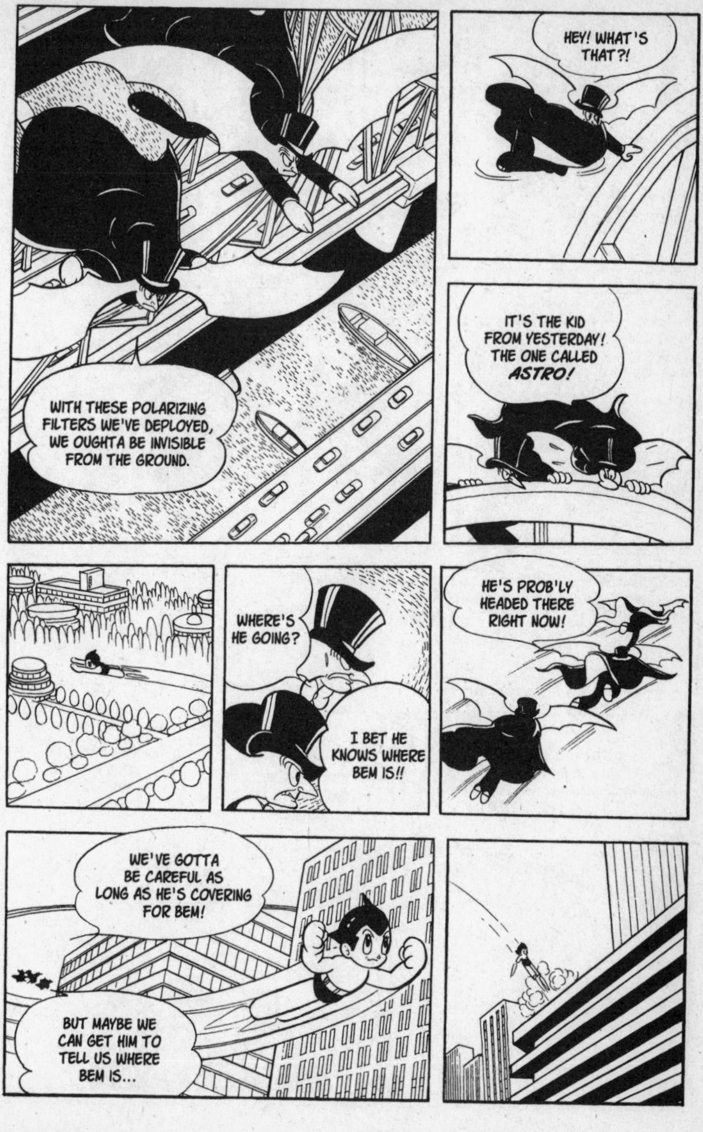
WITH THESE POLARIZING FILTERS WE'VE DEPLOYED, WE OUGHTA BE INVISIBLE FROM THE GROUND.
HEY! WHAT'S THAT?!
IT'S THE KID FROM YESTERDAY! THE ONE CALLED ASTRO!
WHERE'S HE GOING?
I BET HE KNOWS WHERE BEM IS!!
HE'S PROB'LY HEADED THERE RIGHT NOW!
WE'VE GOTTA BE CAREFUL AS LONG AS HE'S COVERING FOR BEM!
BUT MAYBE WE CAN GET HIM TO TELL US WHERE BEM IS...

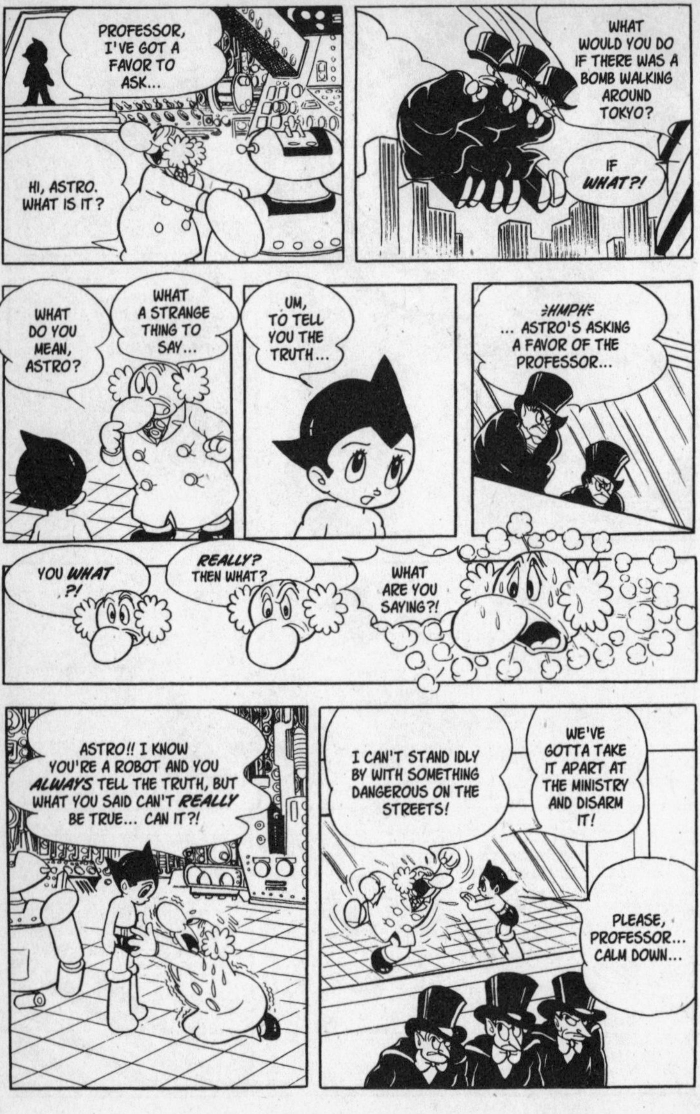
PROFESSOR, I'VE GOT A FAVOR TO ASK...
HI, ASTRO. WHAT IS IT?
WHAT WOULD YOU DO IF THERE WAS A BOMB WALKING AROUND TOKYO?
IF ***WHAT?!***
WHAT DO YOU MEAN, ASTRO?
WHAT A STRANGE THING TO SAY...
UM, TO TELL YOU THE TRUTH...
HMPH ... ASTRO'S ASKING A FAVOR OF THE PROFESSOR...
YOU ***WHAT?!***
REALLY? THEN WHAT?
WHAT ARE YOU SAYING?!
ASTRO!! I KNOW YOU'RE A ROBOT AND YOU ***ALWAYS*** TELL THE TRUTH, BUT WHAT YOU SAID CAN'T ***REALLY*** BE TRUE... CAN IT?!
I CAN'T STAND IDLY BY WITH SOMETHING DANGEROUS ON THE STREETS!
WE'VE GOTTA TAKE IT APART AT THE MINISTRY AND DISARM IT!
PLEASE, PROFESSOR... CALM DOWN...

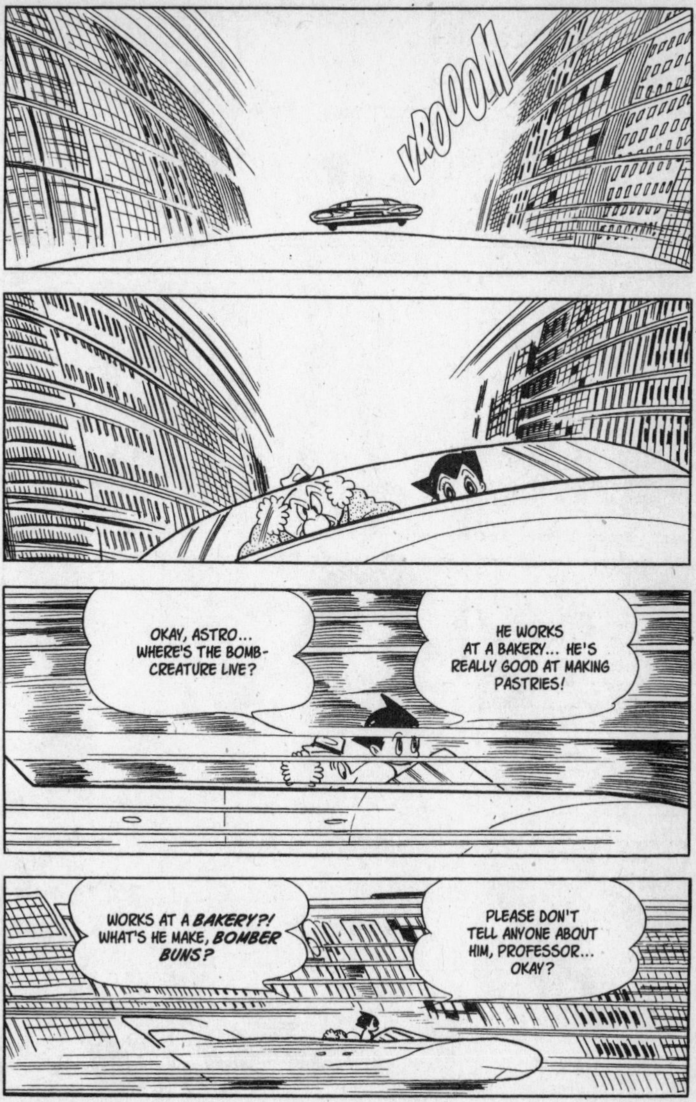
VROOOM
OKAY, ASTRO... WHERE'S THE BOMB-CREATURE LIVE?
HE WORKS AT A BAKERY... HE'S REALLY GOOD AT MAKING PASTRIES!
WORKS AT A *BAKERY*?! WHAT'S HE MAKE, *BOMBER BUNS*?
PLEASE DON'T TELL ANYONE ABOUT HIM, PROFESSOR... OKAY?

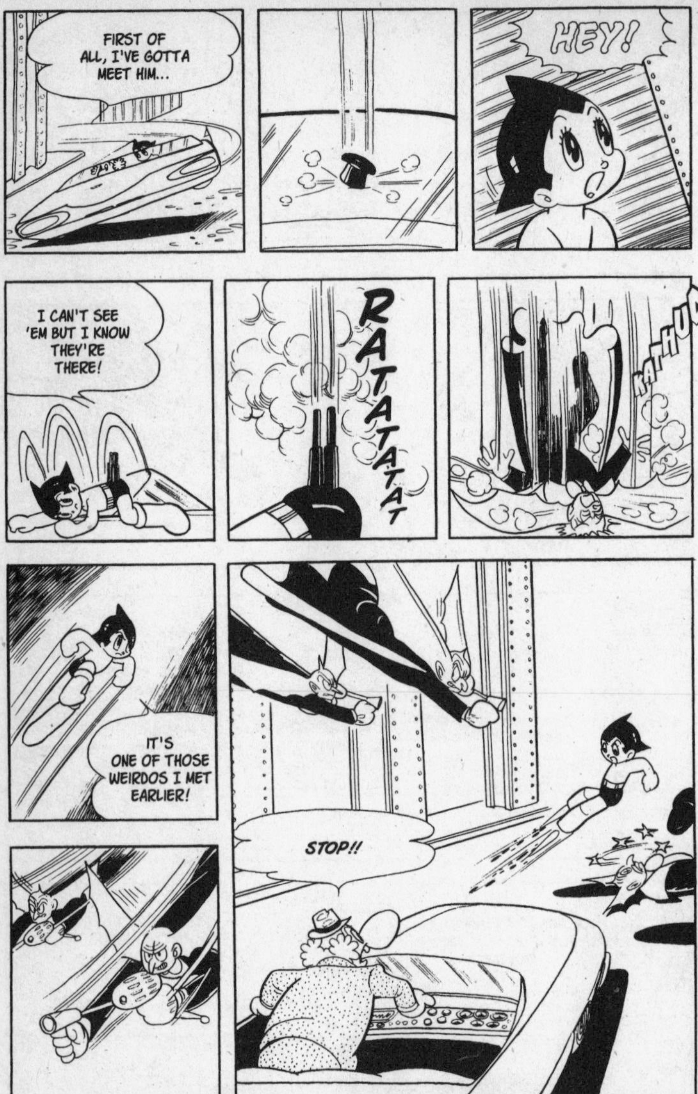
FIRST OF ALL, I'VE GOTTA MEET HIM...
HEY!
I CAN'T SEE 'EM BUT I KNOW THEY'RE THERE!
RATATATATAT
KATHUD
IT'S ONE OF THOSE WEIRDOS I MET EARLIER!
STOP!!

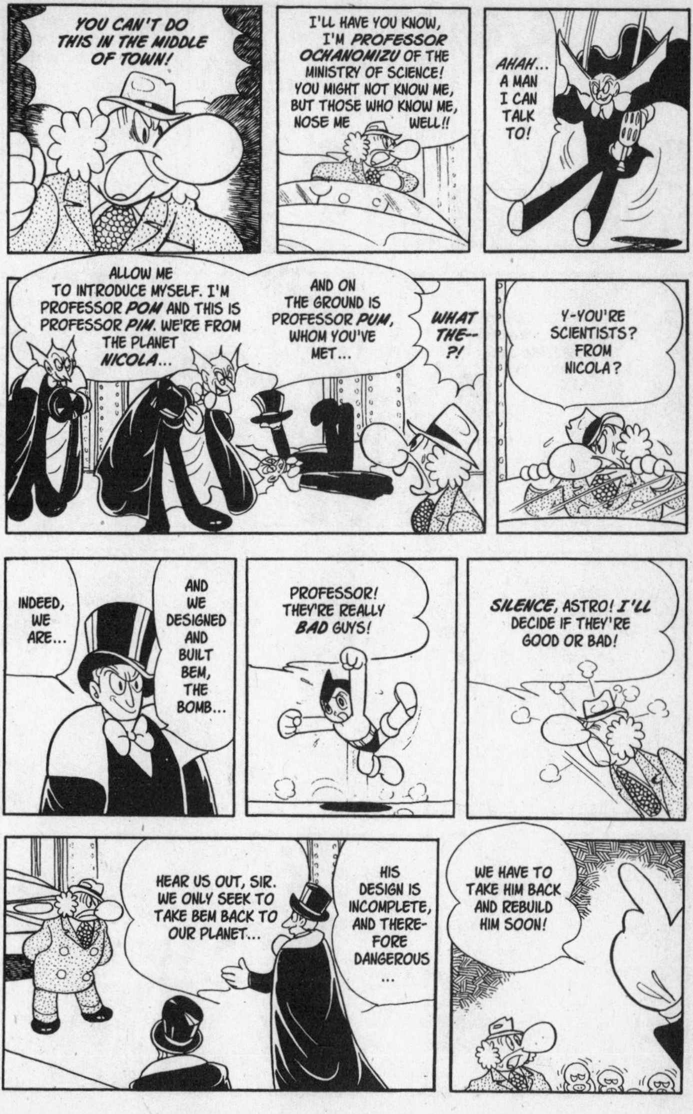
YOU CAN'T DO THIS IN THE MIDDLE OF TOWN!
I'LL HAVE YOU KNOW, I'M PROFESSOR OCHANOMIZU OF THE MINISTRY OF SCIENCE! YOU MIGHT NOT KNOW ME, BUT THOSE WHO KNOW ME, NOSE ME WELL!!
AHAH... A MAN I CAN TALK TO!
ALLOW ME TO INTRODUCE MYSELF. I'M PROFESSOR POM AND THIS IS PROFESSOR PIM. WE'RE FROM THE PLANET NICOLA...
AND ON THE GROUND IS PROFESSOR PUM, WHOM YOU'VE MET...
WHAT THE--?!
Y-YOU'RE SCIENTISTS? FROM NICOLA?
INDEED, WE ARE...
AND WE DESIGNED AND BUILT BEM, THE BOMB...
PROFESSOR! THEY'RE REALLY BAD GUYS!
SILENCE, ASTRO! I'LL DECIDE IF THEY'RE GOOD OR BAD!
HEAR US OUT, SIR. WE ONLY SEEK TO TAKE BEM BACK TO OUR PLANET...
HIS DESIGN IS INCOMPLETE, AND THEREFORE DANGEROUS...
WE HAVE TO TAKE HIM BACK AND REBUILD HIM SOON!

IF YOU'RE REALLY A SCIENTIST, I'M SURE YOU'LL UNDERSTAND...

DON'T BELIEVE THEM, PROFESSOR! THEY'RE *LYING!*

≠HMPH≠... BUT ARE YOU PLANNING TO USE THE BOMB TO WAGE WAR?

WAR? OF *COURSE* NOT! WE KNOW HOW *DANGEROUS* THAT IS!!

IT'S FOR *PEACEFUL PURPOSES* ONLY! WE *SWEAR!*

THEY MAKE SENSE TO ME, ASTRO...

NO, PROFESSOR! *NO!*

REST ASSURED, WE SHALL CAUSE YOU NO TROUBLE

IT'S A DEAL, THEN...

SWEAR YOU'LL NEVER USE IT IN WAR, AND I'LL TAKE YOU AT YOUR WORD AND COOPERATE...

YOU HAVE MY WORD, SIR...

34

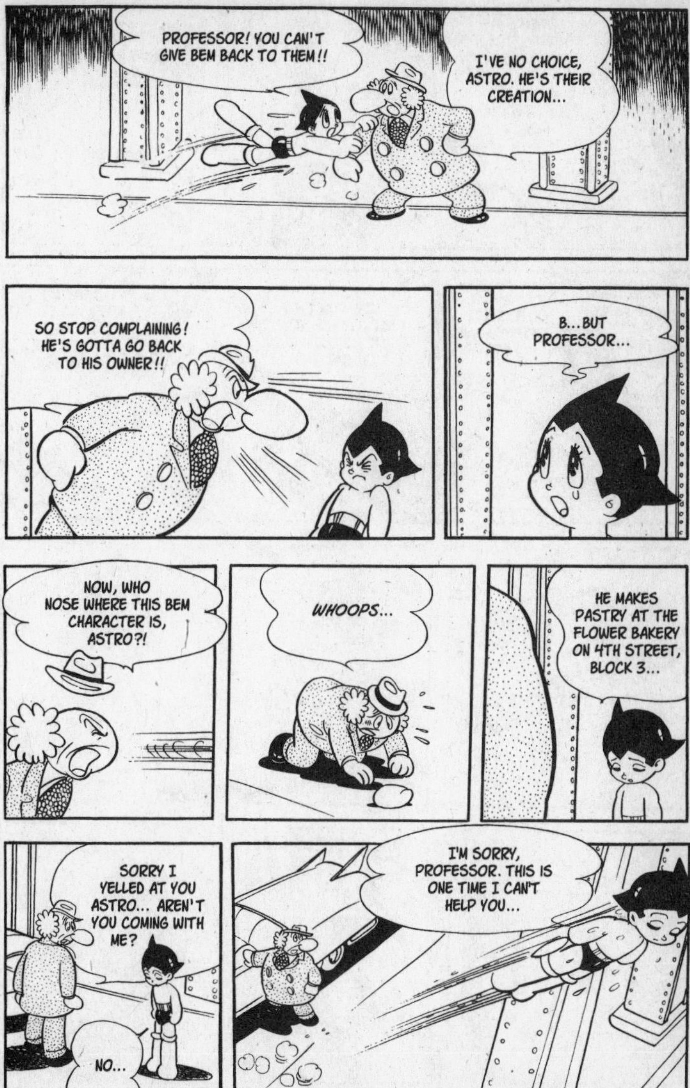
PROFESSOR! YOU CAN'T GIVE BEM BACK TO THEM!!
I'VE NO CHOICE, ASTRO. HE'S THEIR CREATION...
SO STOP COMPLAINING! HE'S GOTTA GO BACK TO HIS OWNER!!
B...BUT PROFESSOR...
NOW, WHO NOSE WHERE THIS BEM CHARACTER IS, ASTRO?!
WHOOPS...
HE MAKES PASTRY AT THE FLOWER BAKERY ON 4TH STREET, BLOCK 3...
SORRY I YELLED AT YOU ASTRO... AREN'T YOU COMING WITH ME?
NO...
I'M SORRY, PROFESSOR. THIS IS ONE TIME I CAN'T HELP YOU...

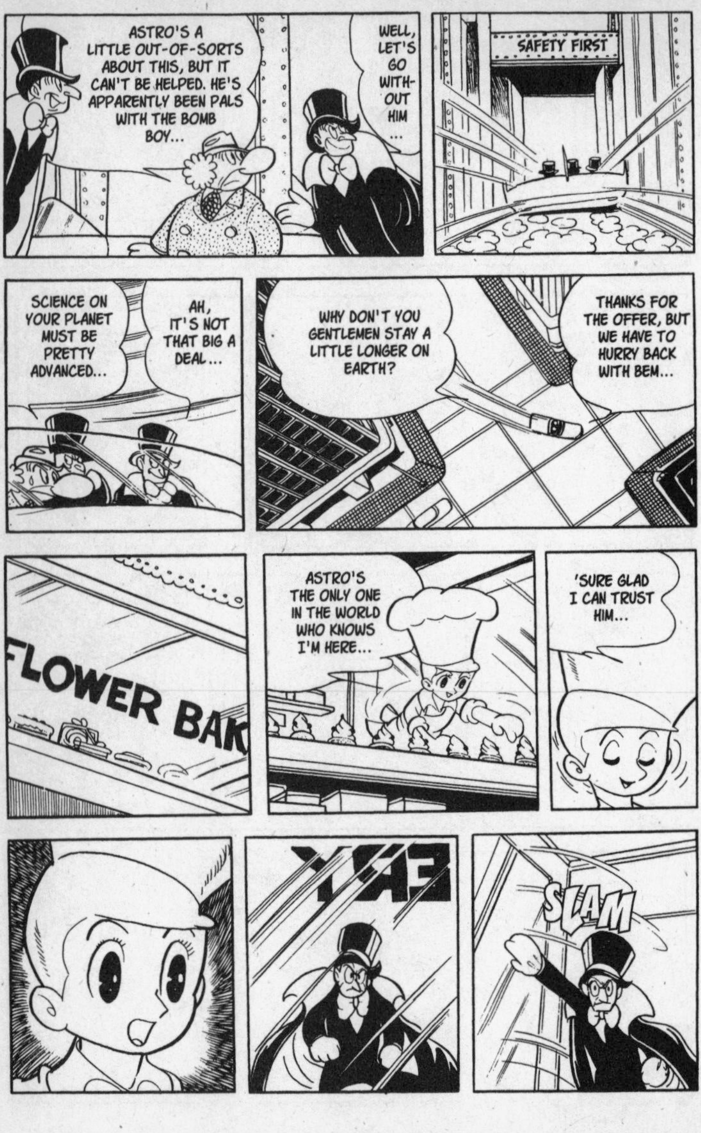
ASTRO'S A LITTLE OUT-OF-SORTS ABOUT THIS, BUT IT CAN'T BE HELPED. HE'S APPARENTLY BEEN PALS WITH THE BOMB BOY...
WELL, LET'S GO WITH-OUT HIM ...
SAFETY FIRST
SCIENCE ON YOUR PLANET MUST BE PRETTY ADVANCED...
AH, IT'S NOT THAT BIG A DEAL...
WHY DON'T YOU GENTLEMEN STAY A LITTLE LONGER ON EARTH?
THANKS FOR THE OFFER, BUT WE HAVE TO HURRY BACK WITH BEM...
FLOWER BAK
ASTRO'S THE ONLY ONE IN THE WORLD WHO KNOWS I'M HERE...
'SURE GLAD I CAN TRUST HIM...
SLAM

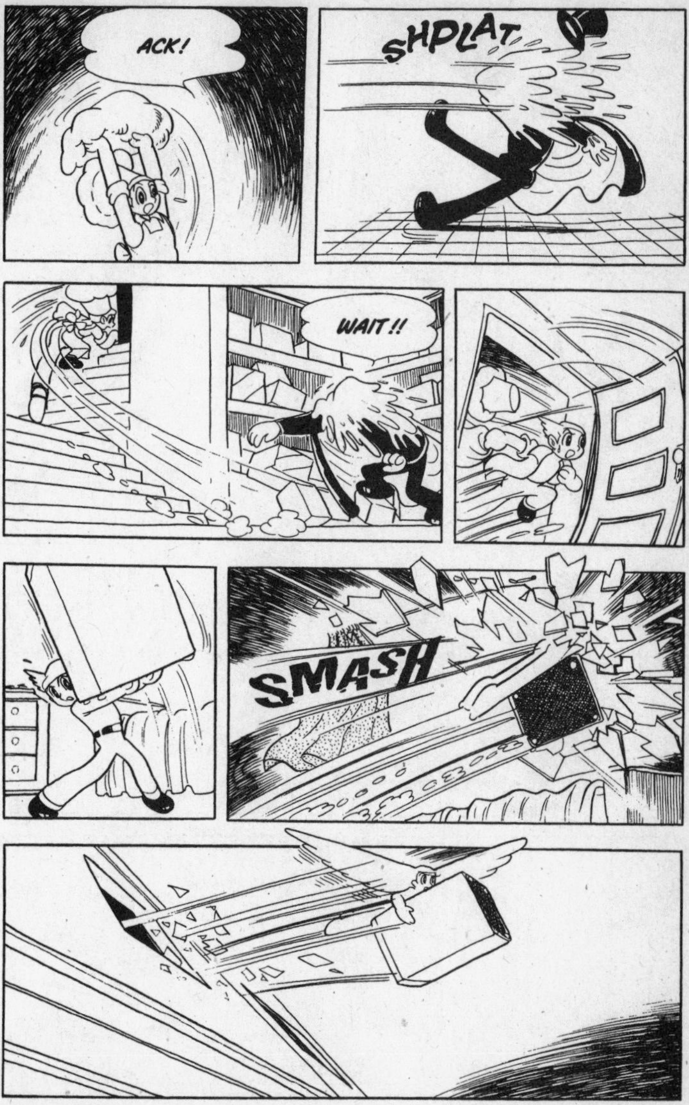

ACK!
SHPLAT
WAIT!!
SMASH

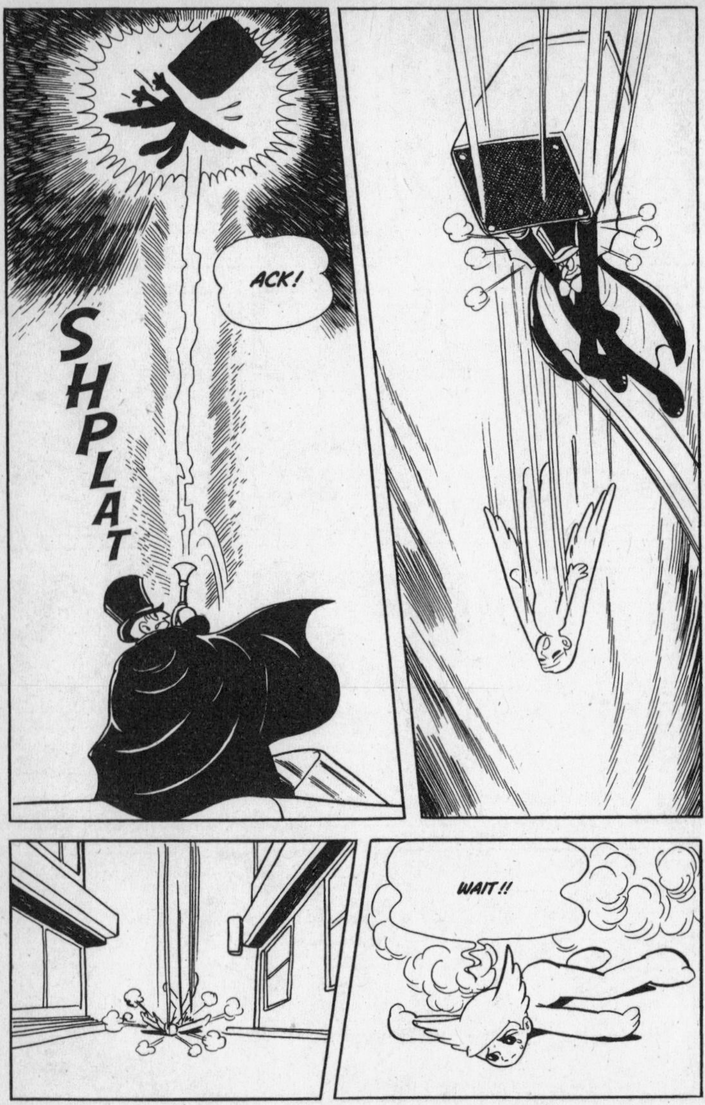
ACK!
SHPLAT
WAIT!!

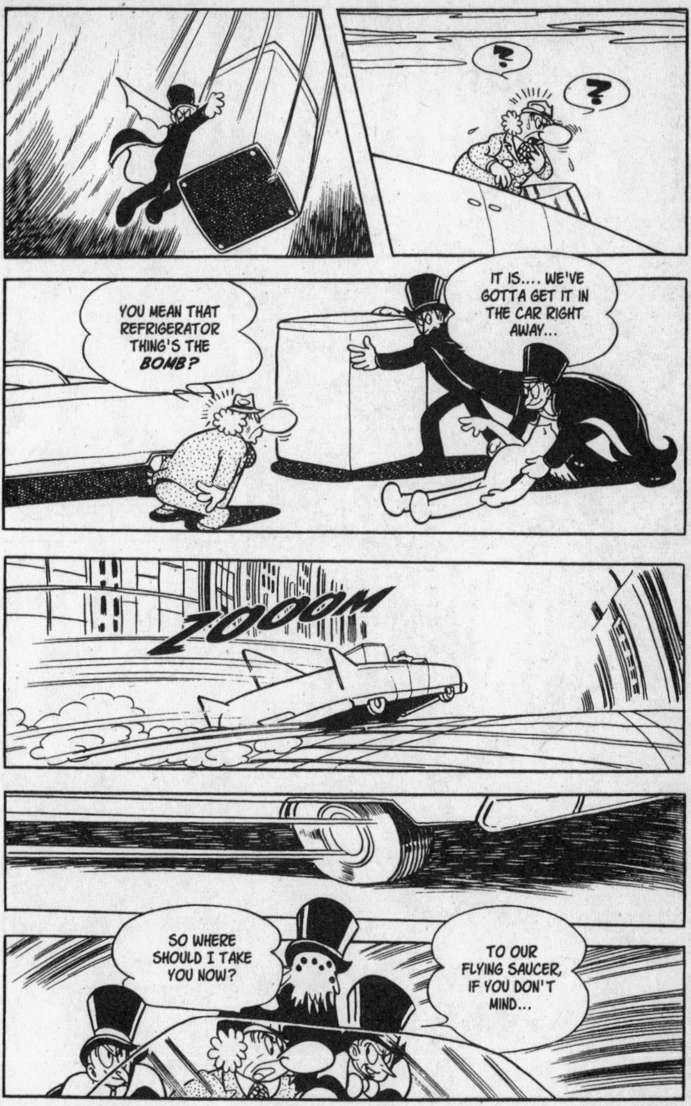
?
?
YOU MEAN THAT REFRIGERATOR THING'S THE *BOMB?*
IT IS.... WE'VE GOTTA GET IT IN THE CAR RIGHT AWAY...
ZOOOOM
SO WHERE SHOULD I TAKE YOU NOW?
TO OUR FLYING SAUCER, IF YOU DON'T MIND...

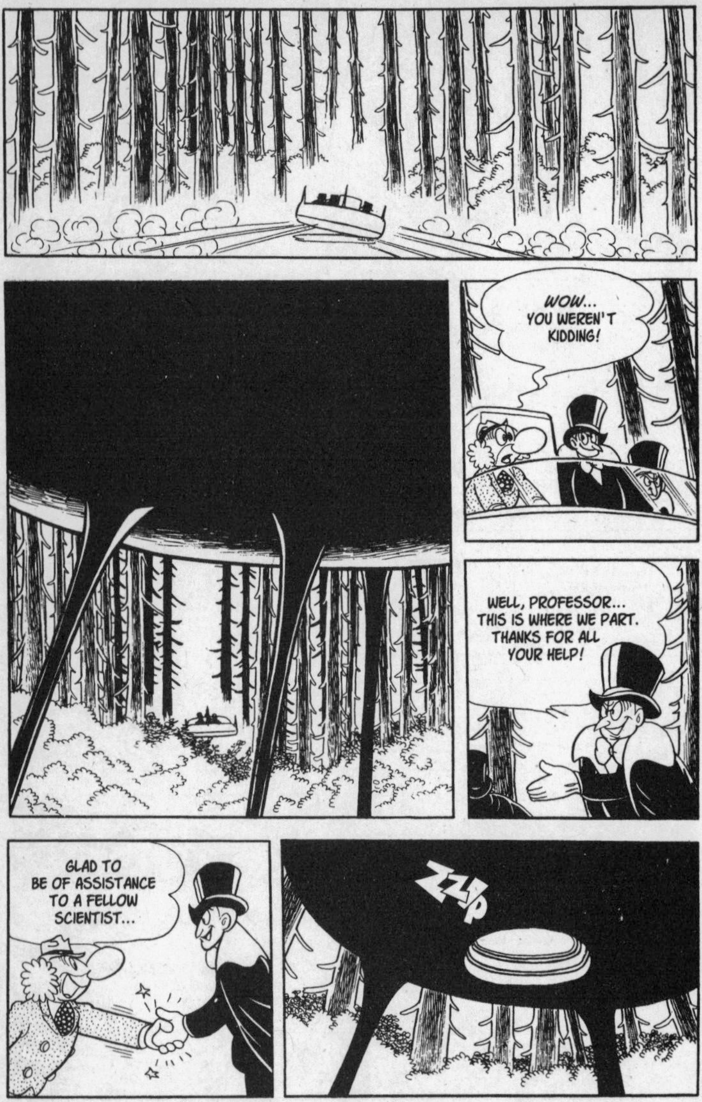
WOW...
YOU WEREN'T
KIDDING!
WELL, PROFESSOR...
THIS IS WHERE WE PART.
THANKS FOR ALL
YOUR HELP!
GLAD TO
BE OF ASSISTANCE
TO A FELLOW
SCIENTIST...
ZZIP

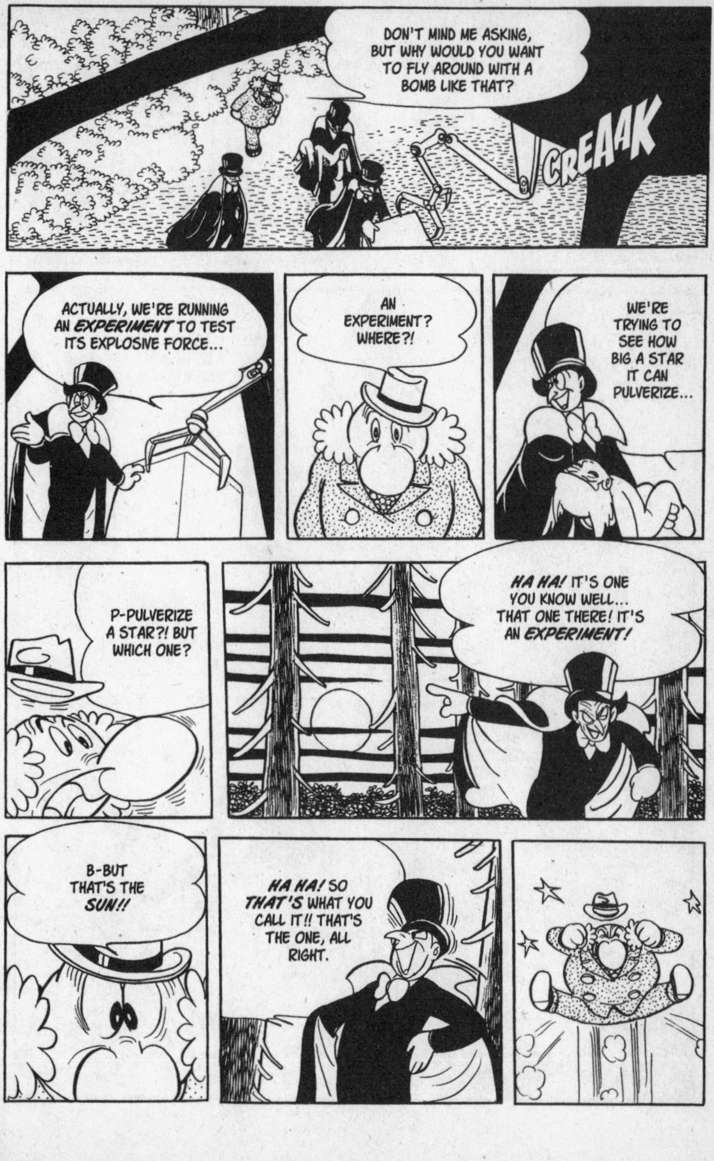
DON'T MIND ME ASKING, BUT WHY WOULD YOU WANT TO FLY AROUND WITH A BOMB LIKE THAT?
CREAAK
ACTUALLY, WE'RE RUNNING AN *EXPERIMENT* TO TEST ITS EXPLOSIVE FORCE...
AN EXPERIMENT? WHERE?!
WE'RE TRYING TO SEE HOW BIG A STAR IT CAN PULVERIZE...
P-PULVERIZE A STAR?! BUT WHICH ONE?
HA HA! IT'S ONE YOU KNOW WELL... THAT ONE THERE! IT'S AN *EXPERIMENT!*
B-BUT THAT'S THE *SUN!!*
HA HA! SO *THAT'S* WHAT YOU CALL IT!! THAT'S THE ONE, ALL RIGHT.

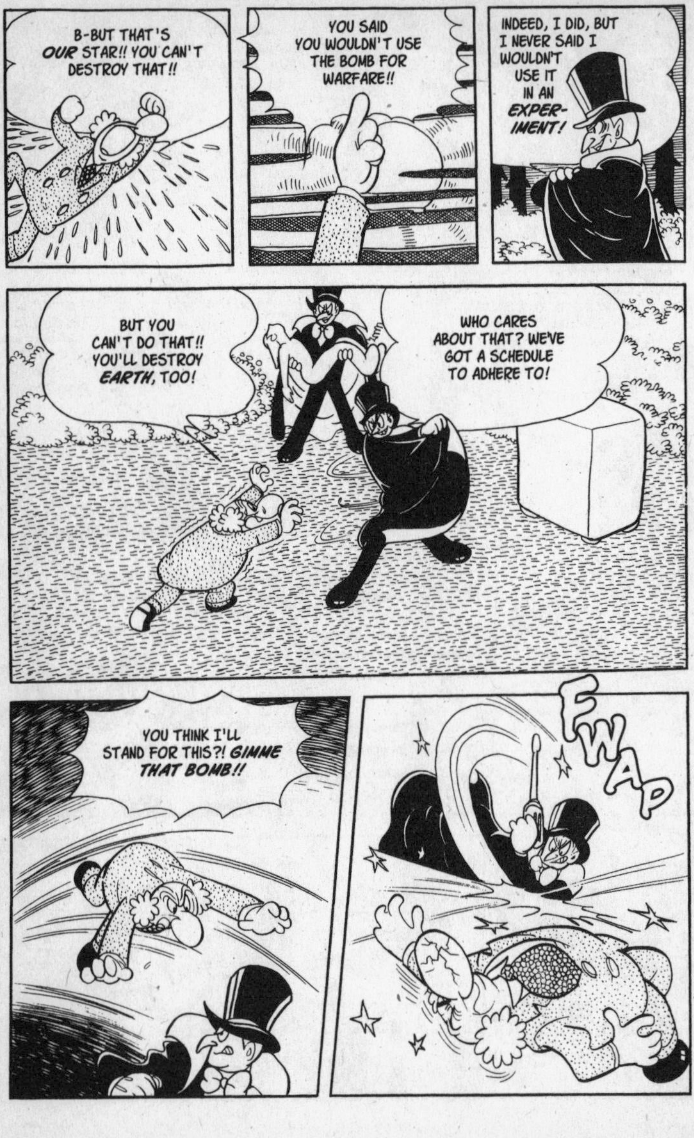
B-BUT THAT'S OUR STAR!! YOU CAN'T DESTROY THAT!!
YOU SAID YOU WOULDN'T USE THE BOMB FOR WARFARE!!
INDEED, I DID, BUT I NEVER SAID I WOULDN'T USE IT IN AN EXPERIMENT!
BUT YOU CAN'T DO THAT!! YOU'LL DESTROY EARTH, TOO!
WHO CARES ABOUT THAT? WE'VE GOT A SCHEDULE TO ADHERE TO!
YOU THINK I'LL STAND FOR THIS?! GIMME THAT BOMB!!
FWAP

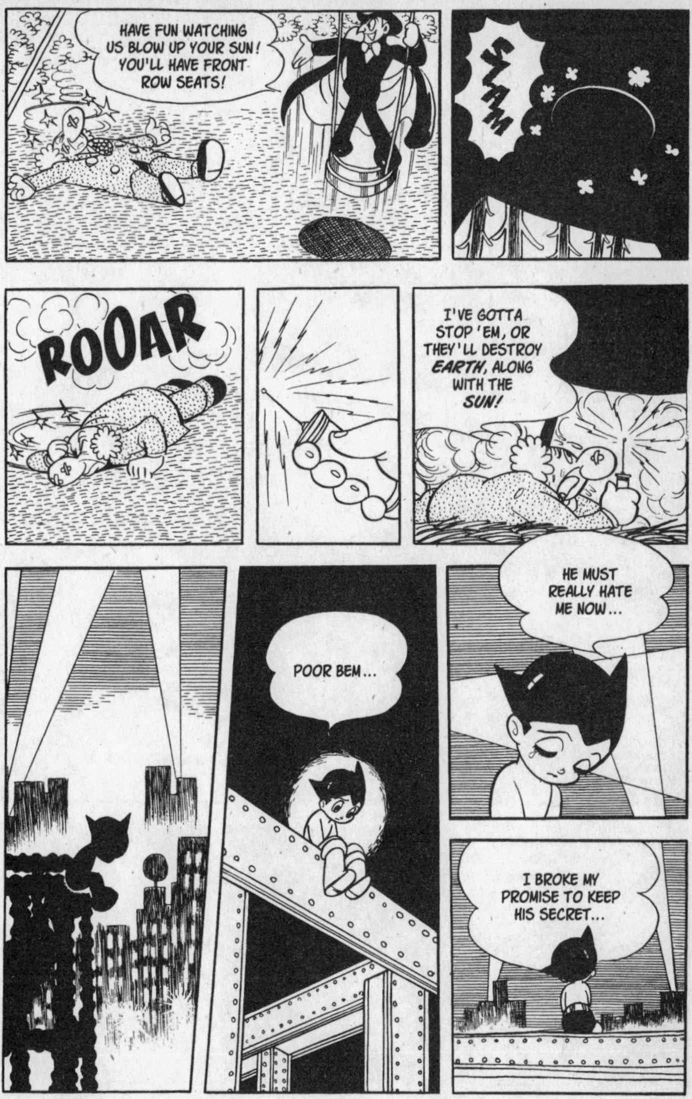
HAVE FUN WATCHING US BLOW UP YOUR SUN! YOU'LL HAVE FRONT ROW SEATS!
SLAM
ROOAR
I'VE GOTTA STOP 'EM, OR THEY'LL DESTROY *EARTH*, ALONG WITH THE *SUN!*
POOR BEM...
HE MUST REALLY HATE ME NOW...
I BROKE MY PROMISE TO KEEP HIS SECRET...

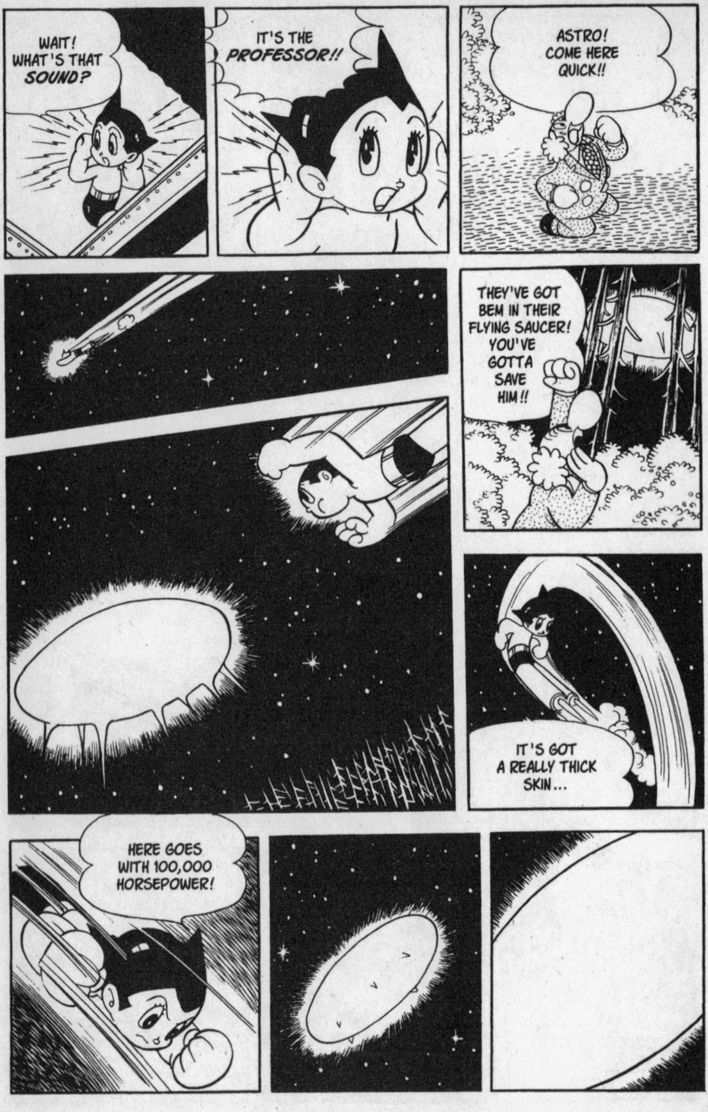
WAIT! WHAT'S THAT SOUND?
IT'S THE PROFESSOR!!
ASTRO! COME HERE QUICK!!
THEY'VE GOT BEM IN THEIR FLYING SAUCER! YOU'VE GOTTA SAVE HIM!!
IT'S GOT A REALLY THICK SKIN...
HERE GOES WITH 100,000 HORSEPOWER!

IT DIDN'T WORK!!

GOTTA TRY SOMETHING ELSE!

THIS MUST BE THE HATCH...

I'LL PRY IT OPEN LIKE SO...

JUST A TAD MORE...

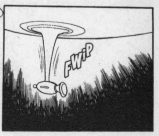

FWiP

45

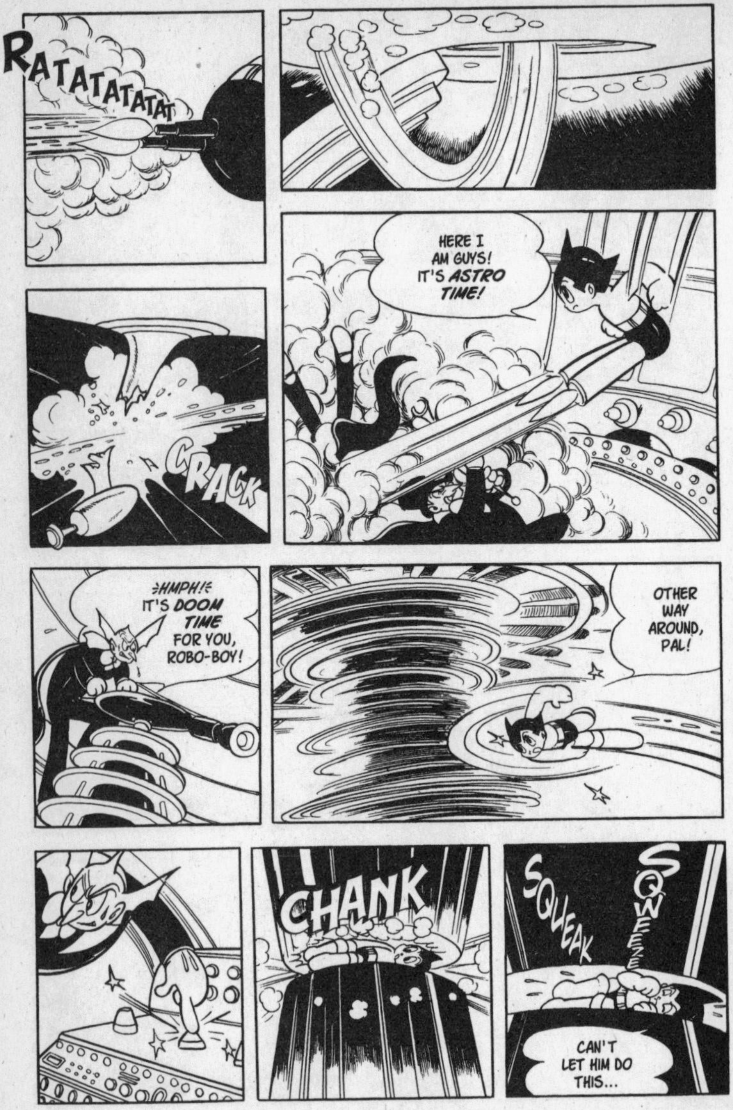
RATATATATATAT
HERE I AM GUYS! IT'S ASTRO TIME!
CRACK
HMPH! IT'S DOOM TIME FOR YOU, ROBO-BOY!
OTHER WAY AROUND, PAL!
CHANK
SQUEAK
SQWEEZE
CAN'T LET HIM DO THIS...

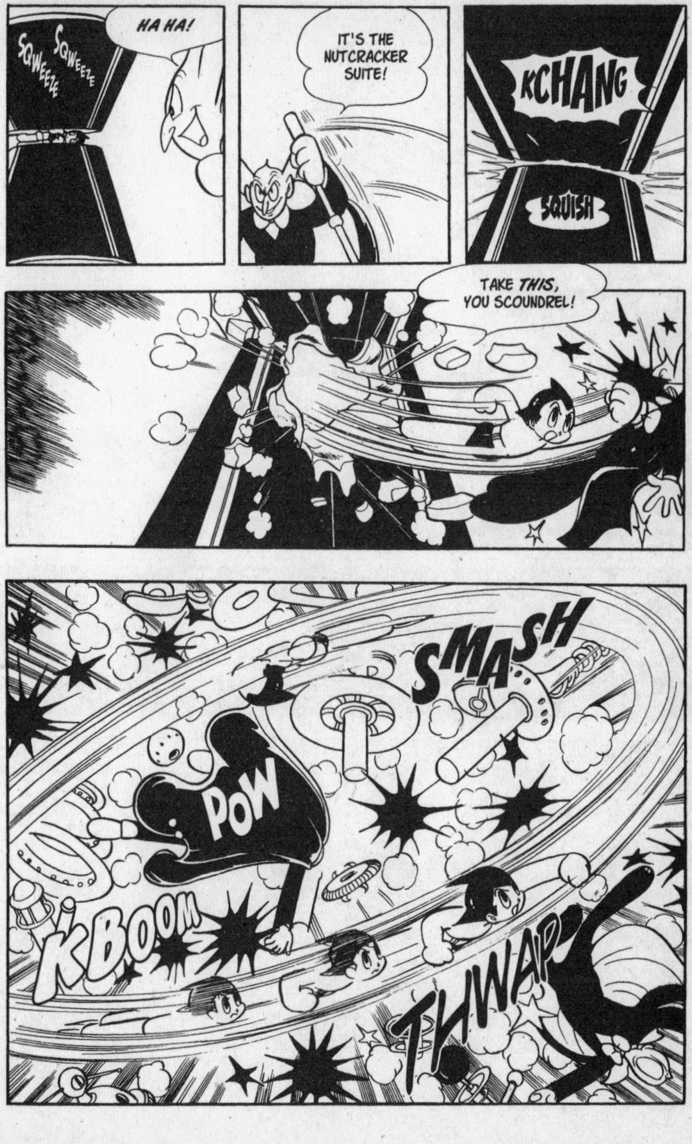
SQWEEZE SQWEEZE
HA HA!
IT'S THE NUTCRACKER SUITE!
KCHANG
SQUISH
TAKE THIS, YOU SCOUNDREL!
SMASH
POW
KBOOM
THWAP

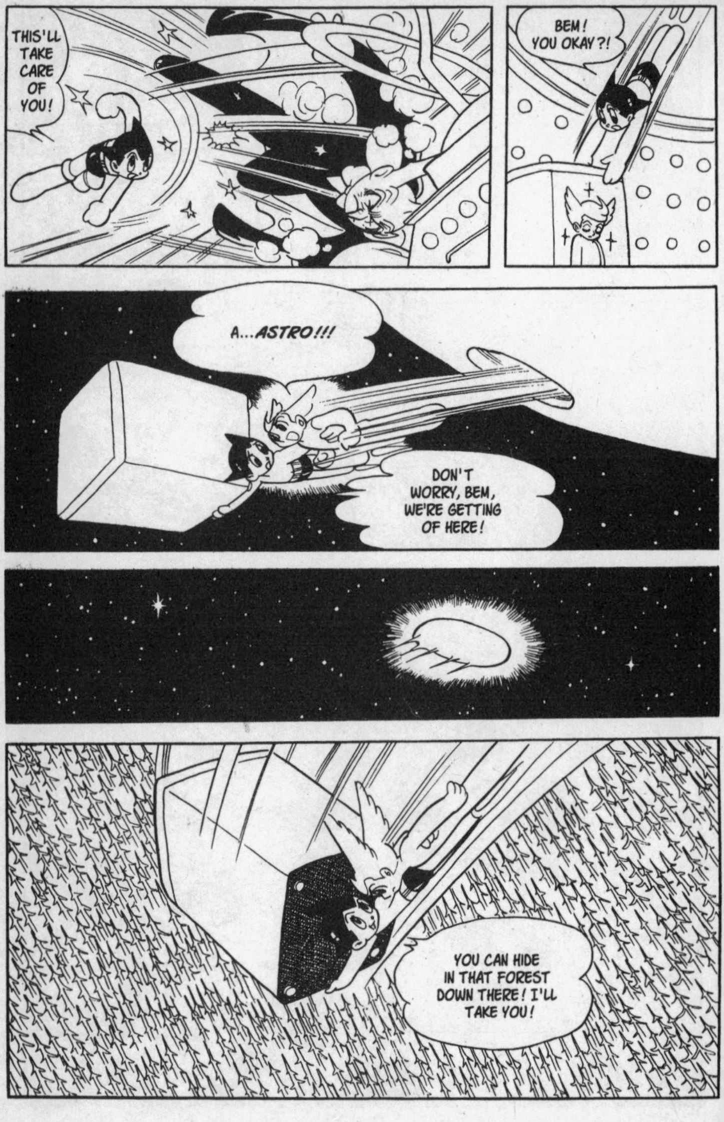
THIS'LL TAKE CARE OF YOU!
BEM! YOU OKAY?!
A...ASTRO!!!
DON'T WORRY, BEM, WE'RE GETTING OF HERE!
YOU CAN HIDE IN THAT FOREST DOWN THERE! I'LL TAKE YOU!

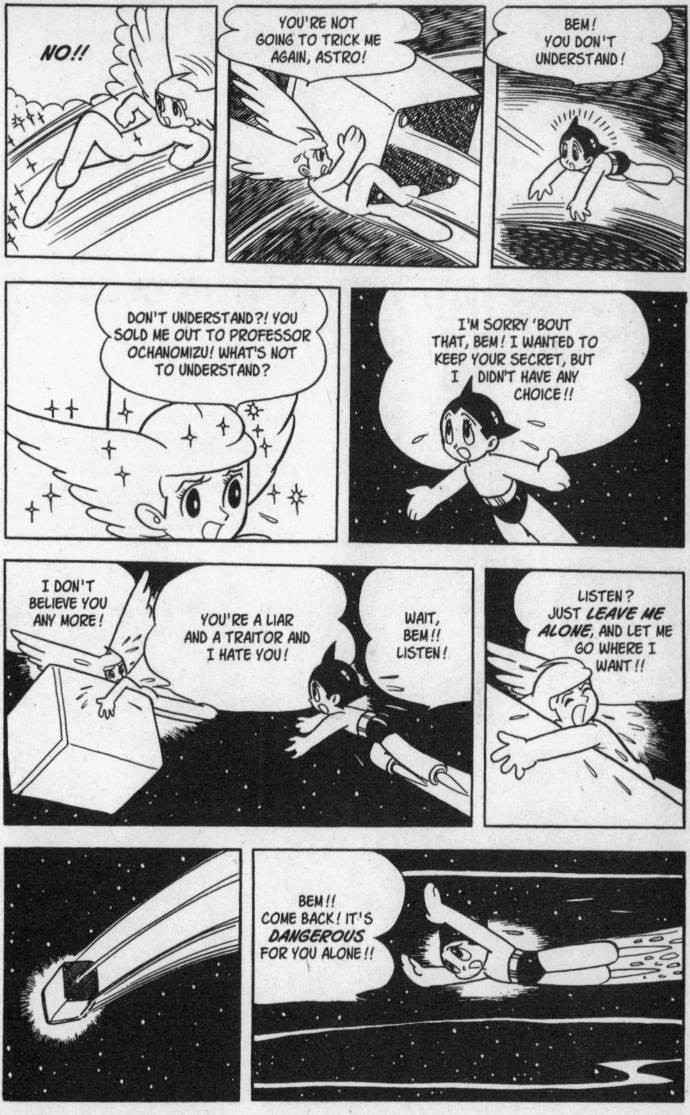

NO!!
YOU'RE NOT GOING TO TRICK ME AGAIN, ASTRO!
BEM! YOU DON'T UNDERSTAND!
DON'T UNDERSTAND?! YOU SOLD ME OUT TO PROFESSOR OCHANOMIZU! WHAT'S NOT TO UNDERSTAND?
I'M SORRY 'BOUT THAT, BEM! I WANTED TO KEEP YOUR SECRET, BUT I DIDN'T HAVE ANY CHOICE!!
I DON'T BELIEVE YOU ANY MORE!
YOU'RE A LIAR AND A TRAITOR AND I HATE YOU!
WAIT, BEM!! LISTEN!
LISTEN? JUST ***LEAVE ME ALONE***, AND LET ME GO WHERE I WANT!!
BEM!! COME BACK! IT'S ***DANGEROUS*** FOR YOU ALONE!!

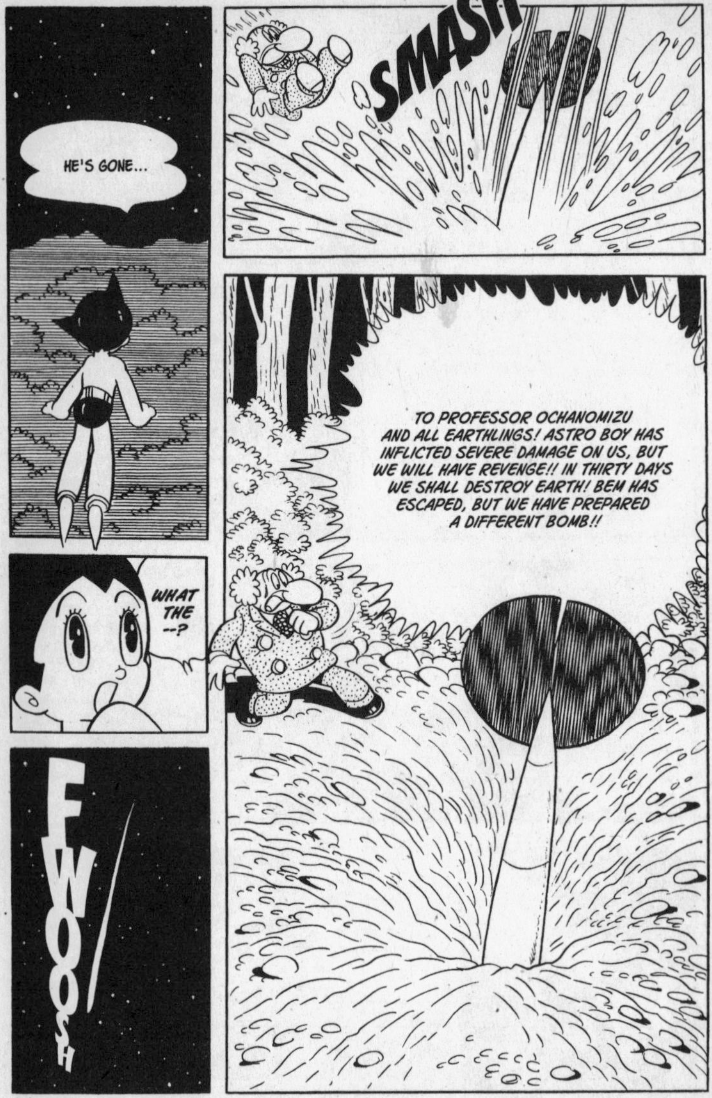
HE'S GONE...
WHAT THE --?
FWOOSH
SMASH
TO PROFESSOR OCHANOMIZU AND ALL EARTHLINGS! ASTRO BOY HAS INFLICTED SEVERE DAMAGE ON US, BUT WE WILL HAVE REVENGE!! IN THIRTY DAYS WE SHALL DESTROY EARTH! BEM HAS ESCAPED, BUT WE HAVE PREPARED A DIFFERENT BOMB!!

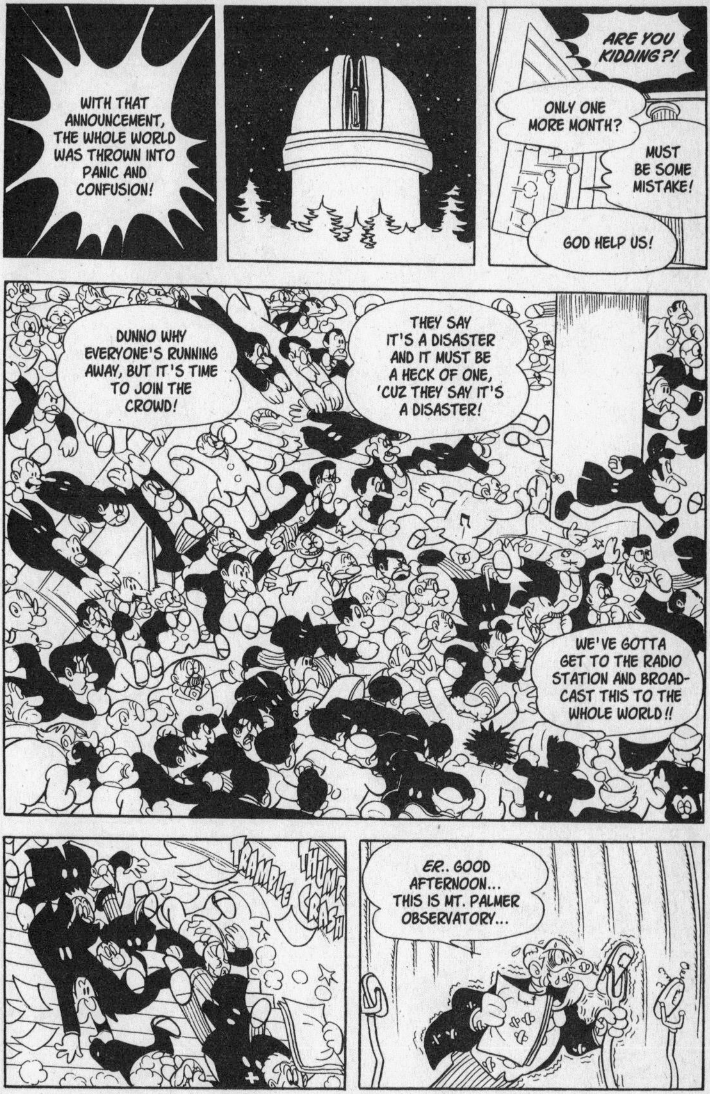
WITH THAT ANNOUNCEMENT, THE WHOLE WORLD WAS THROWN INTO PANIC AND CONFUSION!
ARE YOU KIDDING?!
ONLY ONE MORE MONTH?
MUST BE SOME MISTAKE!
GOD HELP US!
DUNNO WHY EVERYONE'S RUNNING AWAY, BUT IT'S TIME TO JOIN THE CROWD!
THEY SAY IT'S A DISASTER AND IT MUST BE A HECK OF ONE, 'CUZ THEY SAY IT'S A DISASTER!
WE'VE GOTTA GET TO THE RADIO STATION AND BROAD-CAST THIS TO THE WHOLE WORLD!!
TRAMPLE
THUMP
CRASH
ER.. GOOD AFTERNOON... THIS IS MT. PALMER OBSERVATORY...

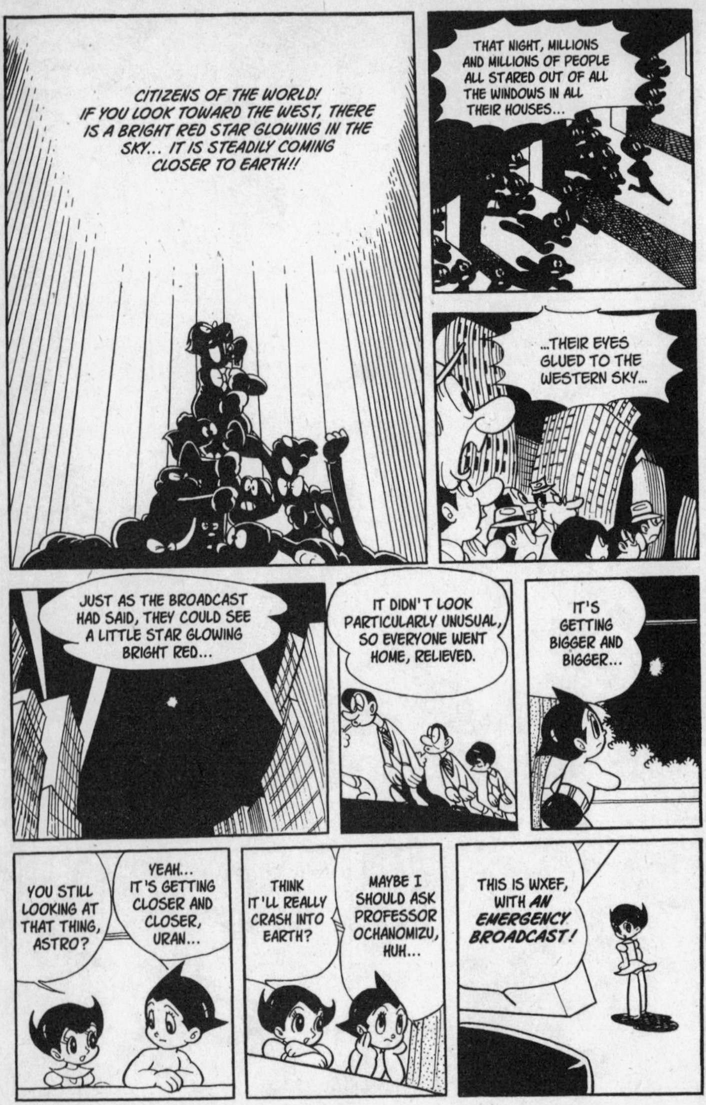

CITIZENS OF THE WORLD! IF YOU LOOK TOWARD THE WEST, THERE IS A BRIGHT RED STAR GLOWING IN THE SKY... IT IS STEADILY COMING CLOSER TO EARTH!!
THAT NIGHT, MILLIONS AND MILLIONS OF PEOPLE ALL STARED OUT OF ALL THE WINDOWS IN ALL THEIR HOUSES...
...THEIR EYES GLUED TO THE WESTERN SKY...
JUST AS THE BROADCAST HAD SAID, THEY COULD SEE A LITTLE STAR GLOWING BRIGHT RED...
IT DIDN'T LOOK PARTICULARLY UNUSUAL, SO EVERYONE WENT HOME, RELIEVED.
IT'S GETTING BIGGER AND BIGGER...
YOU STILL LOOKING AT THAT THING, ASTRO?
YEAH... IT'S GETTING CLOSER AND CLOSER, URAN...
THINK IT'LL REALLY CRASH INTO EARTH?
MAYBE I SHOULD ASK PROFESSOR OCHANOMIZU, HUH...
THIS IS WXEF, WITH AN EMERGENCY BROADCAST!

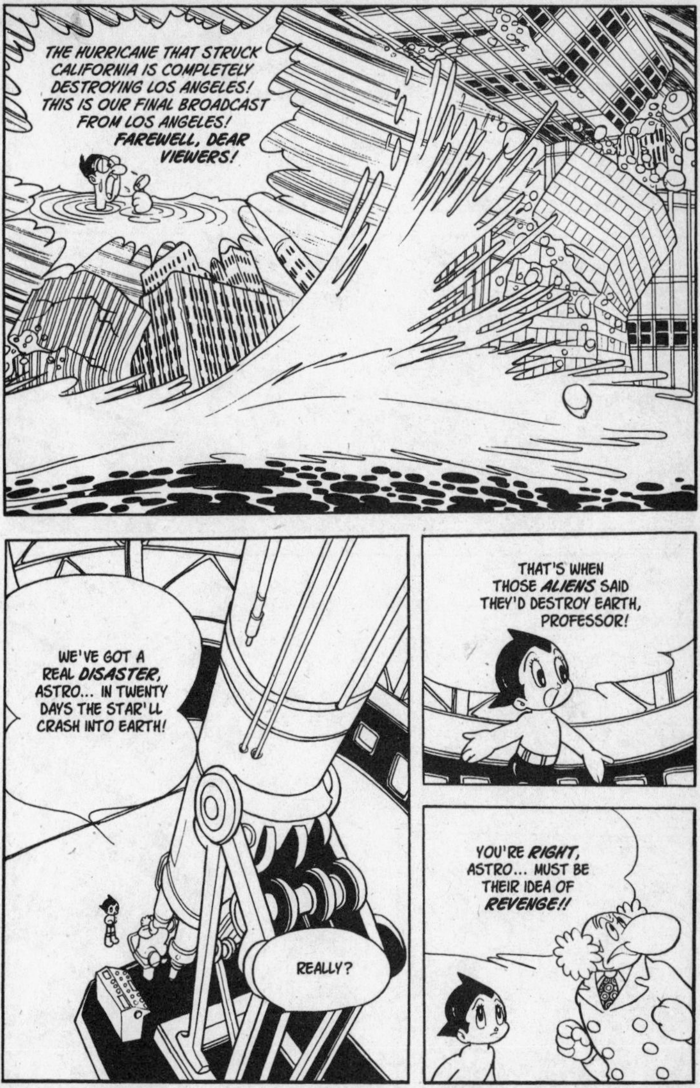
THE HURRICANE THAT STRUCK CALIFORNIA IS COMPLETELY DESTROYING LOS ANGELES! THIS IS OUR FINAL BROADCAST FROM LOS ANGELES! FAREWELL, DEAR VIEWERS!
WE'VE GOT A REAL DISASTER, ASTRO... IN TWENTY DAYS THE STAR'LL CRASH INTO EARTH!
REALLY?
THAT'S WHEN THOSE ALIENS SAID THEY'D DESTROY EARTH, PROFESSOR!
YOU'RE RIGHT, ASTRO... MUST BE THEIR IDEA OF REVENGE!!

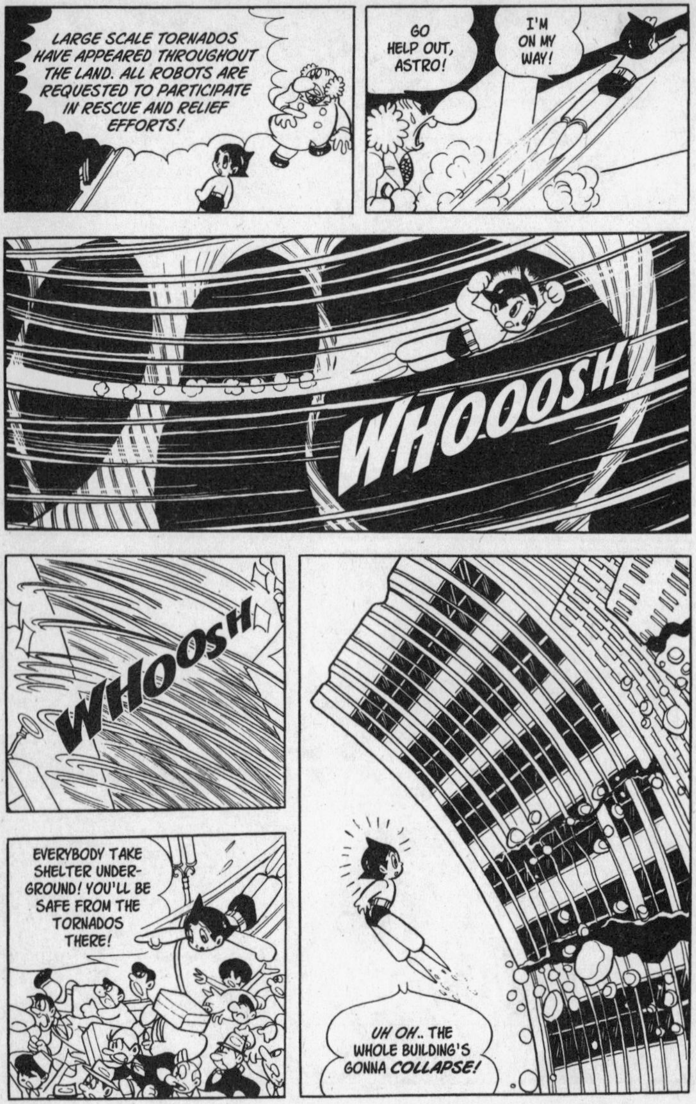
LARGE SCALE TORNADOS HAVE APPEARED THROUGHOUT THE LAND. ALL ROBOTS ARE REQUESTED TO PARTICIPATE IN RESCUE AND RELIEF EFFORTS!
GO HELP OUT, ASTRO!
I'M ON MY WAY!
WHOOOSH
WHOOSH
EVERYBODY TAKE SHELTER UNDER-GROUND! YOU'LL BE SAFE FROM THE TORNADOS THERE!
UH OH.. THE WHOLE BUILDING'S GONNA COLLAPSE!

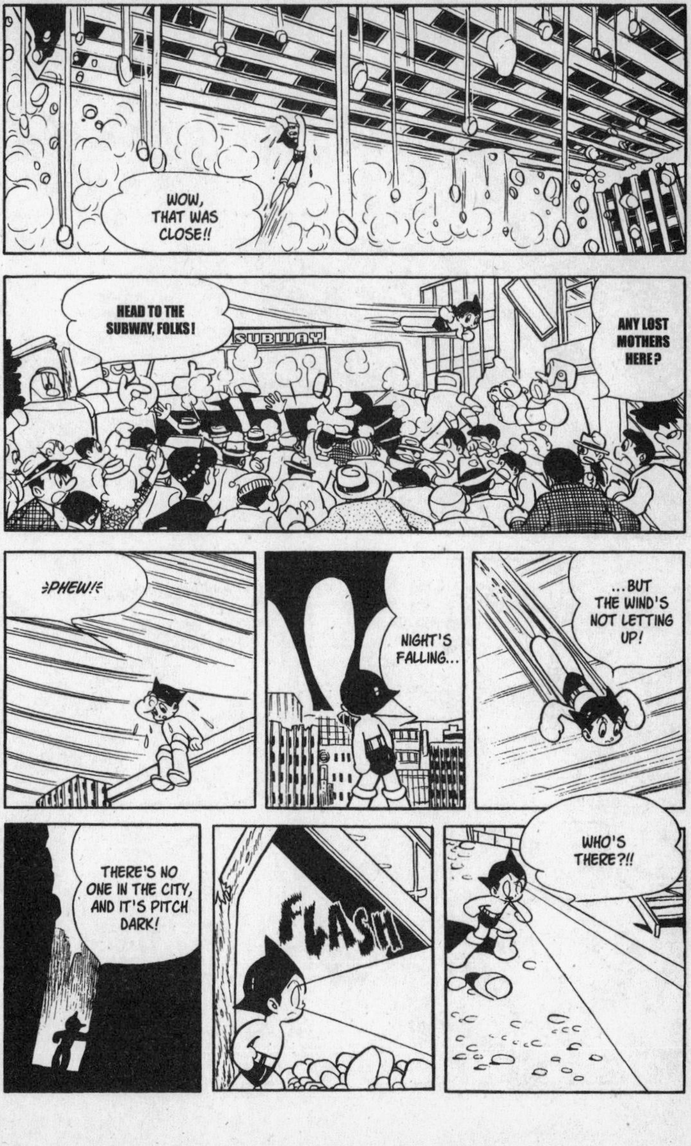
WOW, THAT WAS CLOSE!!
HEAD TO THE SUBWAY, FOLKS!
SUBWAY
ANY LOST MOTHERS HERE?
PHEW!
NIGHT'S FALLING...
...BUT THE WIND'S NOT LETTING UP!
THERE'S NO ONE IN THE CITY, AND IT'S PITCH DARK!
FLASH
WHO'S THERE?!!

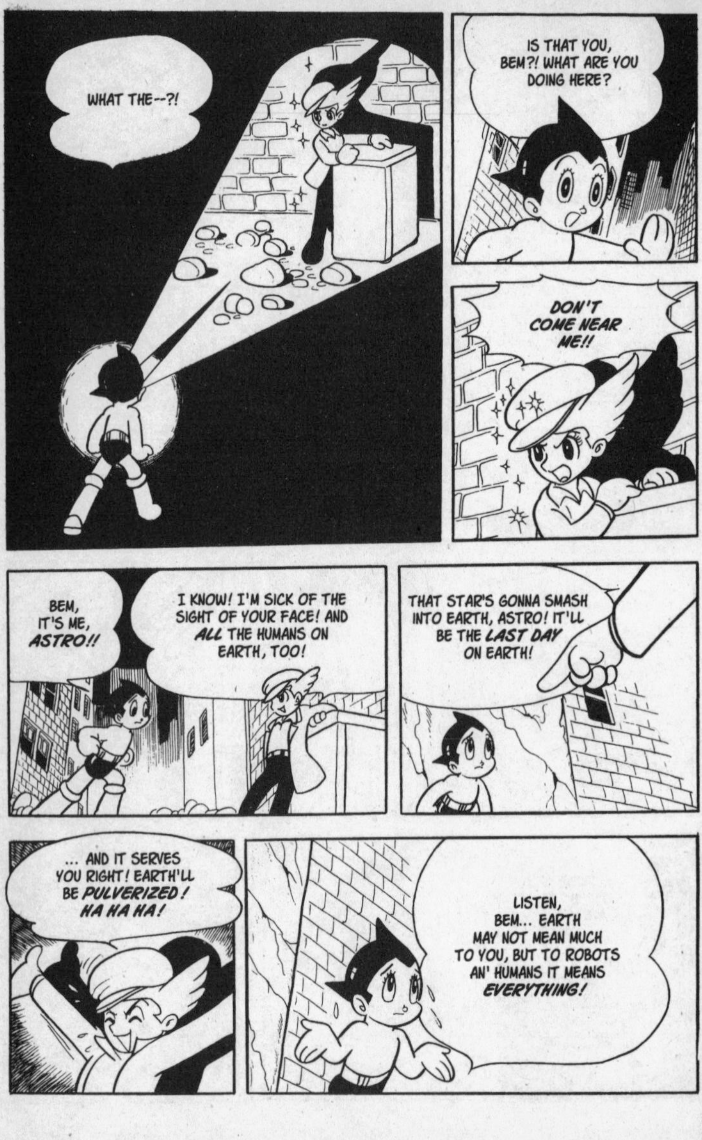
WHAT THE--?!
IS THAT YOU, BEM?! WHAT ARE YOU DOING HERE?
DON'T COME NEAR ME!!
BEM, IT'S ME, ASTRO!!
I KNOW! I'M SICK OF THE SIGHT OF YOUR FACE! AND ALL THE HUMANS ON EARTH, TOO!
THAT STAR'S GONNA SMASH INTO EARTH, ASTRO! IT'LL BE THE LAST DAY ON EARTH!
... AND IT SERVES YOU RIGHT! EARTH'LL BE PULVERIZED! HA HA HA!
LISTEN, BEM... EARTH MAY NOT MEAN MUCH TO YOU, BUT TO ROBOTS AN' HUMANS IT MEANS EVERYTHING!

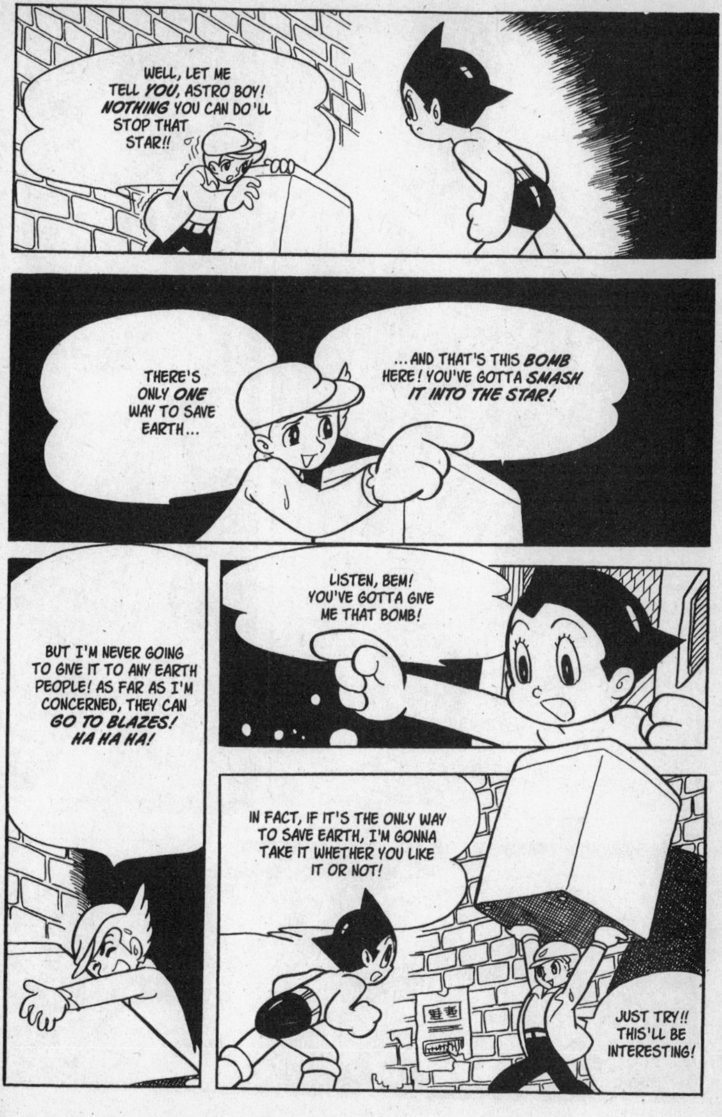
WELL, LET ME TELL YOU, ASTRO BOY! NOTHING YOU CAN DO'LL STOP THAT STAR!!
THERE'S ONLY ONE WAY TO SAVE EARTH...
...AND THAT'S THIS BOMB HERE! YOU'VE GOTTA SMASH IT INTO THE STAR!
BUT I'M NEVER GOING TO GIVE IT TO ANY EARTH PEOPLE! AS FAR AS I'M CONCERNED, THEY CAN GO TO BLAZES! HA HA HA!
LISTEN, BEM! YOU'VE GOTTA GIVE ME THAT BOMB!
IN FACT, IF IT'S THE ONLY WAY TO SAVE EARTH, I'M GONNA TAKE IT WHETHER YOU LIKE IT OR NOT!
JUST TRY!! THIS'LL BE INTERESTING!

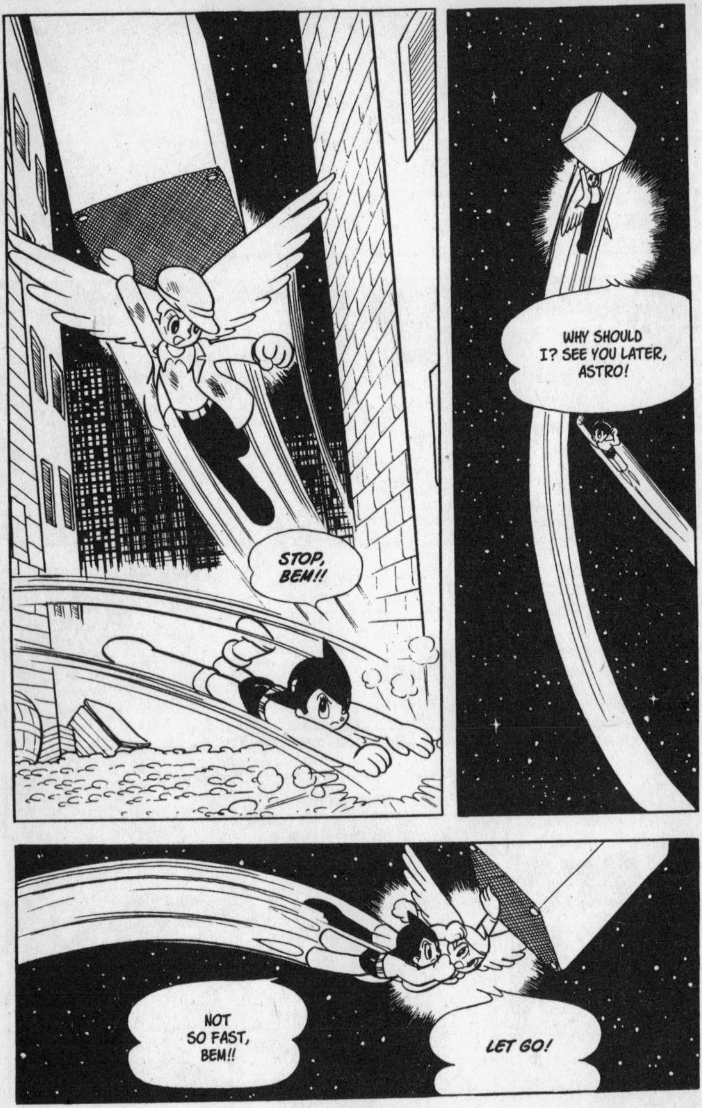
STOP, BEM!!
WHY SHOULD I? SEE YOU LATER, ASTRO!
NOT SO FAST, BEM!!
LET GO!

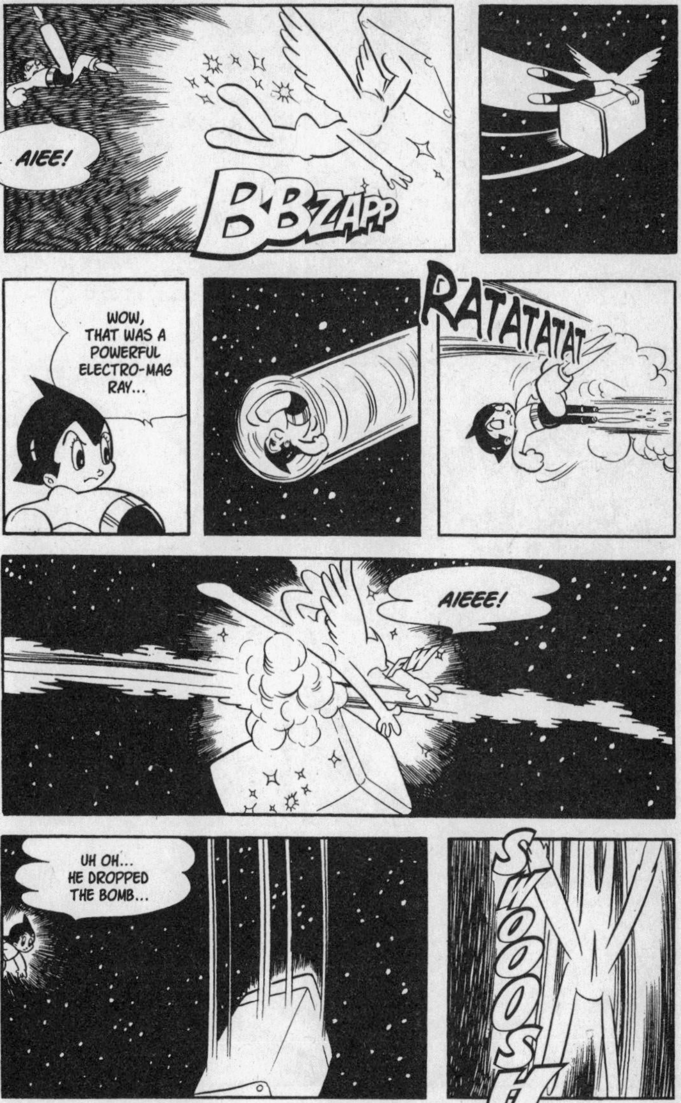
AIEE!
BBZAPP
WOW, THAT WAS A POWERFUL ELECTRO-MAG RAY...
RATATATAT
AIEEE!
UH OH... HE DROPPED THE BOMB...
SWOOOSH

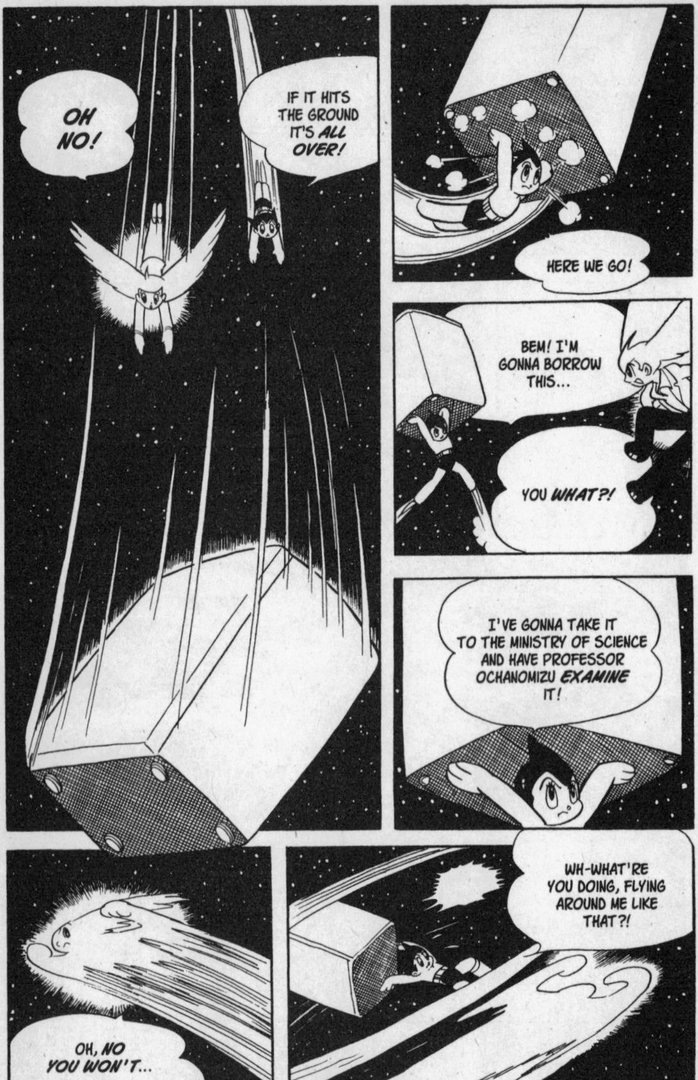

OH NO!
IF IT HITS THE GROUND IT'S ALL OVER!
HERE WE GO!
BEM! I'M GONNA BORROW THIS...
YOU WHAT?!
I'VE GONNA TAKE IT TO THE MINISTRY OF SCIENCE AND HAVE PROFESSOR OCHANOMIZU EXAMINE IT!
OH, NO YOU WON'T...
WH-WHAT'RE YOU DOING, FLYING AROUND ME LIKE THAT?!

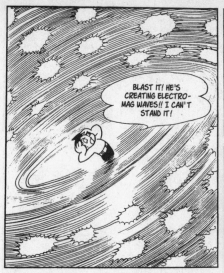

BLAST IT! HE'S CREATING ELECTRO-MAG WAVES!! I CAN'T STAND IT!

SPROING

KERSPLOOOSH

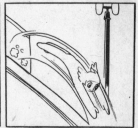

61

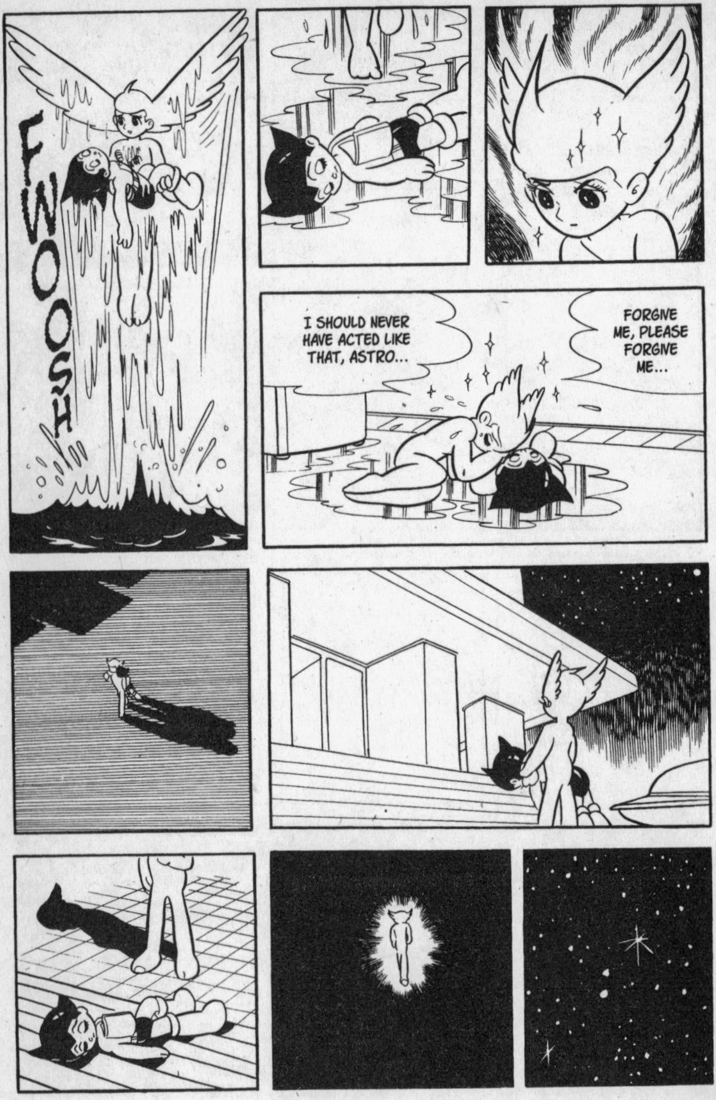
FWOOSH
I SHOULD NEVER HAVE ACTED LIKE THAT, ASTRO...
FORGIVE ME, PLEASE FORGIVE ME...

MY GOLLY GOSH YIKES YOW!!

WHAT HAPPENED TO ASTRO? THINK HE WAS CAUGHT IN A TORNADO?!

NO... HE'S TOO BROKEN UP FOR THAT...

LOOKS LIKE HE WAS CAUGHT IN A POWERFUL *ELECTRO-MAGNETIC* FIELD!

B...BUT WHAT WOULD CREATE IT?!

I DON'T KNOW IF SOMEONE DID THIS DELIBERATELY, BUT IT'S GONNA BE TOUGH TO FIX!!

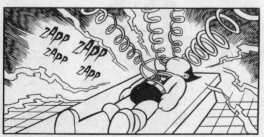

ZAPP ZAPP ZAPP ZAPP

PHEW...

63

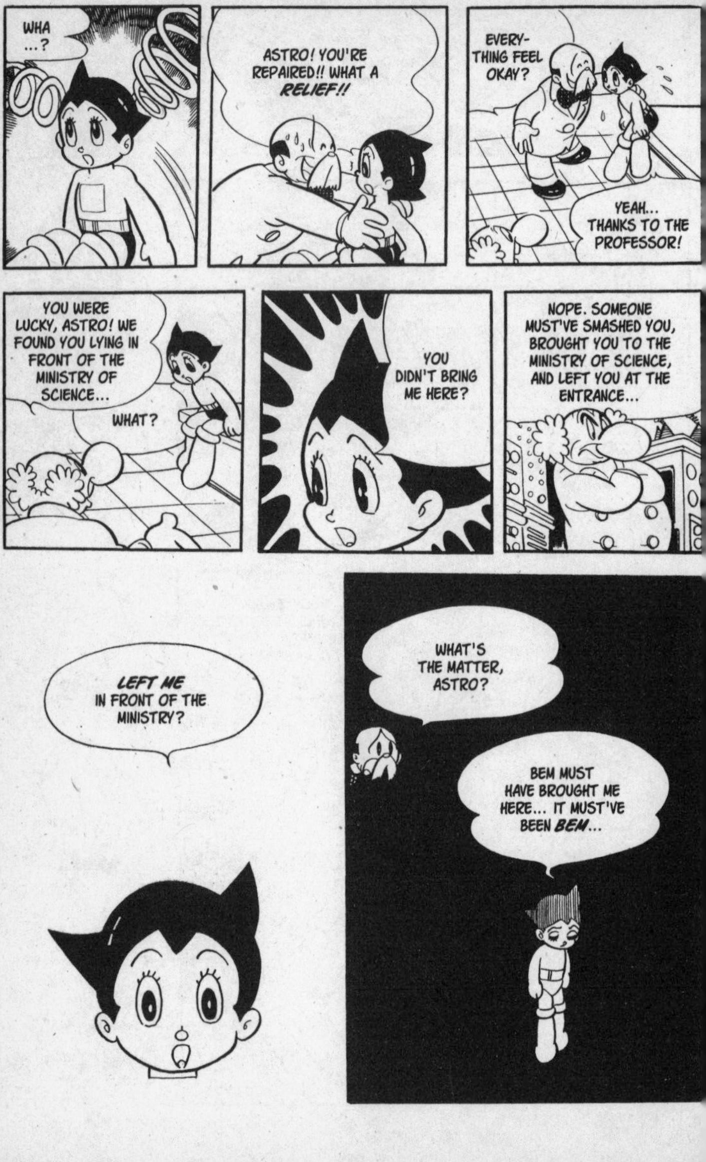
WHA ...?
ASTRO! YOU'RE REPAIRED!! WHAT A *RELIEF!!*
EVERY-THING FEEL OKAY?
YEAH... THANKS TO THE PROFESSOR!
YOU WERE LUCKY, ASTRO! WE FOUND YOU LYING IN FRONT OF THE MINISTRY OF SCIENCE...
WHAT?
YOU DIDN'T BRING ME HERE?
NOPE. SOMEONE MUST'VE SMASHED YOU, BROUGHT YOU TO THE MINISTRY OF SCIENCE, AND LEFT YOU AT THE ENTRANCE...
LEFT ME IN FRONT OF THE MINISTRY?
WHAT'S THE MATTER, ASTRO?
BEM MUST HAVE BROUGHT ME HERE... IT MUST'VE BEEN *BEM*...

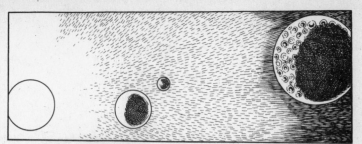

WITH EACH PASSING DAY, THE STRANGE STAR GREW BRIGHTER AND BRIGHTER IN THE WESTERN NIGHT SKY. IT BEGAN TO LOOK LIKE A GIANT EVIL EYE AND TO CAUSE INCREASINGLY VIOLENT CHANGES ON EARTH...

THERE WERE STORMS...

...WITH VIOLENT WINDS UP TO 150 MILES PER HOUR...

POWERFUL EARTHQUAKES SUDDENLY OCCURRED AROUND THE WORLD, CAUSING THE DEATHS OF TENS OF THOUSANDS OF PEOPLE. ALL THESE EVENTS WERE TRIGGERED BY THE STRANGE STAR'S GRAVITY FIELD...

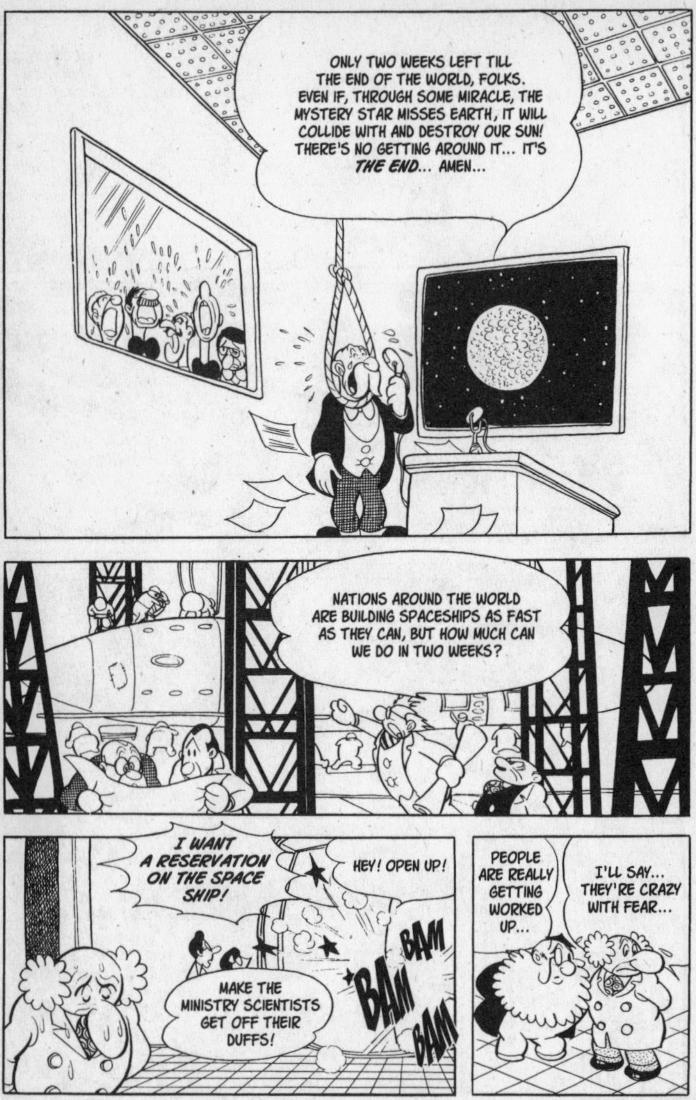
ONLY TWO WEEKS LEFT TILL THE END OF THE WORLD, FOLKS. EVEN IF, THROUGH SOME MIRACLE, THE MYSTERY STAR MISSES EARTH, IT WILL COLLIDE WITH AND DESTROY OUR SUN! THERE'S NO GETTING AROUND IT... IT'S *THE END*... AMEN...
NATIONS AROUND THE WORLD ARE BUILDING SPACESHIPS AS FAST AS THEY CAN, BUT HOW MUCH CAN WE DO IN TWO WEEKS?
I WANT A RESERVATION ON THE SPACE SHIP!
HEY! OPEN UP!
MAKE THE MINISTRY SCIENTISTS GET OFF THEIR DUFFS!
BAM
BAM
BAM
PEOPLE ARE REALLY GETTING WORKED UP...
I'LL SAY... THEY'RE CRAZY WITH FEAR...

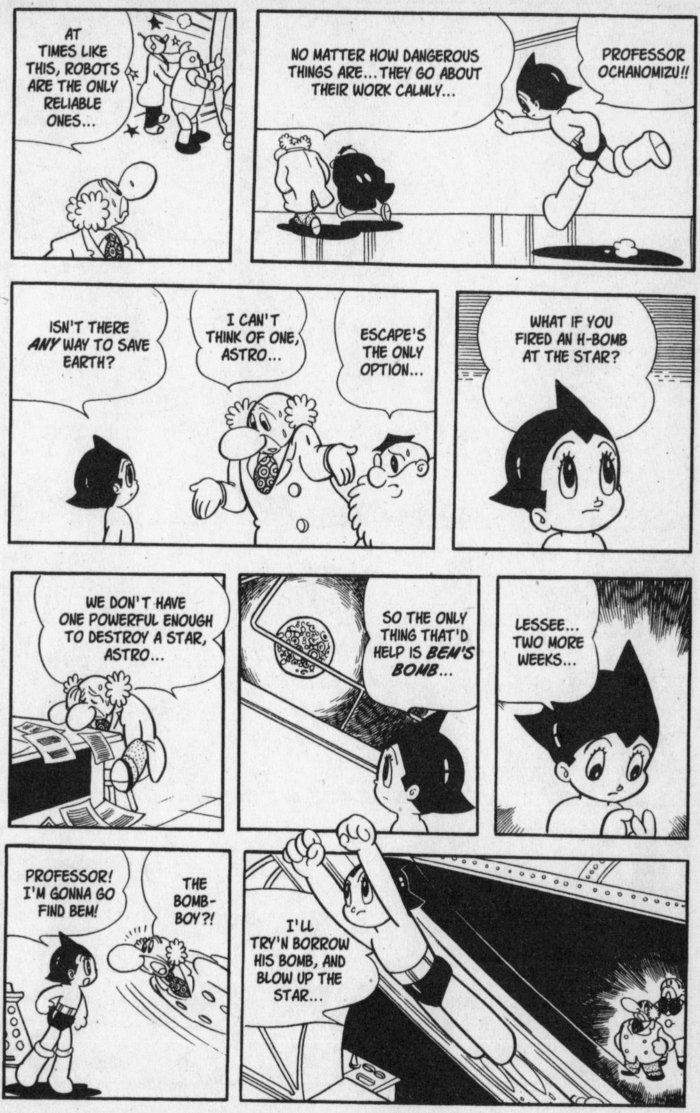

AT TIMES LIKE THIS, ROBOTS ARE THE ONLY RELIABLE ONES...
NO MATTER HOW DANGEROUS THINGS ARE... THEY GO ABOUT THEIR WORK CALMLY...
PROFESSOR OCHANOMIZU!!
ISN'T THERE ANY WAY TO SAVE EARTH?
I CAN'T THINK OF ONE, ASTRO...
ESCAPE'S THE ONLY OPTION...
WHAT IF YOU FIRED AN H-BOMB AT THE STAR?
WE DON'T HAVE ONE POWERFUL ENOUGH TO DESTROY A STAR, ASTRO...
SO THE ONLY THING THAT'D HELP IS BEM'S BOMB...
LESSEE... TWO MORE WEEKS...
PROFESSOR! I'M GONNA GO FIND BEM!
THE BOMB-BOY?!
I'LL TRY'N BORROW HIS BOMB, AND BLOW UP THE STAR...

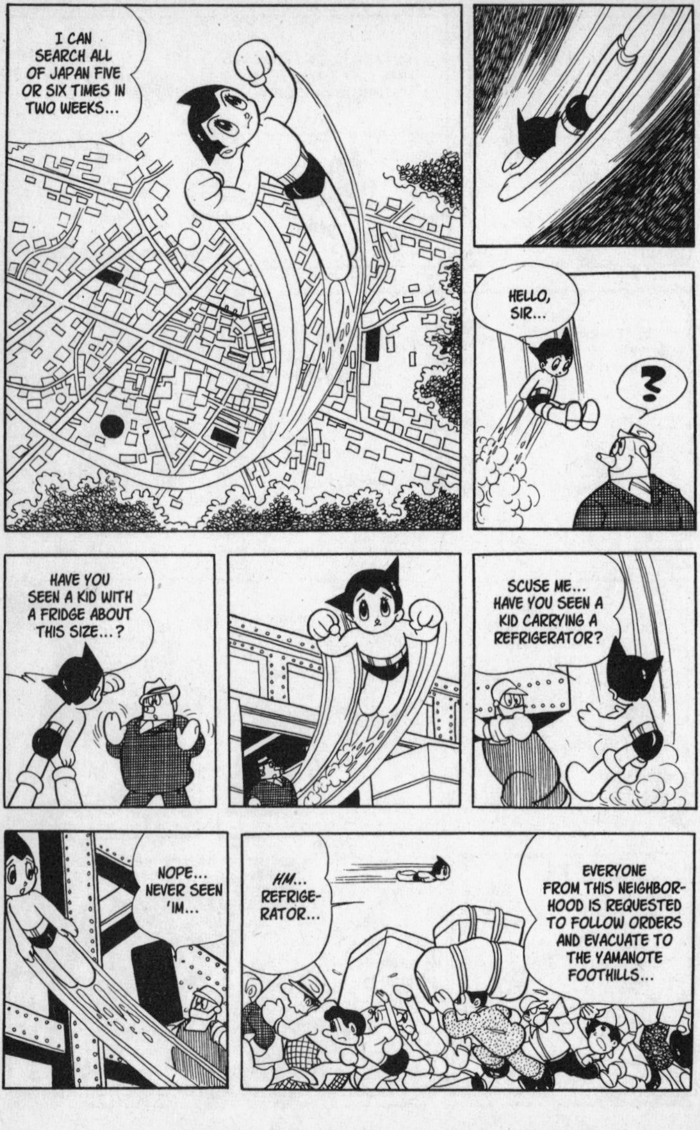
I CAN SEARCH ALL OF JAPAN FIVE OR SIX TIMES IN TWO WEEKS...
HELLO, SIR...
?
HAVE YOU SEEN A KID WITH A FRIDGE ABOUT THIS SIZE...?
SCUSE ME... HAVE YOU SEEN A KID CARRYING A REFRIGERATOR?
NOPE... NEVER SEEN 'IM...
HM... REFRIGE-RATOR...
EVERYONE FROM THIS NEIGHBOR-HOOD IS REQUESTED TO FOLLOW ORDERS AND EVACUATE TO THE YAMANOTE FOOTHILLS...

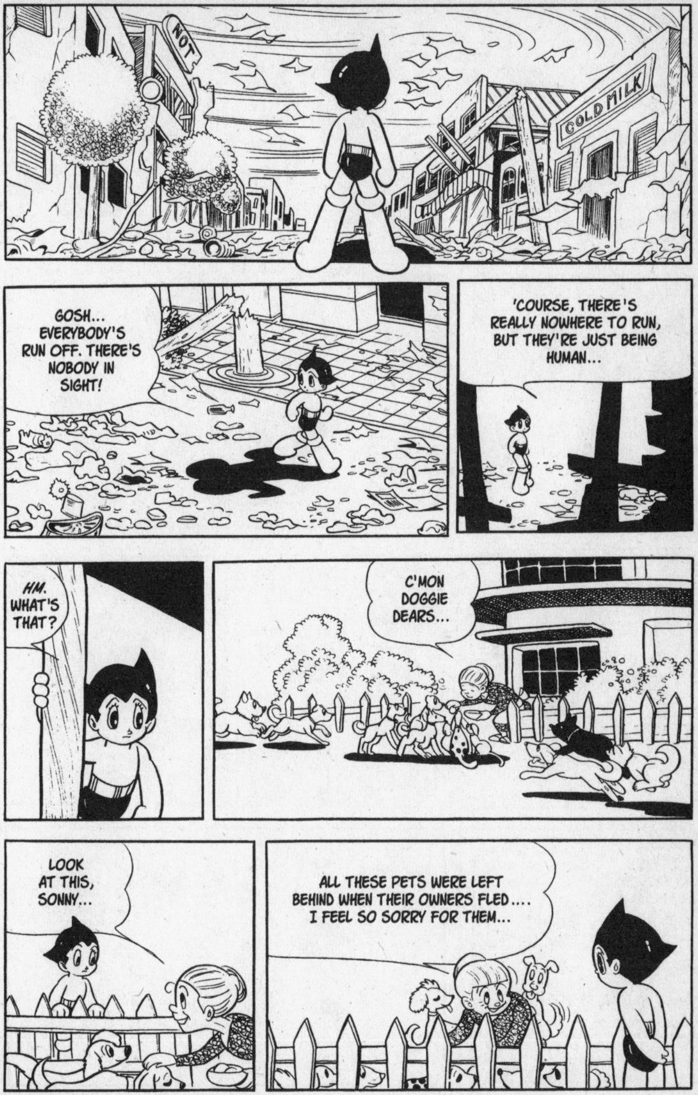
NOT
GOLD MILK
GOSH... EVERYBODY'S RUN OFF. THERE'S NOBODY IN SIGHT!
'COURSE, THERE'S REALLY NOWHERE TO RUN, BUT THEY'RE JUST BEING HUMAN...
HM. WHAT'S THAT?
C'MON DOGGIE DEARS...
LOOK AT THIS, SONNY...
ALL THESE PETS WERE LEFT BEHIND WHEN THEIR OWNERS FLED.... I FEEL SO SORRY FOR THEM...

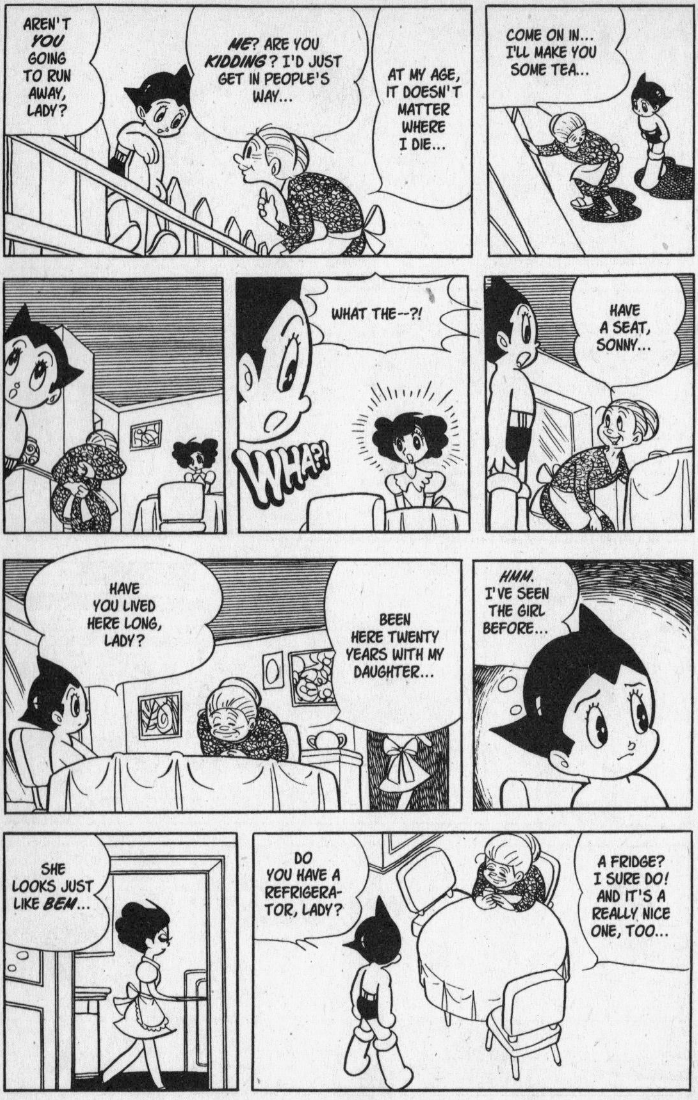

AREN'T *YOU* GOING TO RUN AWAY, LADY?
ME? ARE YOU *KIDDING*? I'D JUST GET IN PEOPLE'S WAY...
AT MY AGE, IT DOESN'T MATTER WHERE I DIE...
COME ON IN... I'LL MAKE YOU SOME TEA...
WHAT THE--?!
WHA?!
HAVE A SEAT, SONNY...
HAVE YOU LIVED HERE LONG, LADY?
BEEN HERE TWENTY YEARS WITH MY DAUGHTER...
HMM. I'VE SEEN THE GIRL BEFORE...
SHE LOOKS JUST LIKE *BEM*...
DO YOU HAVE A REFRIGERA-TOR, LADY?
A FRIDGE? I SURE DO! AND IT'S A REALLY NICE ONE, TOO...

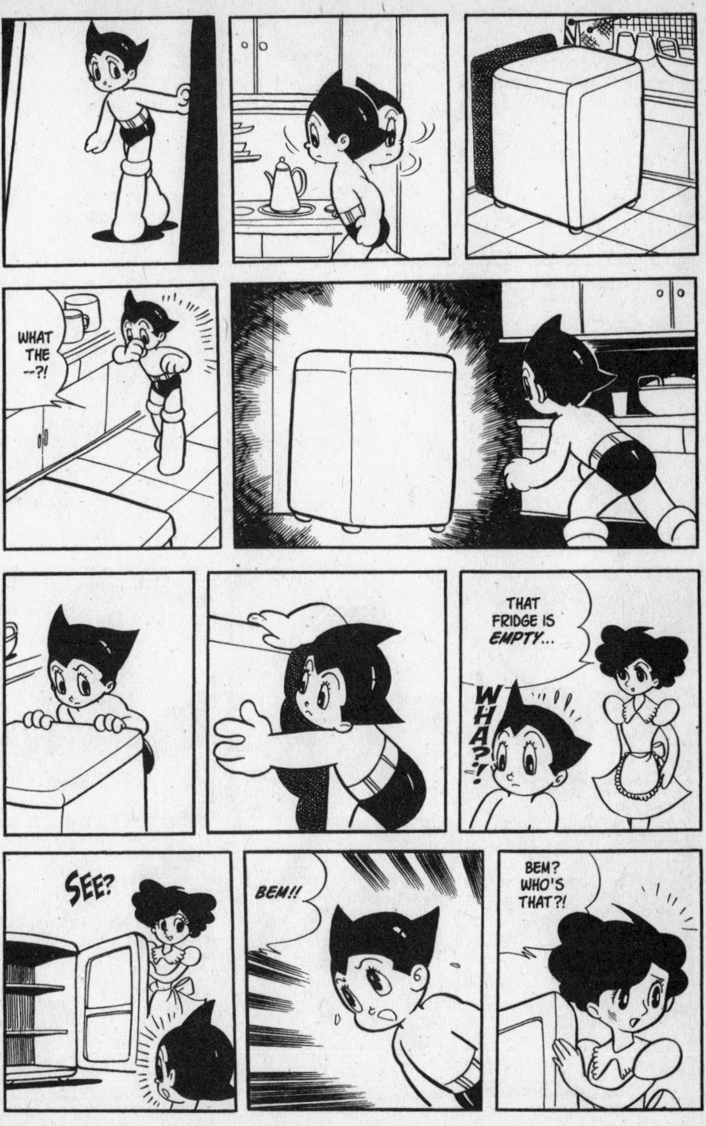
WHAT THE --?!
THAT FRIDGE IS EMPTY...
WHA?!
SEE?
BEM!!
BEM? WHO'S THAT?!

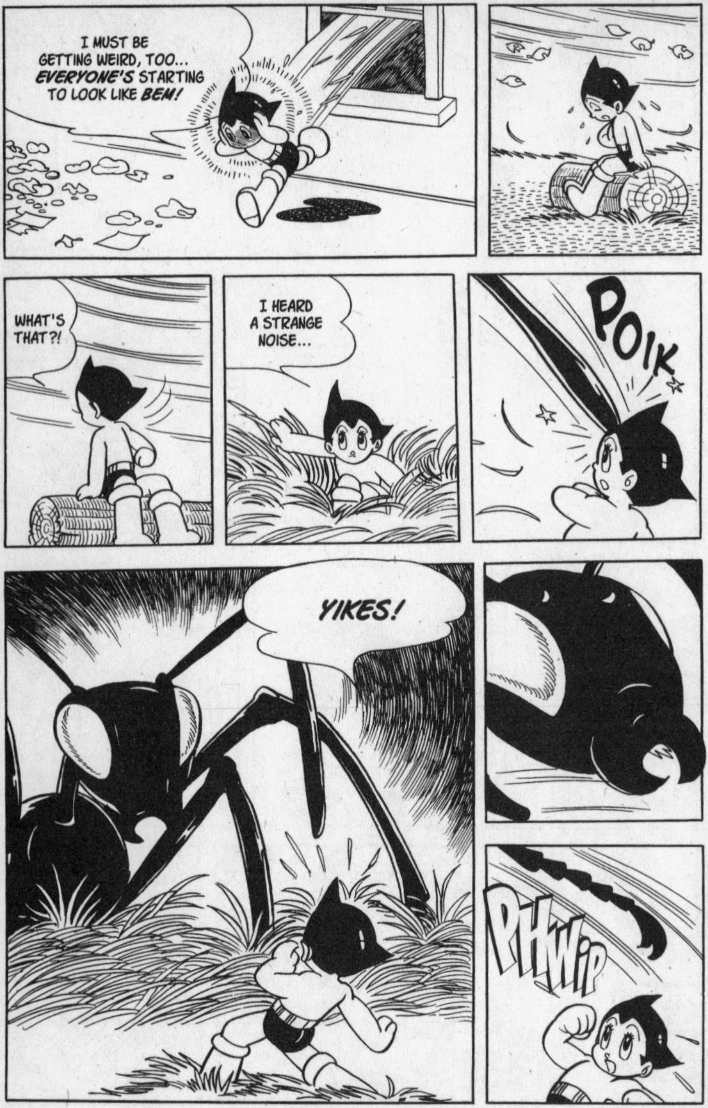
I MUST BE GETTING WEIRD, TOO... EVERYONE'S STARTING TO LOOK LIKE BEM!
WHAT'S THAT?!
I HEARD A STRANGE NOISE...
POIK
YIKES!
PHWIP

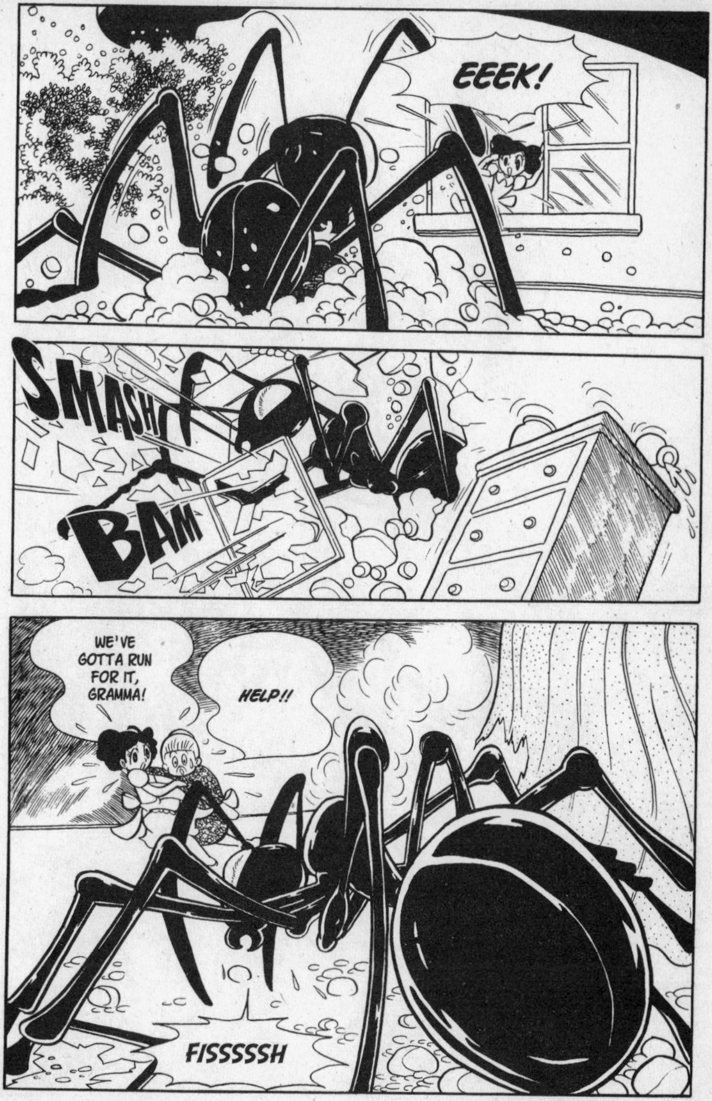
EEEK!
SMASH
BAM
WE'VE GOTTA RUN FOR IT, GRAMMA!
HELP!!
FISSSSSH

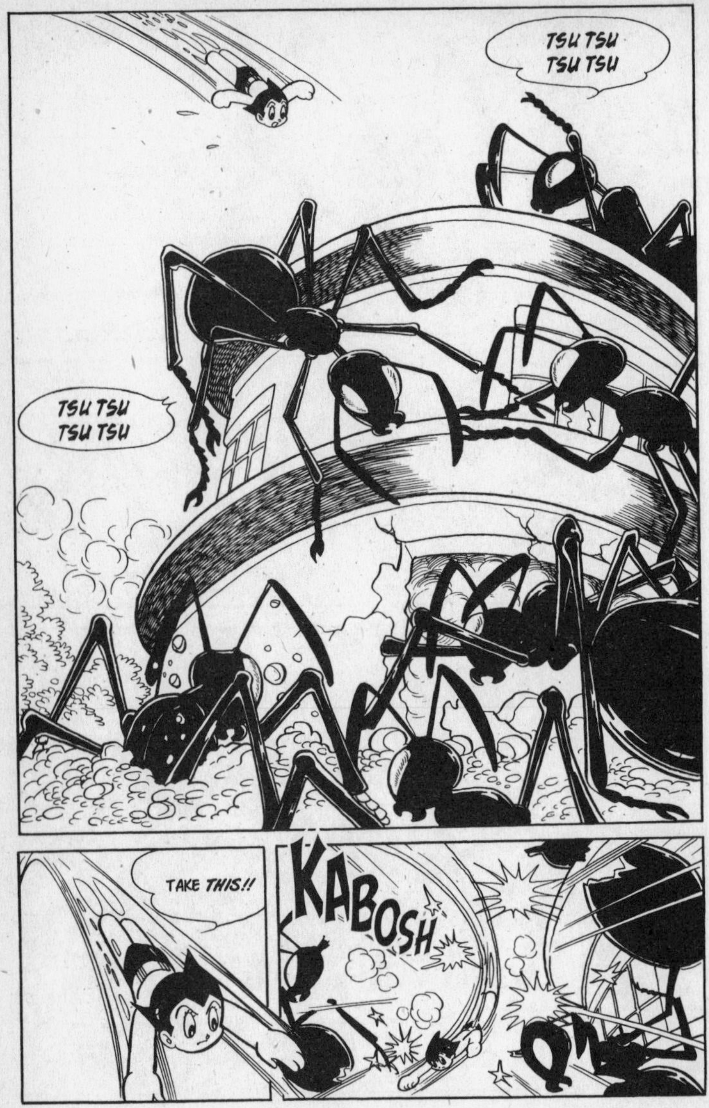
TSU TSU
TSU TSU
TSU TSU
TSU TSU
TAKE THIS!!
KABOSH

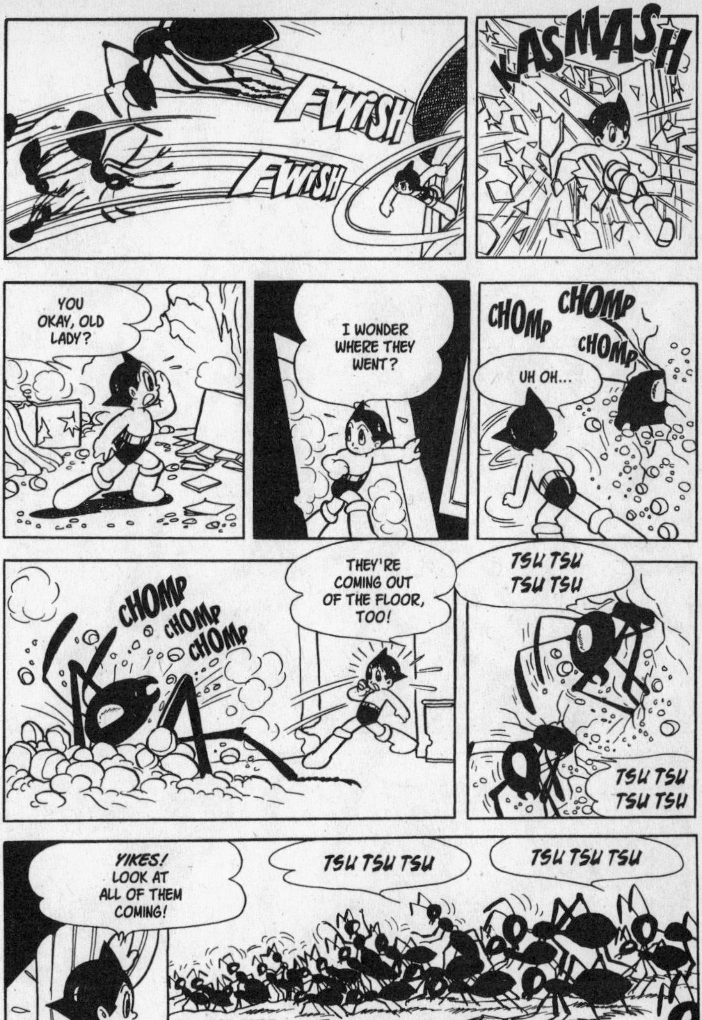
FWISH
FWISH
KASMASH
YOU OKAY, OLD LADY?
I WONDER WHERE THEY WENT?
CHOMP
CHOMP
CHOMP
UH OH...
CHOMP
CHOMP
CHOMP
THEY'RE COMING OUT OF THE FLOOR, TOO!
TSU TSU TSU TSU
TSU TSU TSU TSU
YIKES! LOOK AT ALL OF THEM COMING!
TSU TSU TSU
TSU TSU TSU

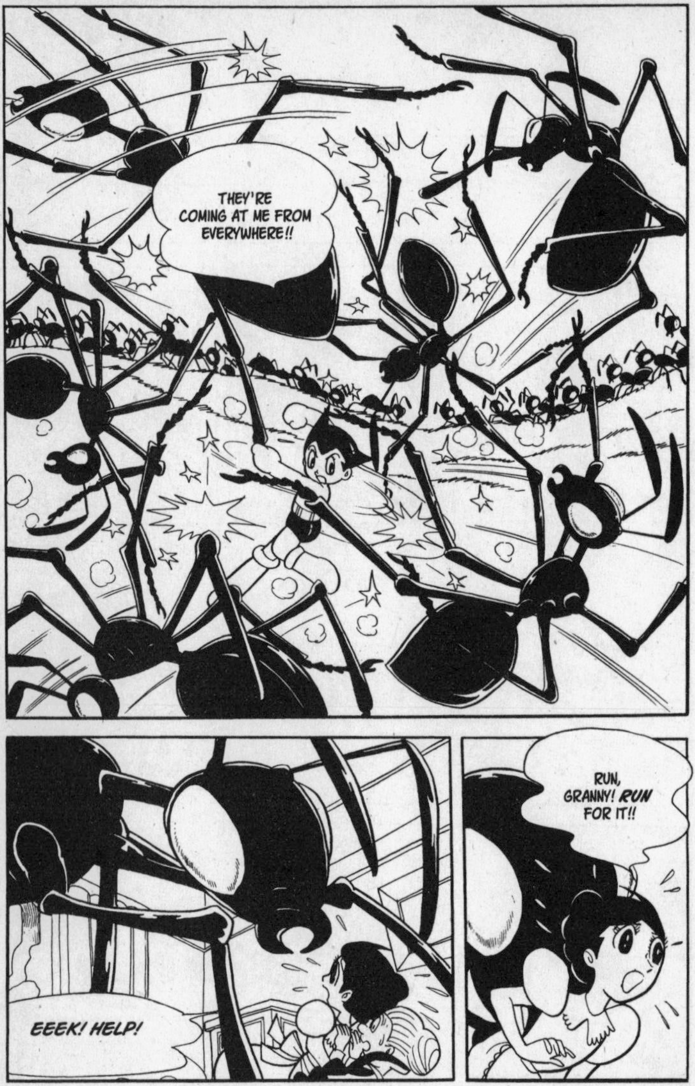
THEY'RE COMING AT ME FROM EVERYWHERE!!
EEEK! HELP!
RUN, GRANNY! *RUN* FOR IT!!

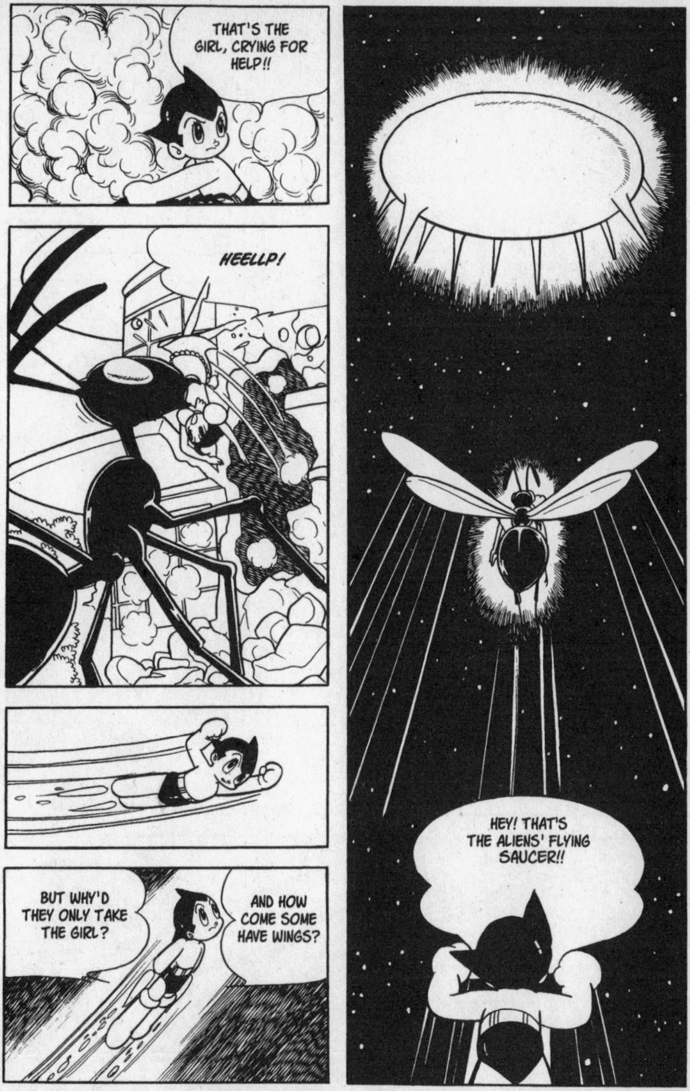
THAT'S THE GIRL, CRYING FOR HELP!!
HEELLP!
BUT WHY'D THEY ONLY TAKE THE GIRL?
AND HOW COME SOME HAVE WINGS?
HEY! THAT'S THE ALIENS' FLYING SAUCER!!

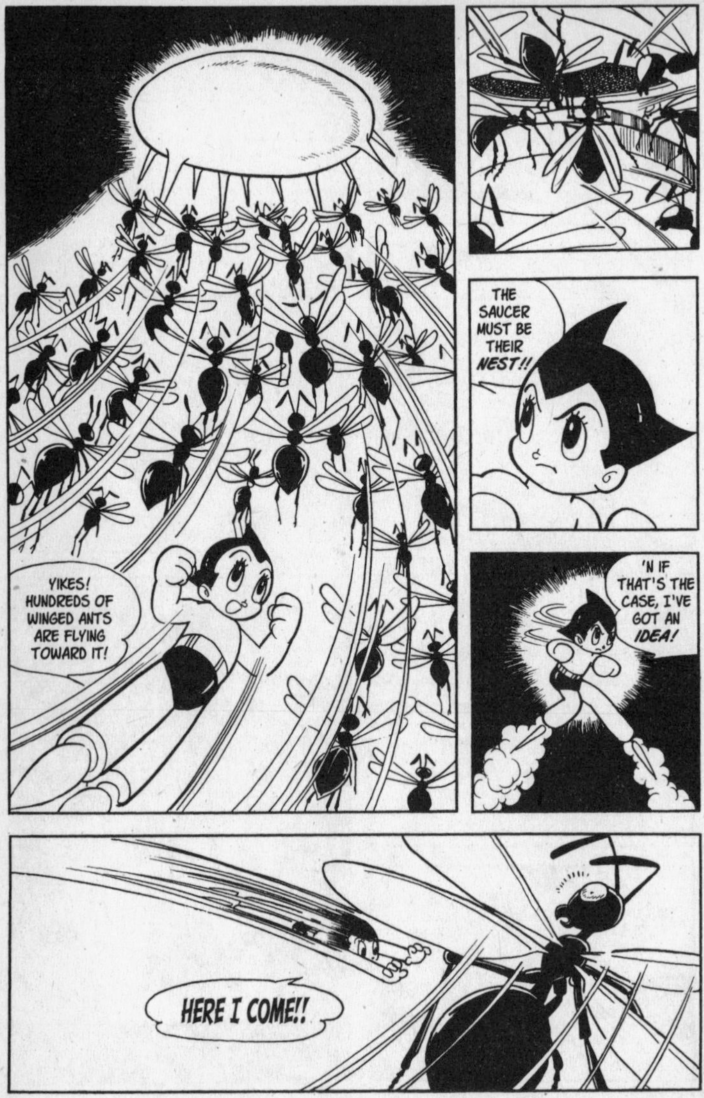
YIKES! HUNDREDS OF WINGED ANTS ARE FLYING TOWARD IT!
THE SAUCER MUST BE THEIR NEST!!
'N IF THAT'S THE CASE, I'VE GOT AN IDEA!
HERE I COME!!

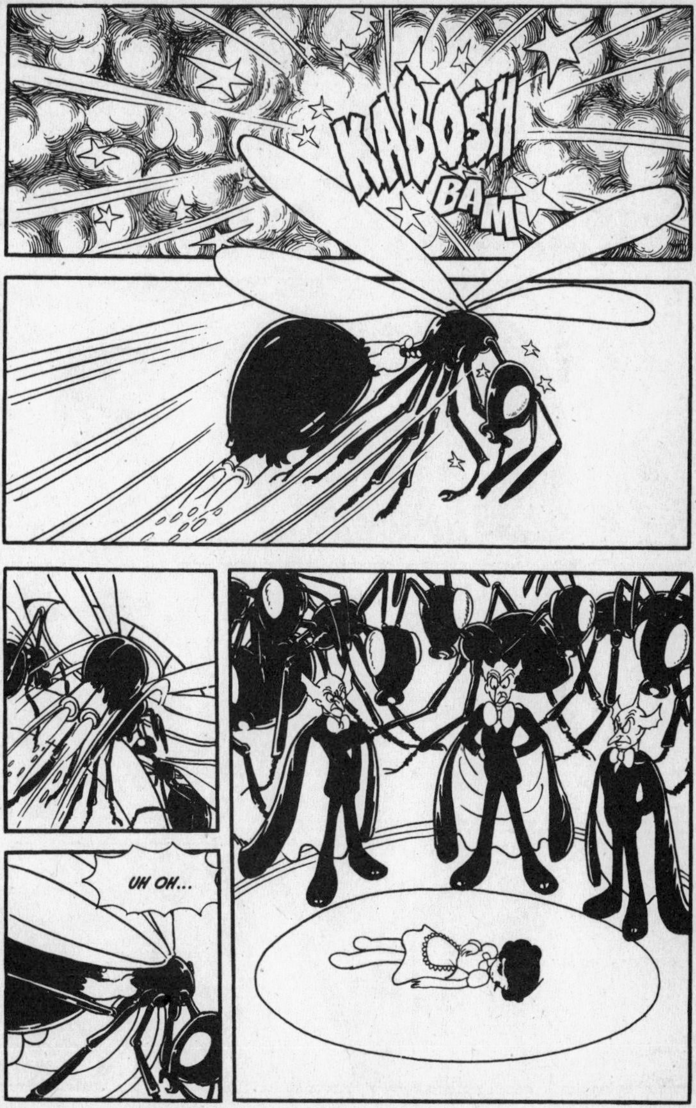
KABOSH
BAM!
UH OH...

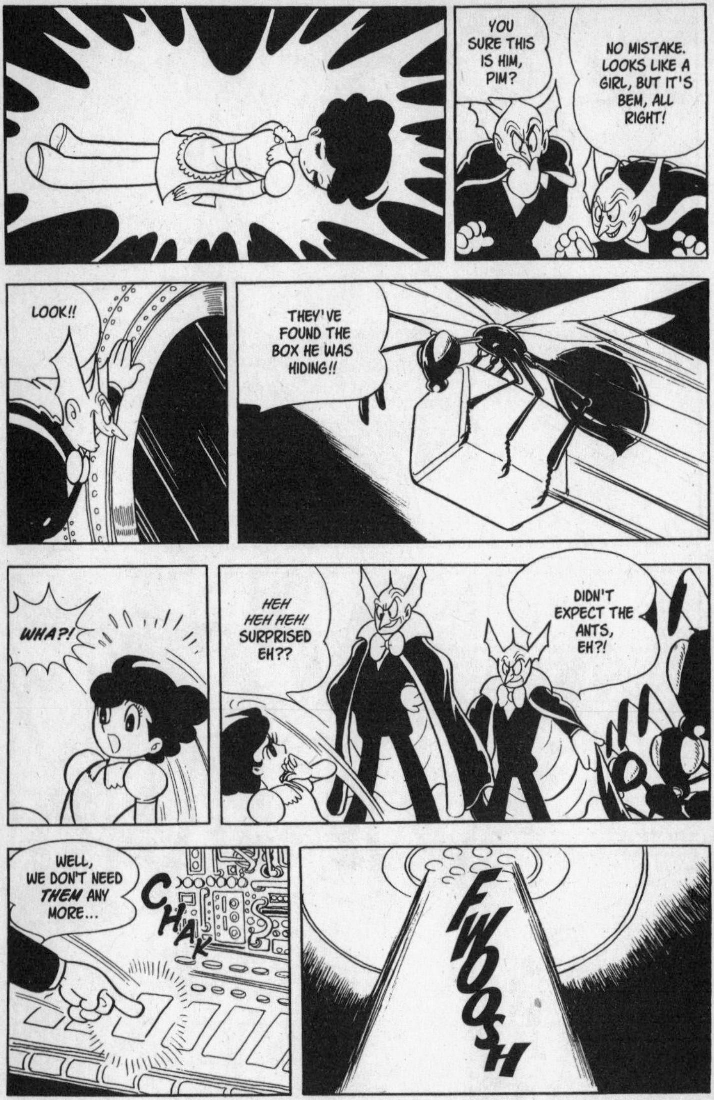
YOU SURE THIS IS HIM, PIM?
NO MISTAKE. LOOKS LIKE A GIRL, BUT IT'S BEM, ALL RIGHT!
LOOK!!
THEY'VE FOUND THE BOX HE WAS HIDING!!
WHA?!
HEH HEH HEH! SURPRISED EH??
DIDN'T EXPECT THE ANTS, EH?!
WELL, WE DON'T NEED *THEM* ANY MORE...
CHAK
FWOOSH

FLASH

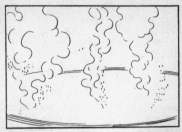

WE FOUND OUT WHERE YOU WERE HIDING, INJECTED *SUPER GROWTH HORMONES* INTO A NEARBY ANT HIVE, AND ENLARGED 'EM!!

THEN WE HIJACKED THEIR BRAINWAVES AND HAD 'EM BRING YOU BACK HERE!! AND THEY BROUGHT THE BOX, TOO!!

YOU DON'T NEED THIS ANY-MORE!

YOU'RE A *BOMB* THAT *WE* MADE!

WHY'D YOU RUN AWAY TO EARTH, ANYWAY?!

YEAH... EARTH'LL BE GONE IN TWO OR THREE DAYS! WHAT'S IT TO YOU?!!

....
....

LEMME SHOW YOU SOMETHING! *WE* SENT THAT STAR TO CRASH INTO EARTH *AND* THE SUN!

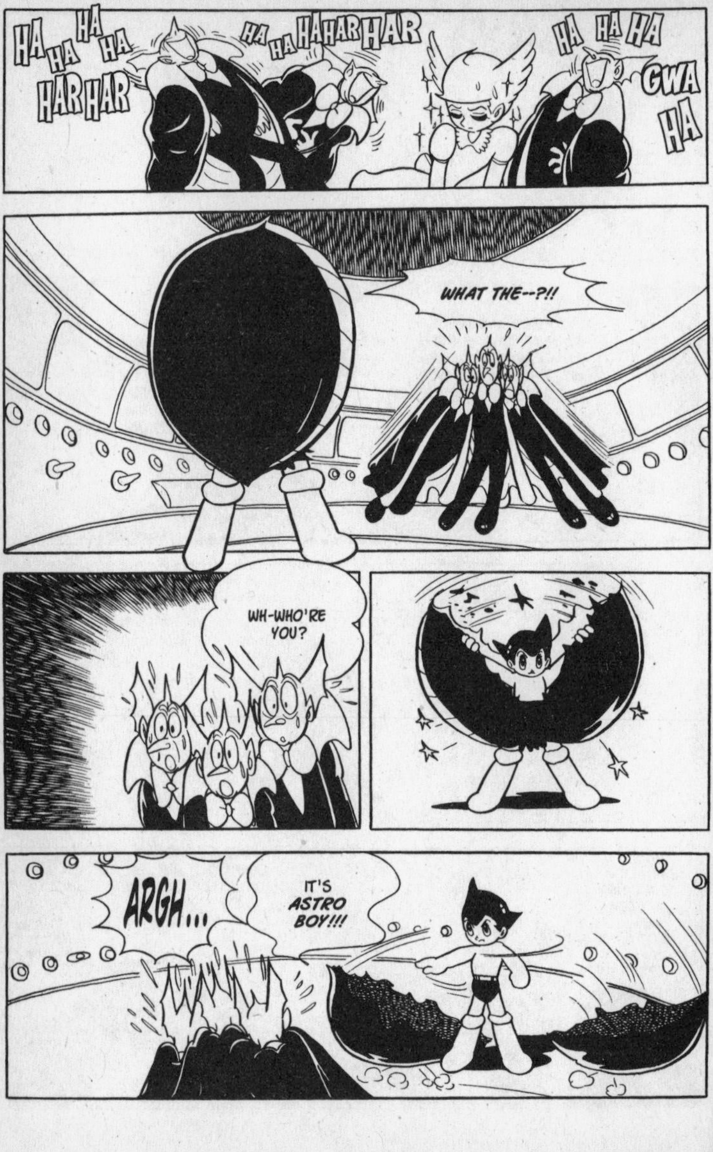
HA HA HA HA HAR HAR
HA HA HAHAR HAR
HA HA HA
GWA HA
WHAT THE--?!!
WH-WHO'RE YOU?
ARGH...
IT'S ASTRO BOY!!!

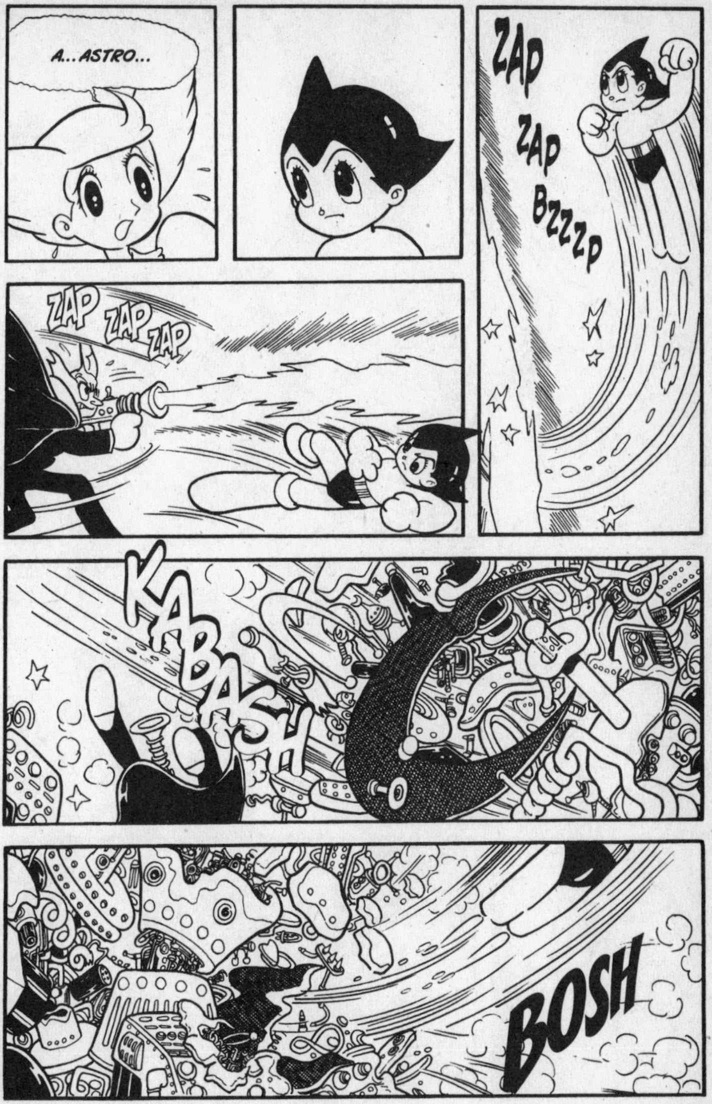
A...ASTRO...
ZAP
ZAP
BZZZZP
ZAP ZAP ZAP
KABASH
BOSH

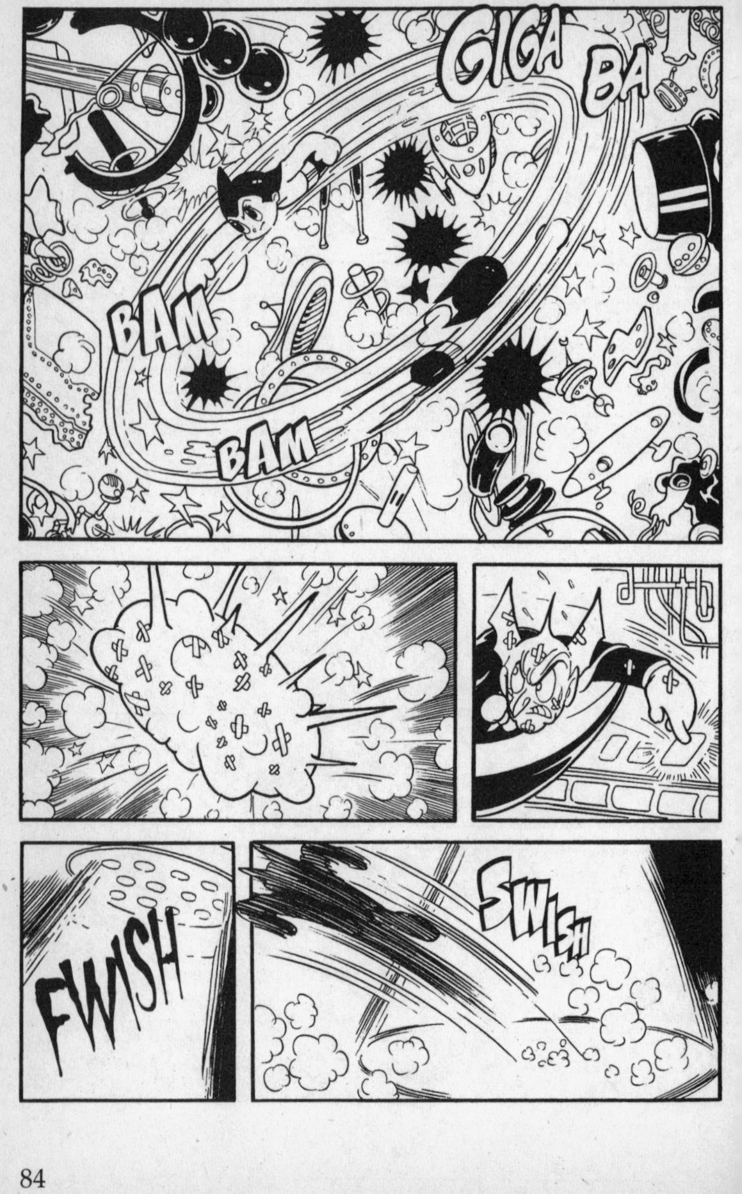
GIGA
BA
BAM
BAM
FWISH
SWISH

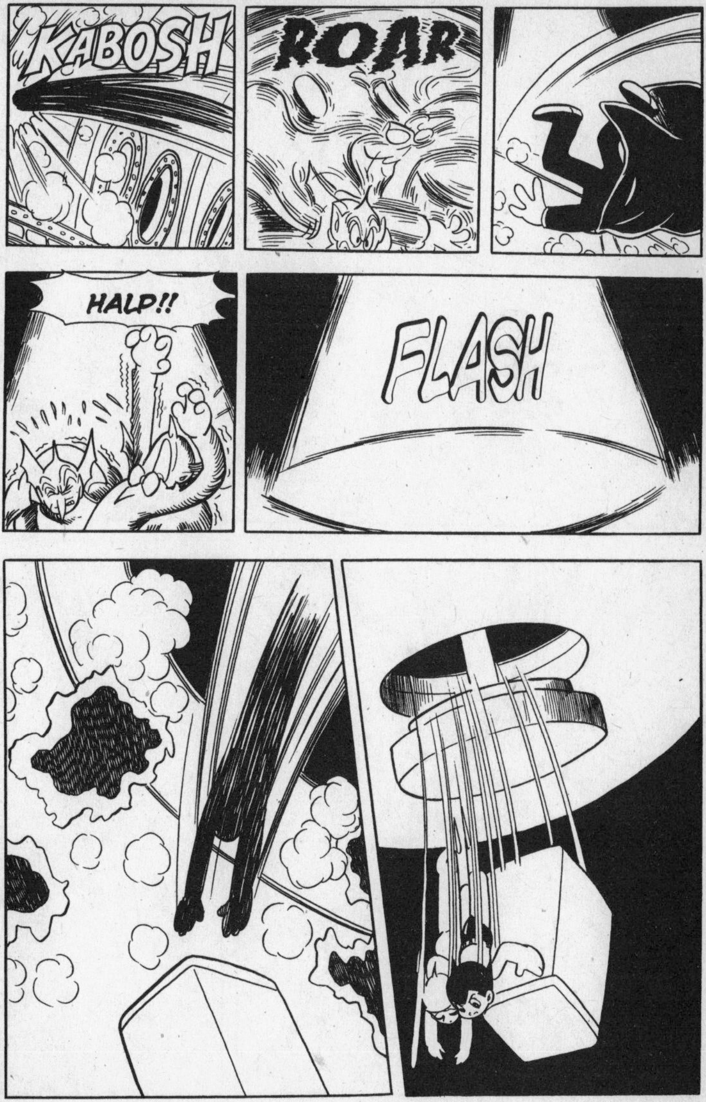
KABOSH
ROAR
HALP!!
FLASH

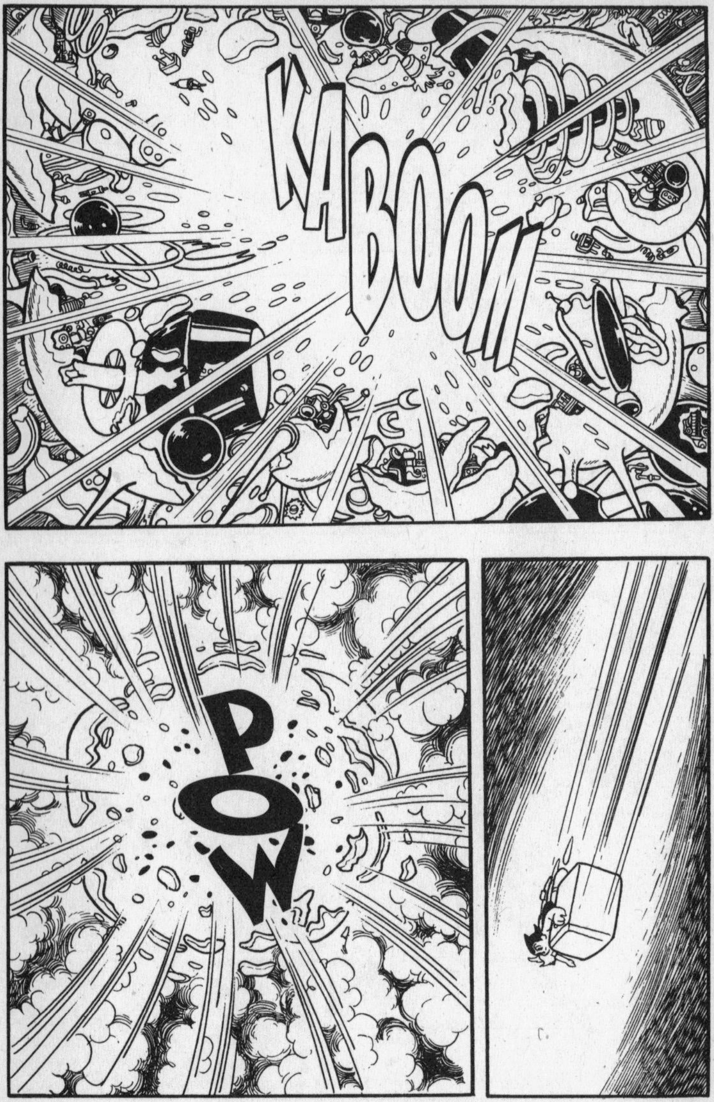
KABOOM
POW

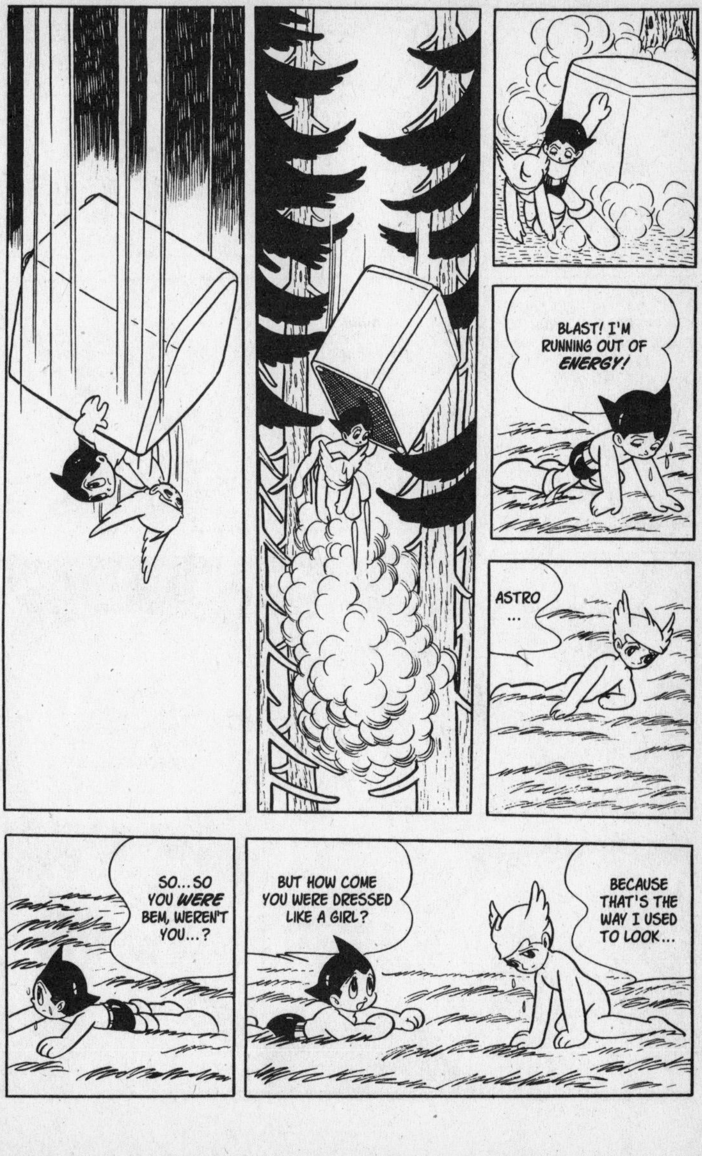

BLAST! I'M RUNNING OUT OF *ENERGY!*
ASTRO ...
SO...SO YOU ***WERE*** BEM, WEREN'T YOU...?
BUT HOW COME YOU WERE DRESSED LIKE A GIRL?
BECAUSE THAT'S THE WAY I USED TO LOOK...

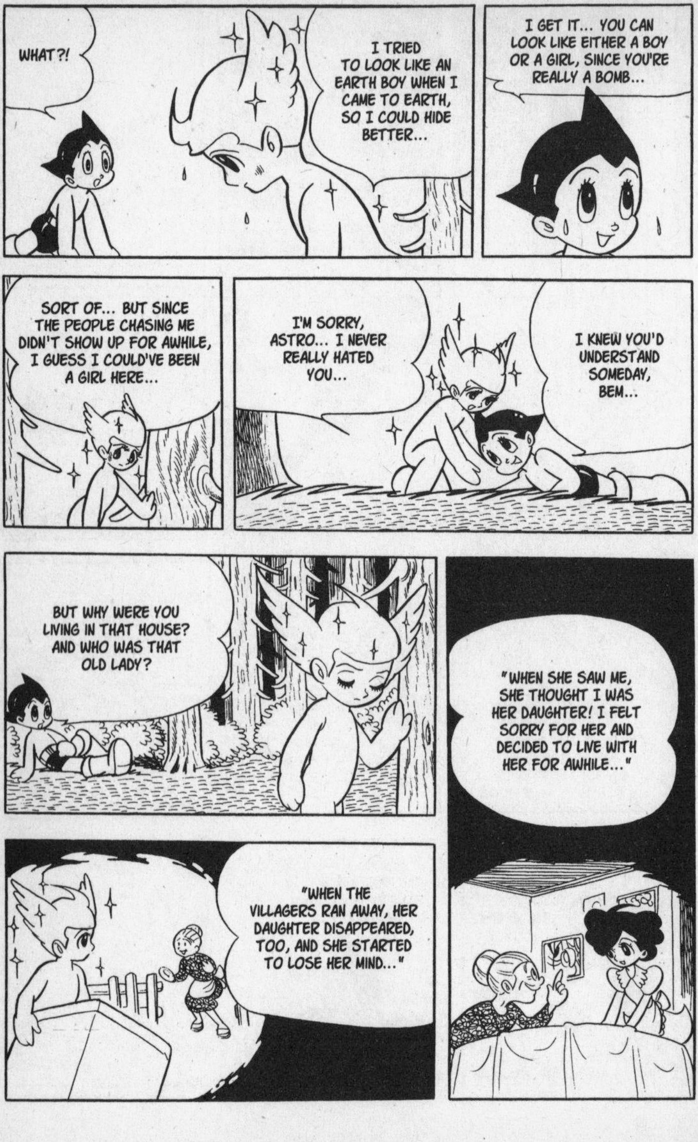
WHAT?!
I TRIED TO LOOK LIKE AN EARTH BOY WHEN I CAME TO EARTH, SO I COULD HIDE BETTER...
I GET IT... YOU CAN LOOK LIKE EITHER A BOY OR A GIRL, SINCE YOU'RE REALLY A BOMB...
SORT OF... BUT SINCE THE PEOPLE CHASING ME DIDN'T SHOW UP FOR AWHILE, I GUESS I COULD'VE BEEN A GIRL HERE...
I'M SORRY, ASTRO... I NEVER REALLY HATED YOU...
I KNEW YOU'D UNDERSTAND SOMEDAY, BEM...
BUT WHY WERE YOU LIVING IN THAT HOUSE? AND WHO WAS THAT OLD LADY?
"WHEN SHE SAW ME, SHE THOUGHT I WAS HER DAUGHTER! I FELT SORRY FOR HER AND DECIDED TO LIVE WITH HER FOR AWHILE..."
"WHEN THE VILLAGERS RAN AWAY, HER DAUGHTER DISAPPEARED, TOO, AND SHE STARTED TO LOSE HER MIND..."

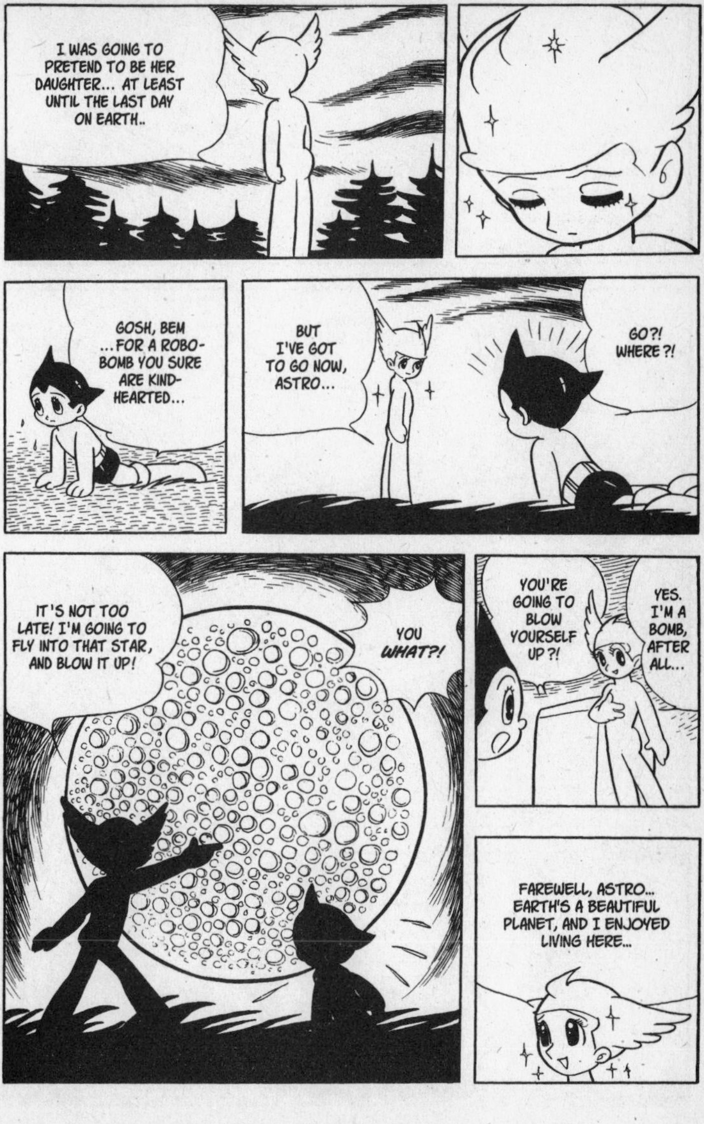
I WAS GOING TO PRETEND TO BE HER DAUGHTER... AT LEAST UNTIL THE LAST DAY ON EARTH..
GOSH, BEM ...FOR A ROBO-BOMB YOU SURE ARE KIND-HEARTED...
BUT I'VE GOT TO GO NOW, ASTRO...
GO?! WHERE?!
IT'S NOT TOO LATE! I'M GOING TO FLY INTO THAT STAR, AND BLOW IT UP!
YOU *WHAT?!*
YOU'RE GOING TO BLOW YOURSELF UP?!
YES. I'M A BOMB, AFTER ALL...
FAREWELL, ASTRO... EARTH'S A BEAUTIFUL PLANET, AND I ENJOYED LIVING HERE...

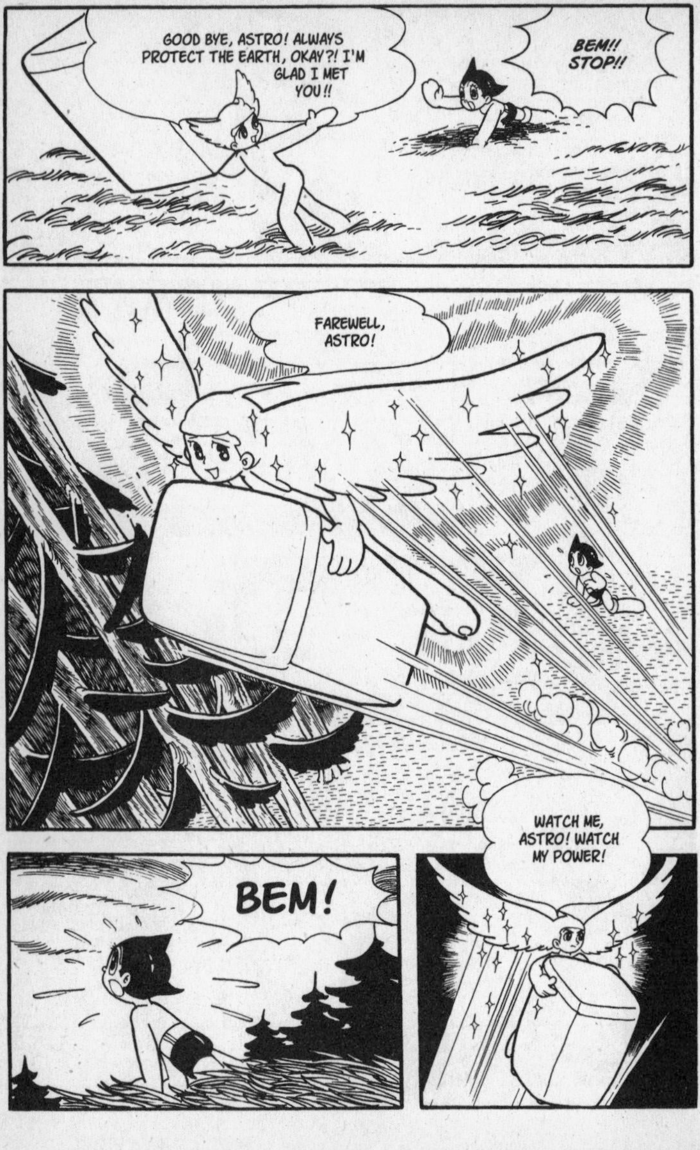
GOOD BYE, ASTRO! ALWAYS PROTECT THE EARTH, OKAY?! I'M GLAD I MET YOU!!
BEM!! STOP!!
FAREWELL, ASTRO!
BEM!
WATCH ME, ASTRO! WATCH MY POWER!

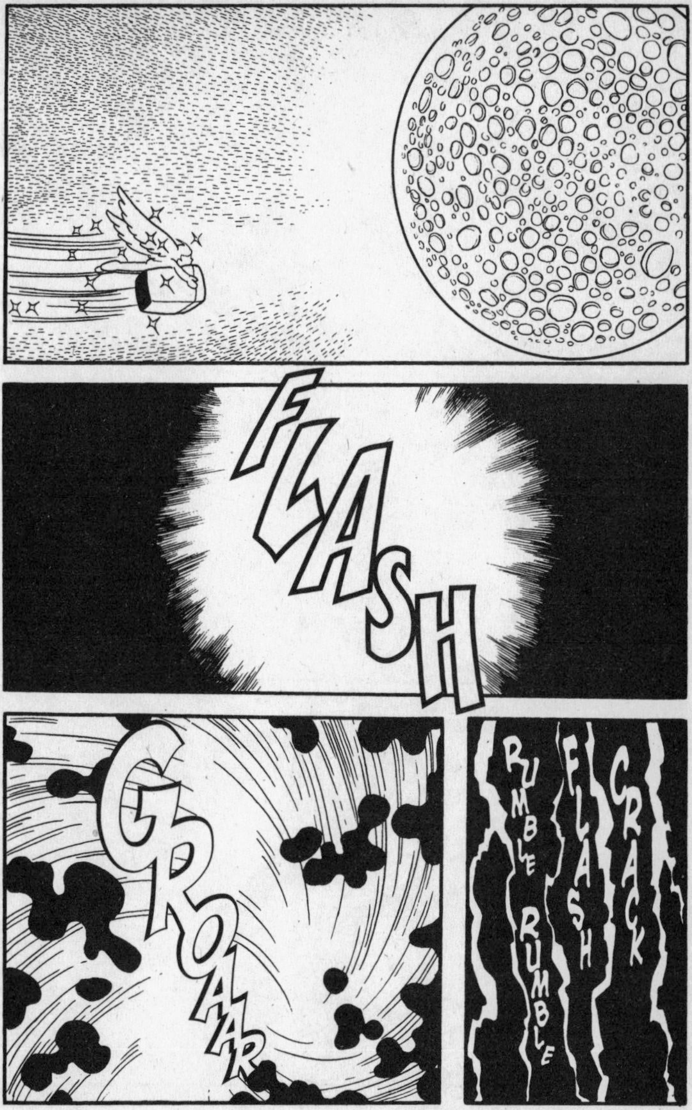
FLASH
GROOAAR
RUMBLE RUMBLE
FLASH
CRACK

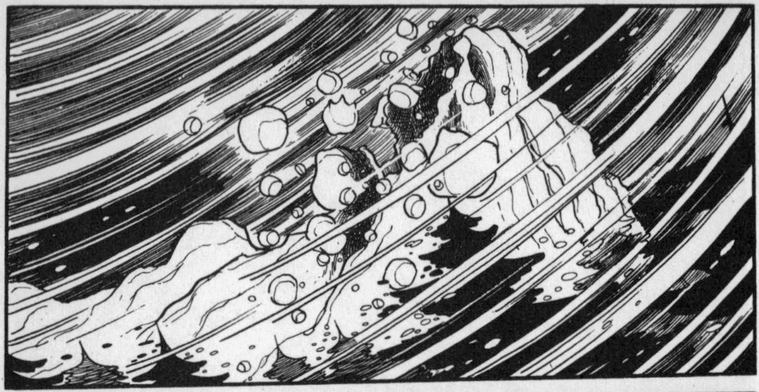
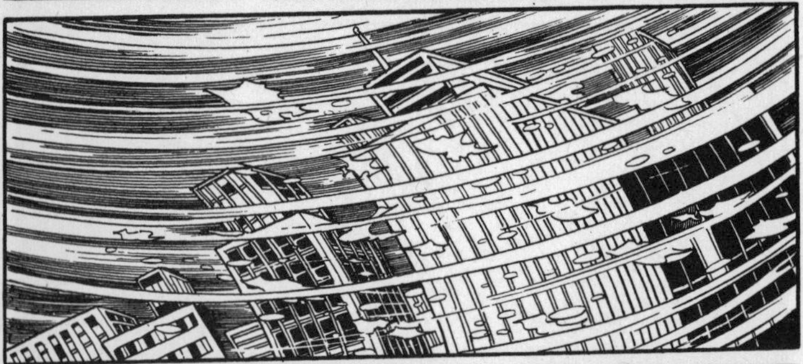
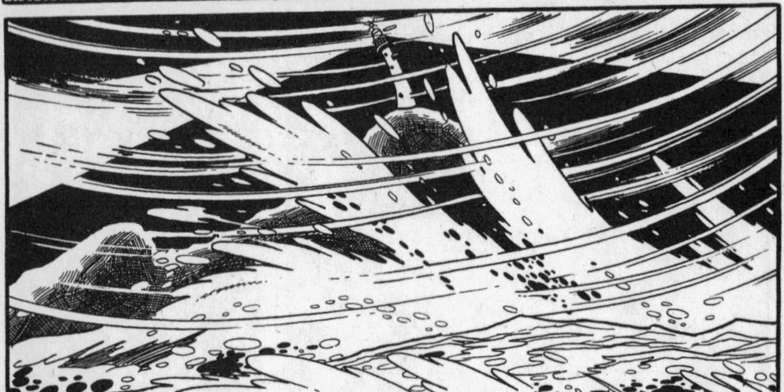

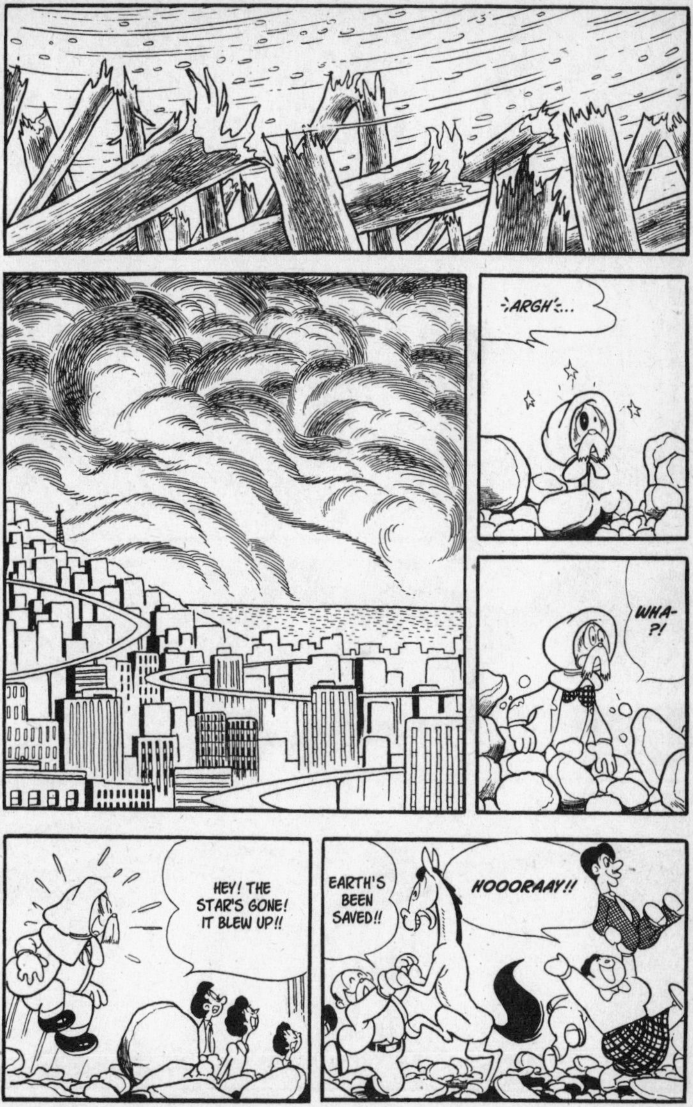
ARGH...
WHA-?!
HEY! THE STAR'S GONE! IT BLEW UP!!
EARTH'S BEEN SAVED!!
HOOORAAY!!

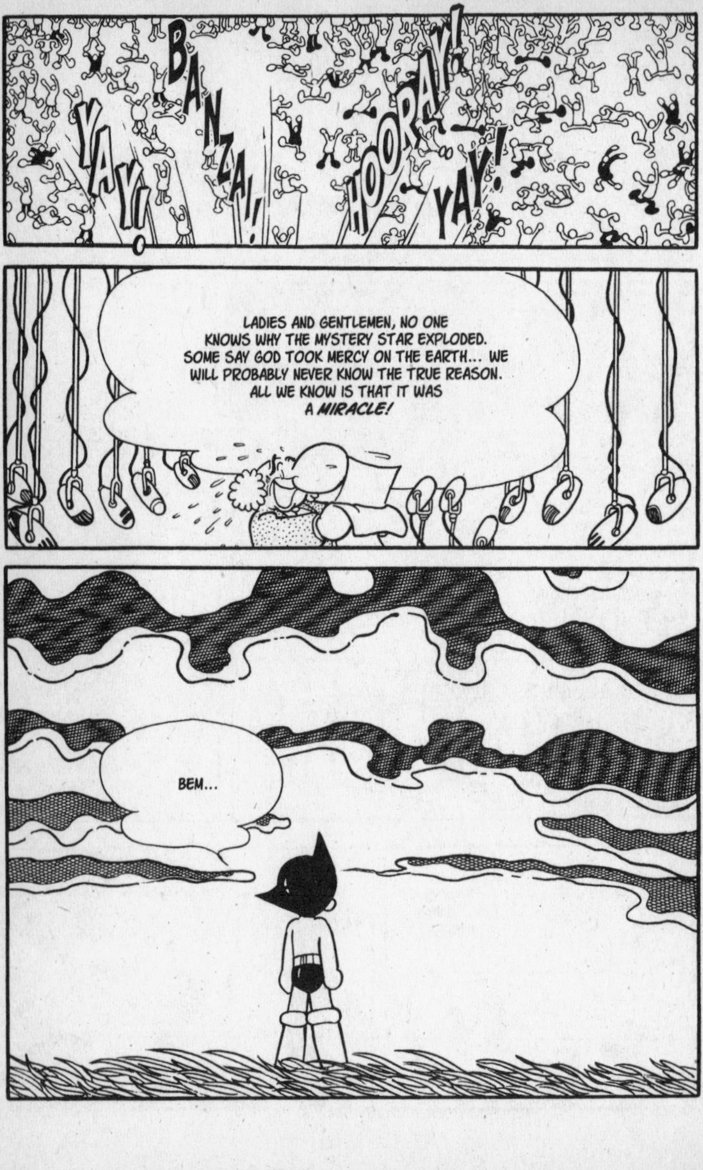
YAY!
BANZAI!!
HOORAY!
YAY!
LADIES AND GENTLEMEN, NO ONE KNOWS WHY THE MYSTERY STAR EXPLODED. SOME SAY GOD TOOK MERCY ON THE EARTH... WE WILL PROBABLY NEVER KNOW THE TRUE REASON. ALL WE KNOW IS THAT IT WAS A MIRACLE!
BEM...

SUBTERRANEAN TANK

First serialized from October to November
1959 in *Shonen* magazine.

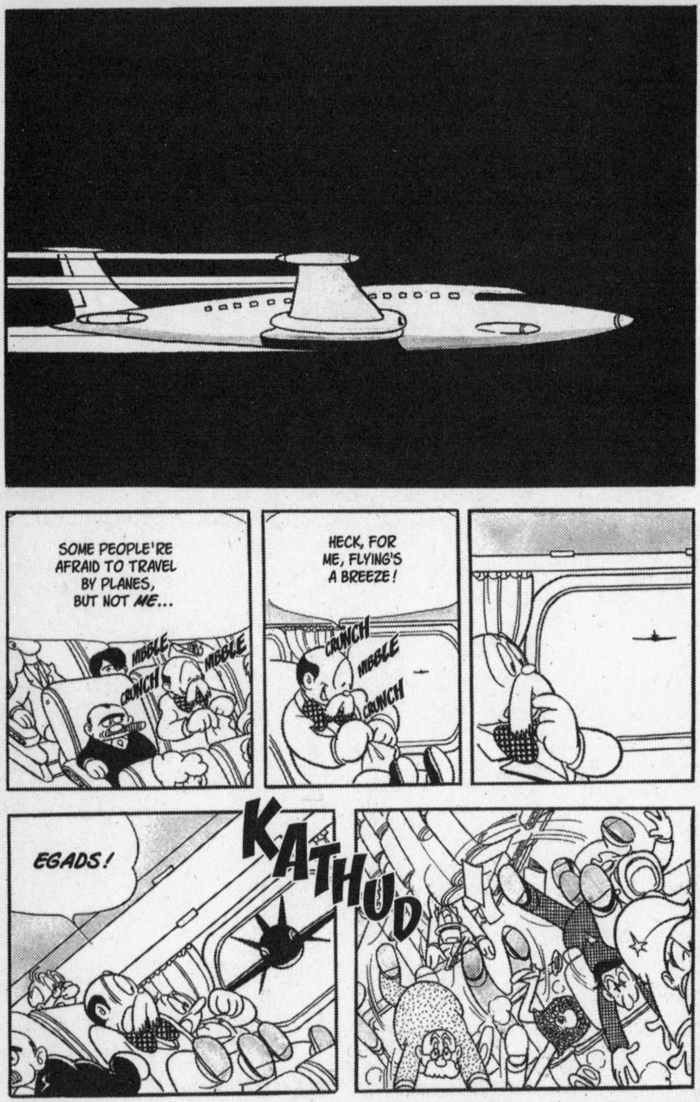
SOME PEOPLE'RE AFRAID TO TRAVEL BY PLANES, BUT NOT *ME*...
NIBBLE
CRUNCH
NIBBLE
HECK, FOR ME, FLYING'S A BREEZE!
CRUNCH
NIBBLE
CRUNCH
EGADS!
KATHUD

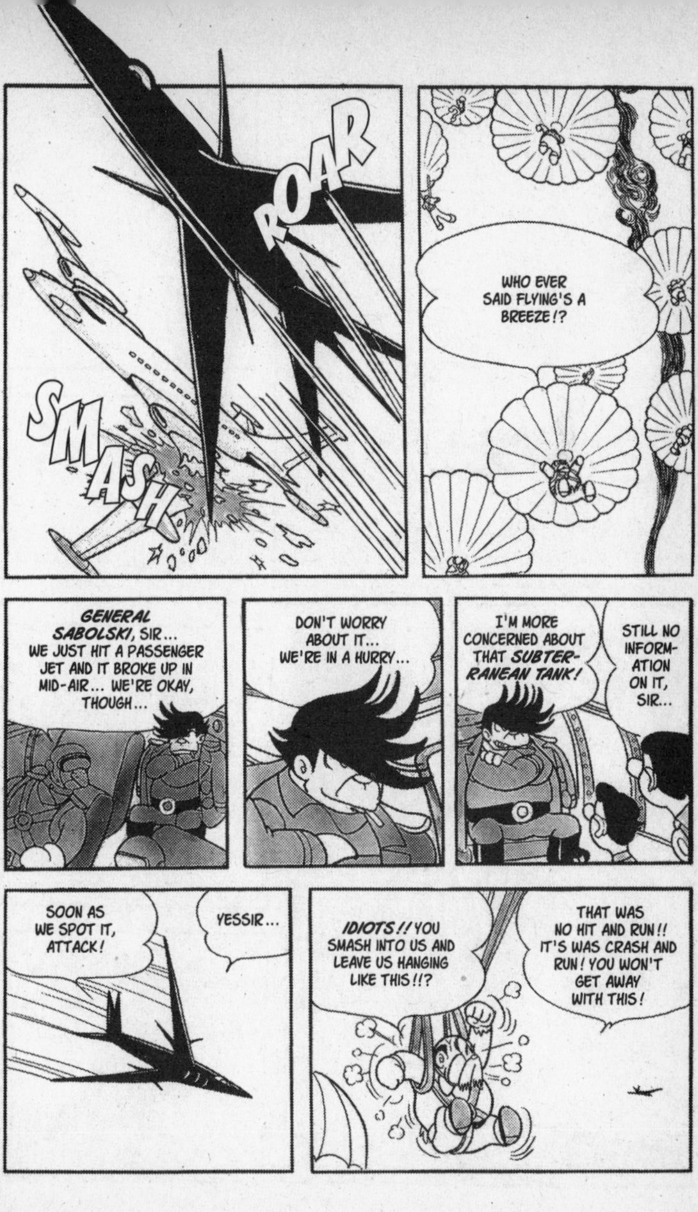
ROAR
SMASH
WHO EVER SAID FLYING'S A BREEZE!?
GENERAL SABOLSKI, SIR... WE JUST HIT A PASSENGER JET AND IT BROKE UP IN MID-AIR... WE'RE OKAY, THOUGH...
DON'T WORRY ABOUT IT... WE'RE IN A HURRY...
I'M MORE CONCERNED ABOUT THAT SUBTER-RANEAN TANK!
STILL NO INFORM-ATION ON IT, SIR...
SOON AS WE SPOT IT, ATTACK!
YESSIR...
IDIOTS!! YOU SMASH INTO US AND LEAVE US HANGING LIKE THIS!!?
THAT WAS NO HIT AND RUN!! IT'S WAS CRASH AND RUN! YOU WON'T GET AWAY WITH THIS!

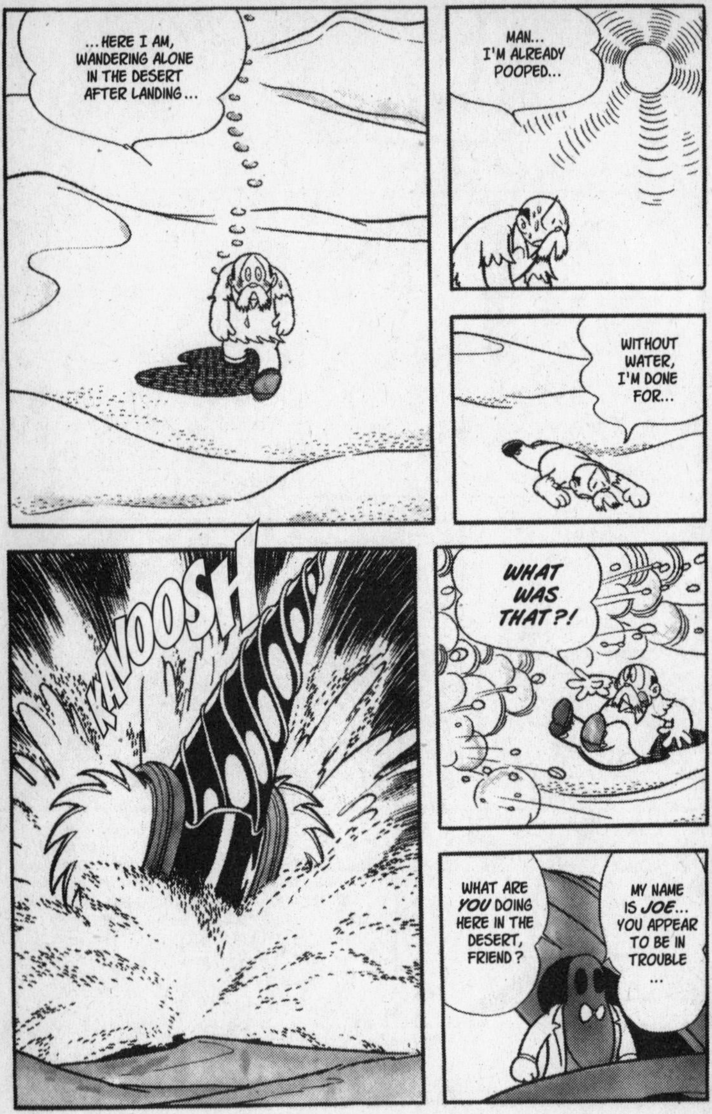
...HERE I AM, WANDERING ALONE IN THE DESERT AFTER LANDING...
MAN... I'M ALREADY POOPED...
WITHOUT WATER, I'M DONE FOR...
KAVOOSH
WHAT WAS THAT?!
WHAT ARE YOU DOING HERE IN THE DESERT, FRIEND?
MY NAME IS JOE... YOU APPEAR TO BE IN TROUBLE ...

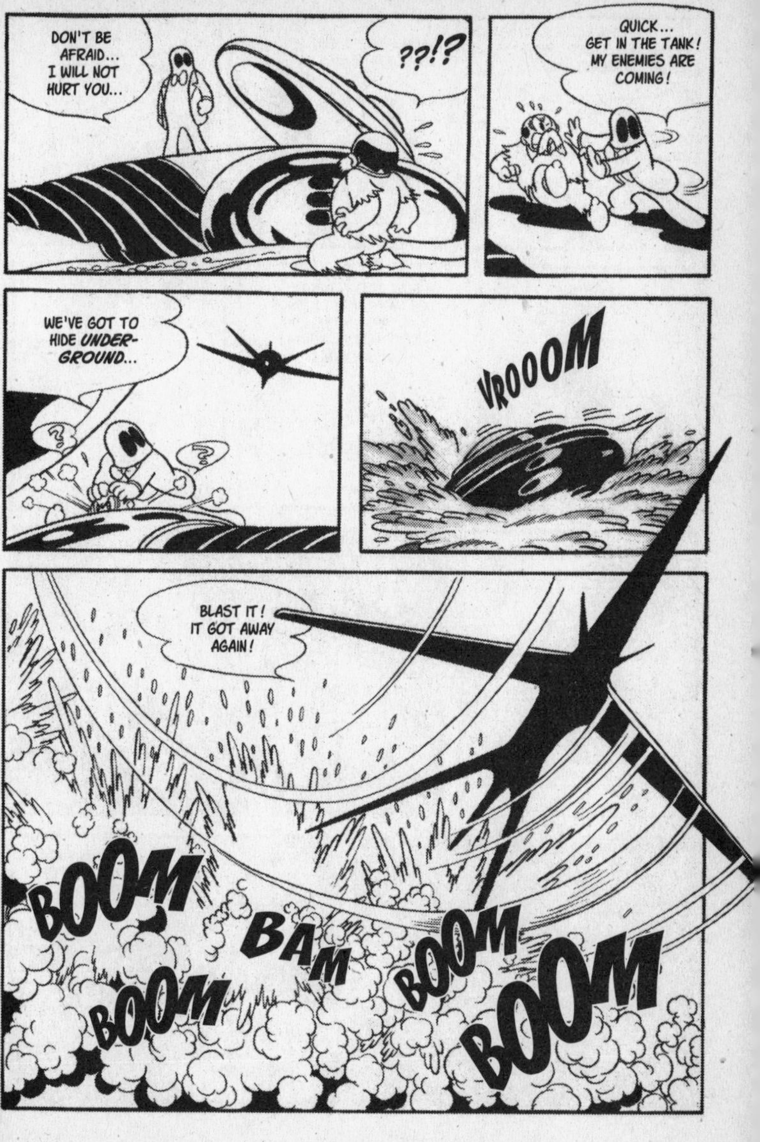

DON'T BE AFRAID... I WILL NOT HURT YOU...
??!?
QUICK... GET IN THE TANK! MY ENEMIES ARE COMING!
WE'VE GOT TO HIDE UNDER-GROUND...
VROOOM
BLAST IT! IT GOT AWAY AGAIN!
BOOM
BOOM
BAM
BOOM
BOOM

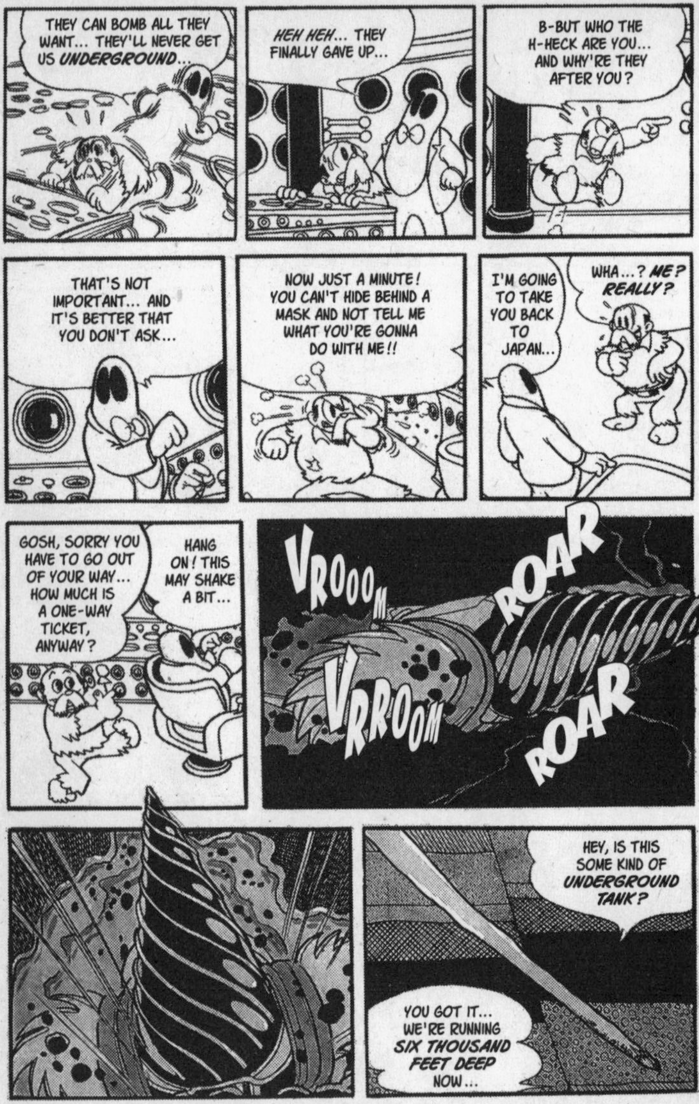
THEY CAN BOMB ALL THEY WANT... THEY'LL NEVER GET US *UNDERGROUND*...
HEH HEH... THEY FINALLY GAVE UP...
B-BUT WHO THE H-HECK ARE YOU... AND WHY'RE THEY AFTER YOU?
THAT'S NOT IMPORTANT... AND IT'S BETTER THAT YOU DON'T ASK...
NOW JUST A MINUTE! YOU CAN'T HIDE BEHIND A MASK AND NOT TELL ME WHAT YOU'RE GONNA DO WITH ME!!
I'M GOING TO TAKE YOU BACK TO JAPAN...
WHA...? *ME? REALLY?*
GOSH, SORRY YOU HAVE TO GO OUT OF YOUR WAY... HOW MUCH IS A ONE-WAY TICKET, ANYWAY?
HANG ON! THIS MAY SHAKE A BIT...
VROOOM
ROAR
VRROOM
ROAR
HEY, IS THIS SOME KIND OF *UNDERGROUND TANK?*
YOU GOT IT... WE'RE RUNNING *SIX THOUSAND FEET DEEP* NOW...

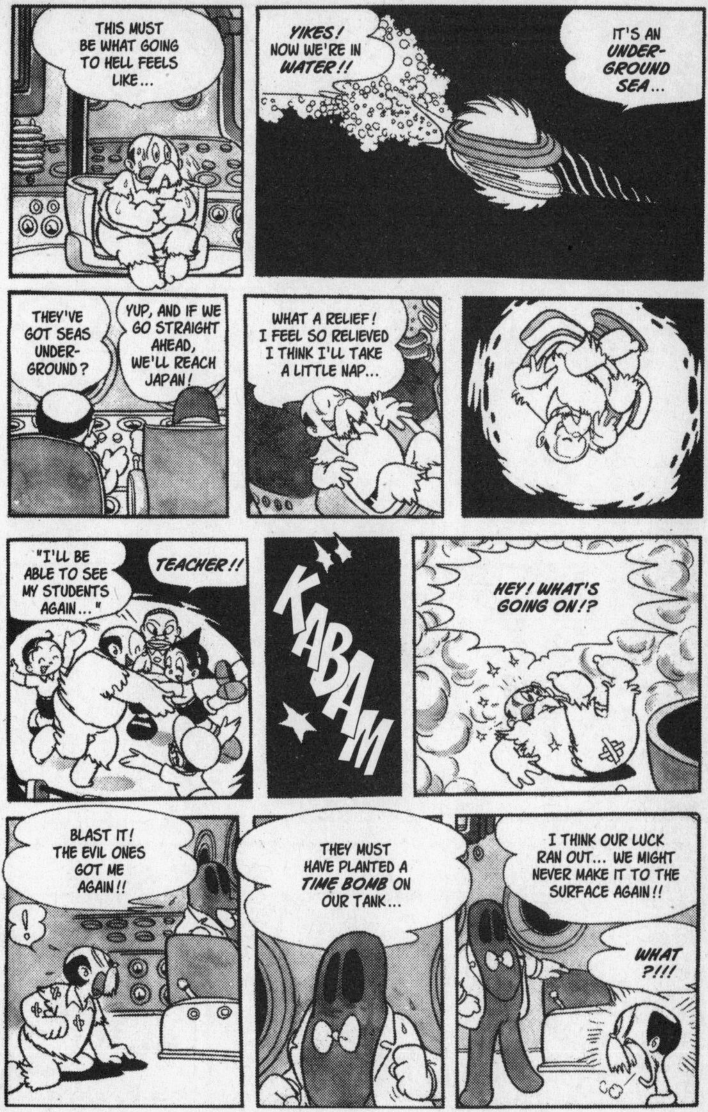
THIS MUST BE WHAT GOING TO HELL FEELS LIKE...
YIKES! NOW WE'RE IN WATER!!
IT'S AN UNDER-GROUND SEA...
THEY'VE GOT SEAS UNDER-GROUND?
YUP, AND IF WE GO STRAIGHT AHEAD, WE'LL REACH JAPAN!
WHAT A RELIEF! I FEEL SO RELIEVED I THINK I'LL TAKE A LITTLE NAP...
"I'LL BE ABLE TO SEE MY STUDENTS AGAIN..."
TEACHER!!
KABAM
HEY! WHAT'S GOING ON!?
BLAST IT! THE EVIL ONES GOT ME AGAIN!!
!
THEY MUST HAVE PLANTED A TIME BOMB ON OUR TANK...
I THINK OUR LUCK RAN OUT... WE MIGHT NEVER MAKE IT TO THE SURFACE AGAIN!!
WHAT ?!!!

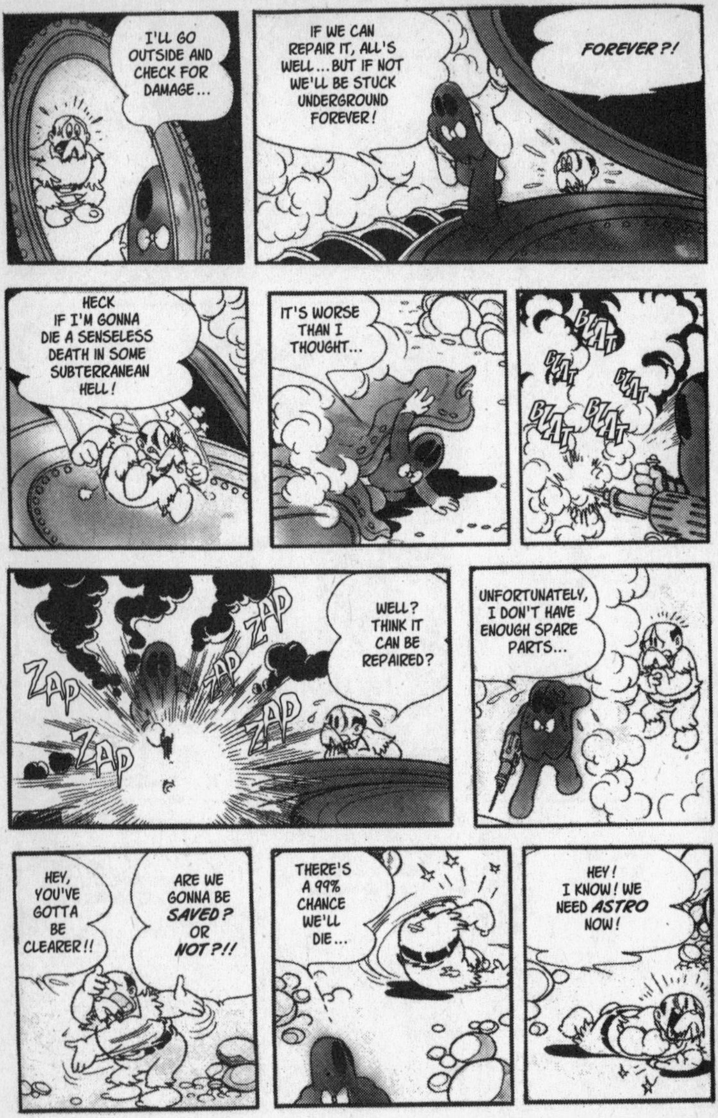
I'LL GO OUTSIDE AND CHECK FOR DAMAGE...
IF WE CAN REPAIR IT, ALL'S WELL...BUT IF NOT WE'LL BE STUCK UNDERGROUND FOREVER!
FOREVER?!
HECK IF I'M GONNA DIE A SENSELESS DEATH IN SOME SUBTERRANEAN HELL!
IT'S WORSE THAN I THOUGHT...
BLAT
BLAT
BLAT
BLAT
BLAT
ZAP
ZAP
ZAP
ZAP
ZAP
WELL? THINK IT CAN BE REPAIRED?
UNFORTUNATELY, I DON'T HAVE ENOUGH SPARE PARTS...
HEY, YOU'VE GOTTA BE CLEARER!!
ARE WE GONNA BE **SAVED?** OR **NOT?!!**
THERE'S A 99% CHANCE WE'LL DIE...
HEY! I KNOW! WE NEED **ASTRO** NOW!

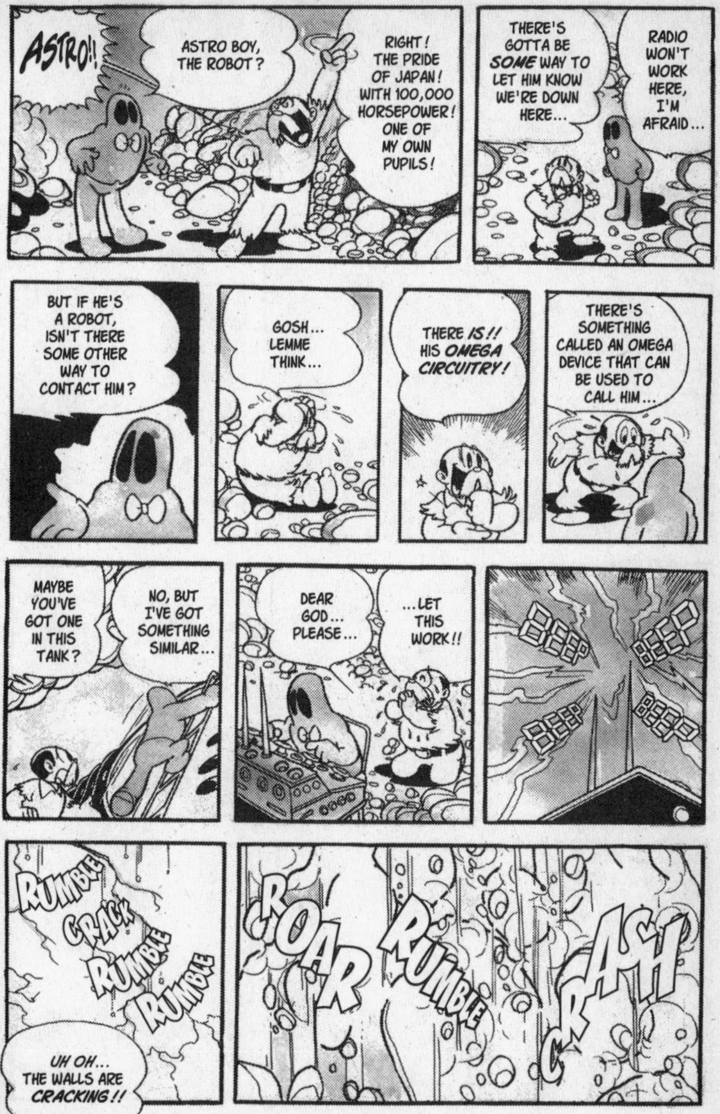
ASTRO!!
ASTRO BOY, THE ROBOT?
RIGHT! THE PRIDE OF JAPAN! WITH 100,000 HORSEPOWER! ONE OF MY OWN PUPILS!
THERE'S GOTTA BE SOME WAY TO LET HIM KNOW WE'RE DOWN HERE...
RADIO WON'T WORK HERE, I'M AFRAID...
BUT IF HE'S A ROBOT, ISN'T THERE SOME OTHER WAY TO CONTACT HIM?
GOSH... LEMME THINK...
THERE IS!! HIS OMEGA CIRCUITRY!
THERE'S SOMETHING CALLED AN OMEGA DEVICE THAT CAN BE USED TO CALL HIM...
MAYBE YOU'VE GOT ONE IN THIS TANK?
NO, BUT I'VE GOT SOMETHING SIMILAR...
DEAR GOD... PLEASE...
...LET THIS WORK!!
BEEP
BEEP
BEEP
BEEP
RUMBLE
CRACK
RUMBLE
RUMBLE
UH OH... THE WALLS ARE CRACKING!!
ROAR
RUMBLE
CRASH

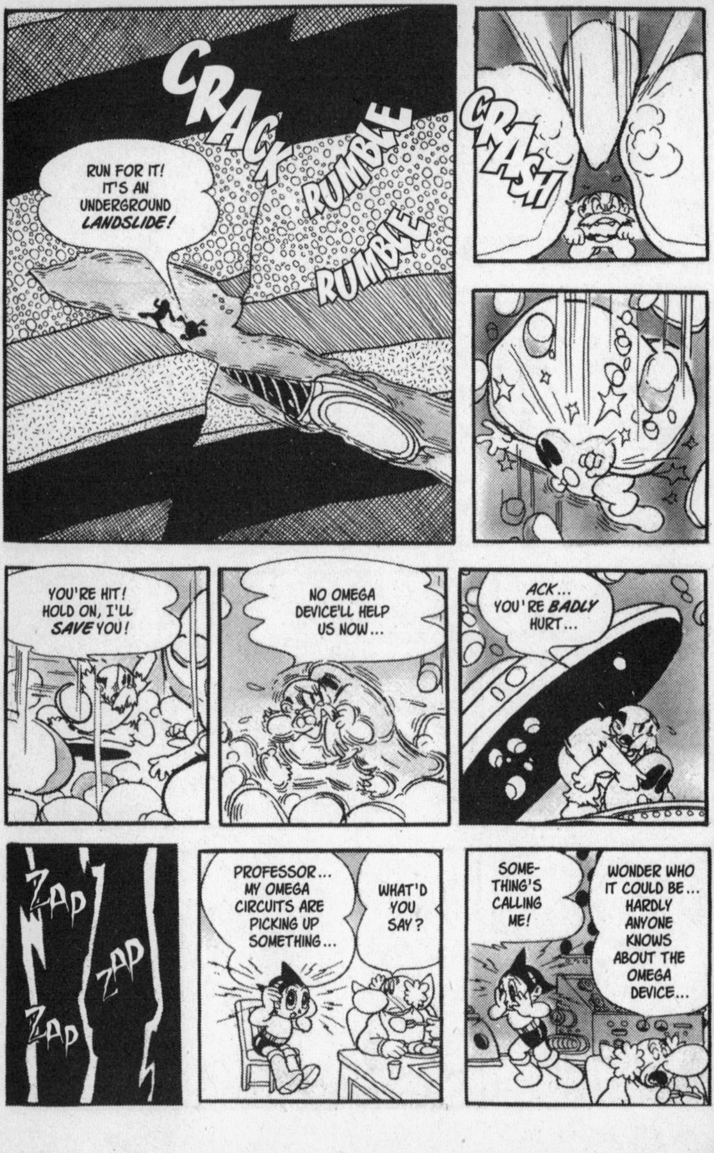

CRACK
RUN FOR IT! IT'S AN UNDERGROUND LANDSLIDE!
RUMBLE
RUMBLE
CRASH
YOU'RE HIT! HOLD ON, I'LL SAVE YOU!
NO OMEGA DEVICE'LL HELP US NOW...
ACK... YOU'RE BADLY HURT...
ZAP
ZAP
ZAP
PROFESSOR... MY OMEGA CIRCUITS ARE PICKING UP SOMETHING...
WHAT'D YOU SAY?
SOME-THING'S CALLING ME!
WONDER WHO IT COULD BE... HARDLY ANYONE KNOWS ABOUT THE OMEGA DEVICE...

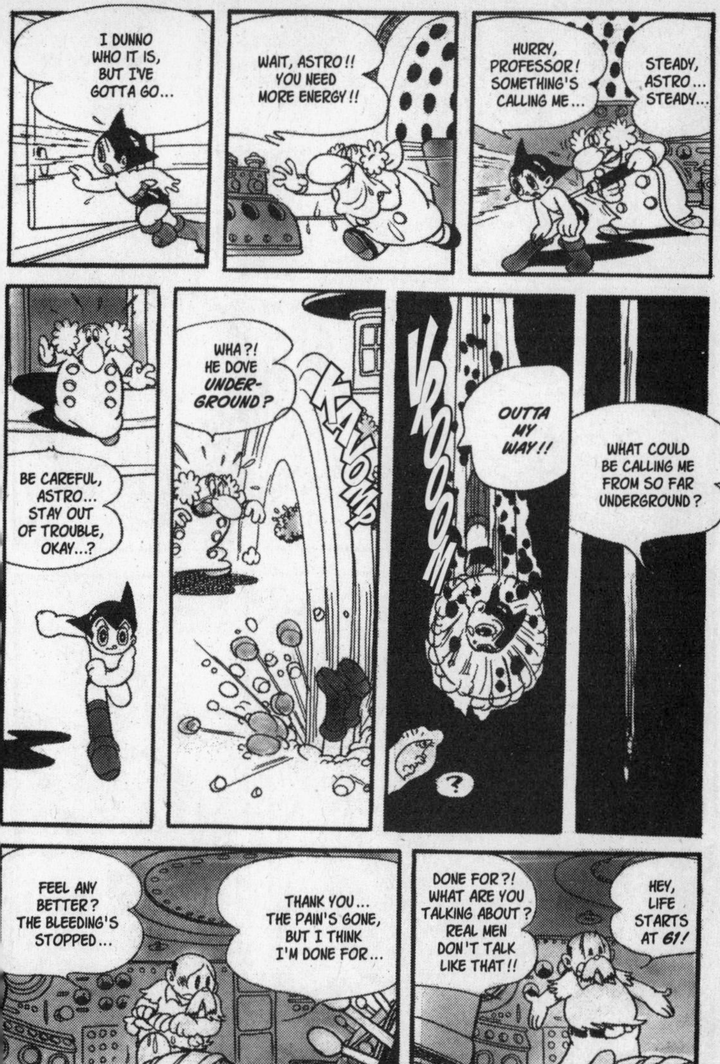
I DUNNO WHO IT IS, BUT I'VE GOTTA GO...
WAIT, ASTRO!! YOU NEED MORE ENERGY!!
HURRY, PROFESSOR! SOMETHING'S CALLING ME...
STEADY, ASTRO... STEADY...
BE CAREFUL, ASTRO... STAY OUT OF TROUBLE, OKAY...?
WHA?! HE DOVE UNDERGROUND?
KAVOMP
VROOOOOM
OUTTA MY WAY!!
?
WHAT COULD BE CALLING ME FROM SO FAR UNDERGROUND?
FEEL ANY BETTER? THE BLEEDING'S STOPPED...
THANK YOU... THE PAIN'S GONE, BUT I THINK I'M DONE FOR...
DONE FOR?! WHAT ARE YOU TALKING ABOUT? REAL MEN DON'T TALK LIKE THAT!!
HEY, LIFE STARTS AT 61!

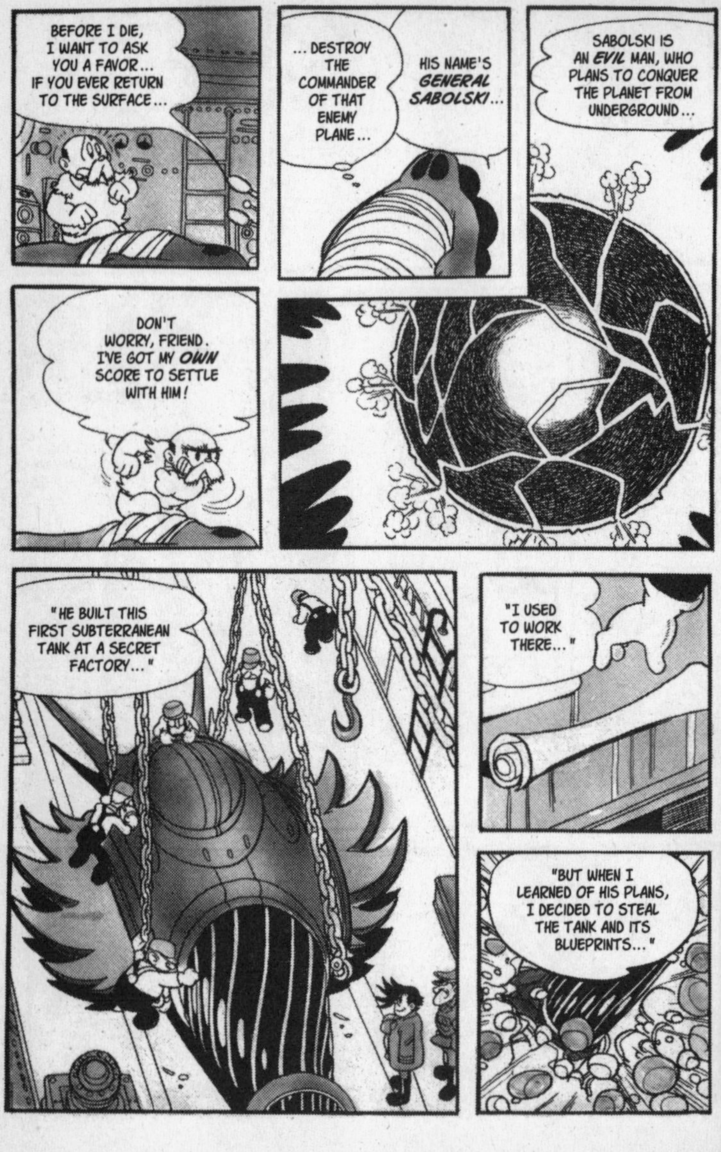
BEFORE I DIE, I WANT TO ASK YOU A FAVOR... IF YOU EVER RETURN TO THE SURFACE...
... DESTROY THE COMMANDER OF THAT ENEMY PLANE...
HIS NAME'S GENERAL SABOLSKI...
SABOLSKI IS AN EVIL MAN, WHO PLANS TO CONQUER THE PLANET FROM UNDERGROUND...
DON'T WORRY, FRIEND. I'VE GOT MY OWN SCORE TO SETTLE WITH HIM!
"HE BUILT THIS FIRST SUBTERRANEAN TANK AT A SECRET FACTORY..."
"I USED TO WORK THERE..."
"BUT WHEN I LEARNED OF HIS PLANS, I DECIDED TO STEAL THE TANK AND ITS BLUEPRINTS..."

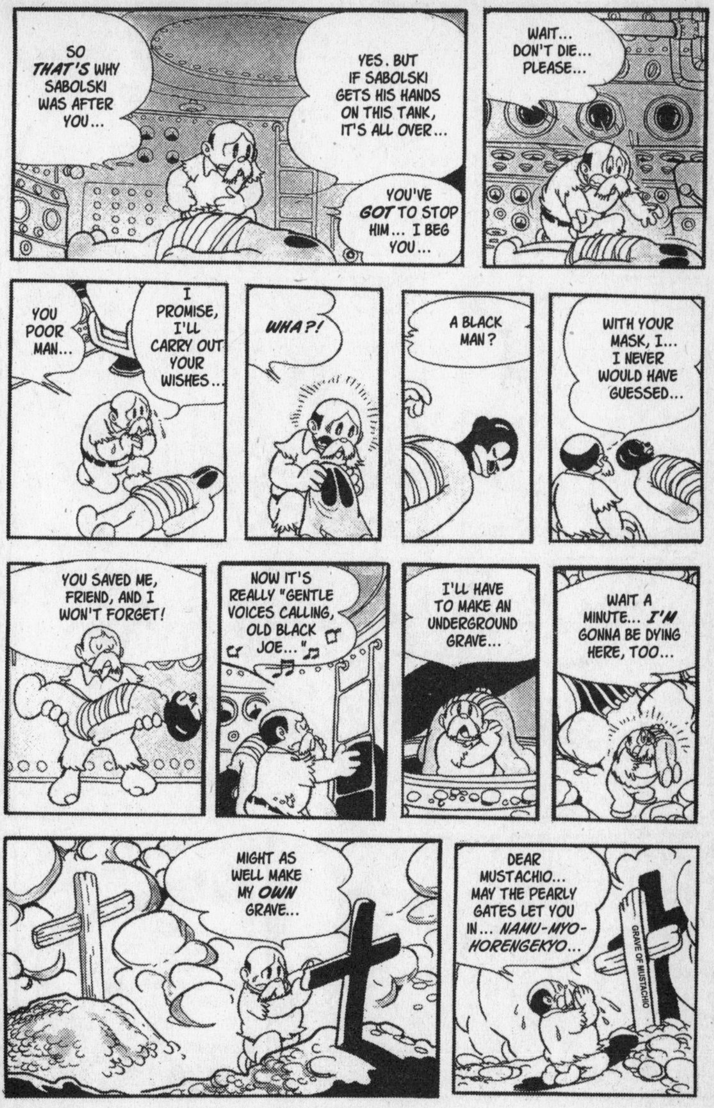

SO THAT'S WHY SABOLSKI WAS AFTER YOU...
YES. BUT IF SABOLSKI GETS HIS HANDS ON THIS TANK, IT'S ALL OVER...
YOU'VE GOT TO STOP HIM... I BEG YOU...
WAIT... DON'T DIE... PLEASE...
YOU POOR MAN...
I PROMISE, I'LL CARRY OUT YOUR WISHES...
WHA?!
A BLACK MAN?
WITH YOUR MASK, I... I NEVER WOULD HAVE GUESSED...
YOU SAVED ME, FRIEND, AND I WON'T FORGET!
NOW IT'S REALLY "GENTLE VOICES CALLING, OLD BLACK JOE..."
I'LL HAVE TO MAKE AN UNDERGROUND GRAVE...
WAIT A MINUTE... I'M GONNA BE DYING HERE, TOO...
MIGHT AS WELL MAKE MY OWN GRAVE...
DEAR MUSTACHIO... MAY THE PEARLY GATES LET YOU IN... NAMU-MYO-HORENGEKYO...
GRAVE OF MUSTACHIO

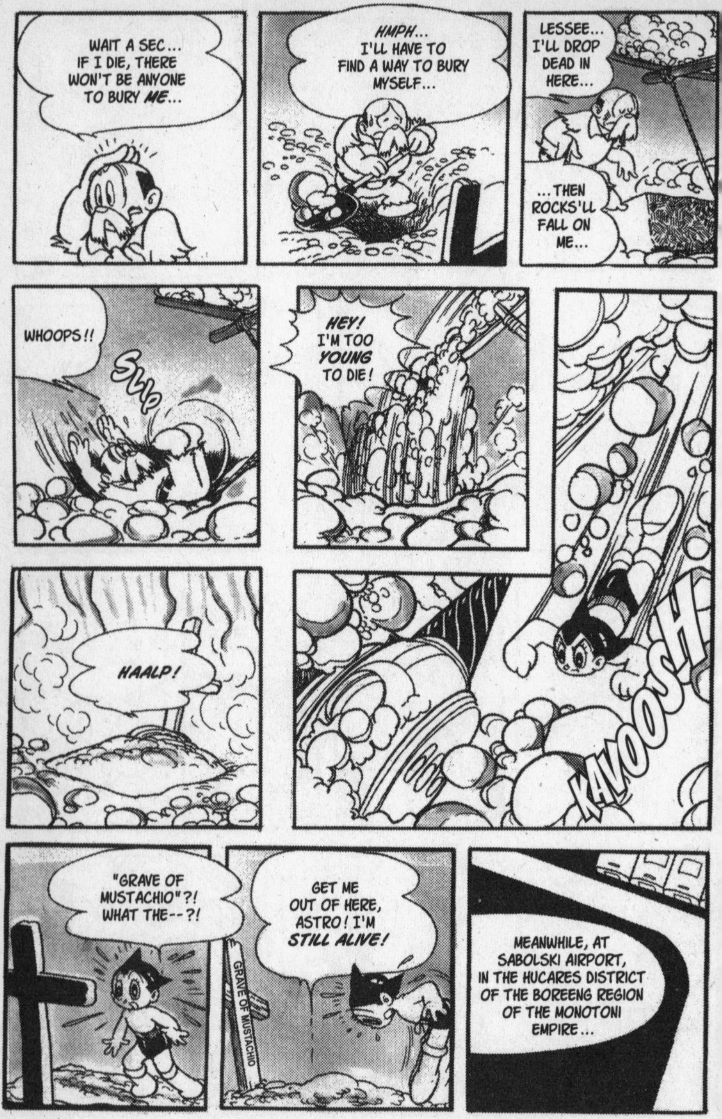
WAIT A SEC...
IF I DIE, THERE WON'T BE ANYONE TO BURY ***ME***...
HMPH... I'LL HAVE TO FIND A WAY TO BURY MYSELF...
LESSEE... I'LL DROP DEAD IN HERE...
...THEN ROCKS'LL FALL ON ME...
WHOOPS!!
SLIP
HEY! I'M TOO ***YOUNG*** TO DIE!
HAALP!
KAVOOSH
"GRAVE OF MUSTACHIO"?! WHAT THE--?!
GET ME OUT OF HERE, ASTRO! I'M ***STILL ALIVE!***
GRAVE OF MUSTACHIO
MEANWHILE, AT SABOLSKI AIRPORT, IN THE HUCARES DISTRICT OF THE BOREENG REGION OF THE MONOTONI EMPIRE...

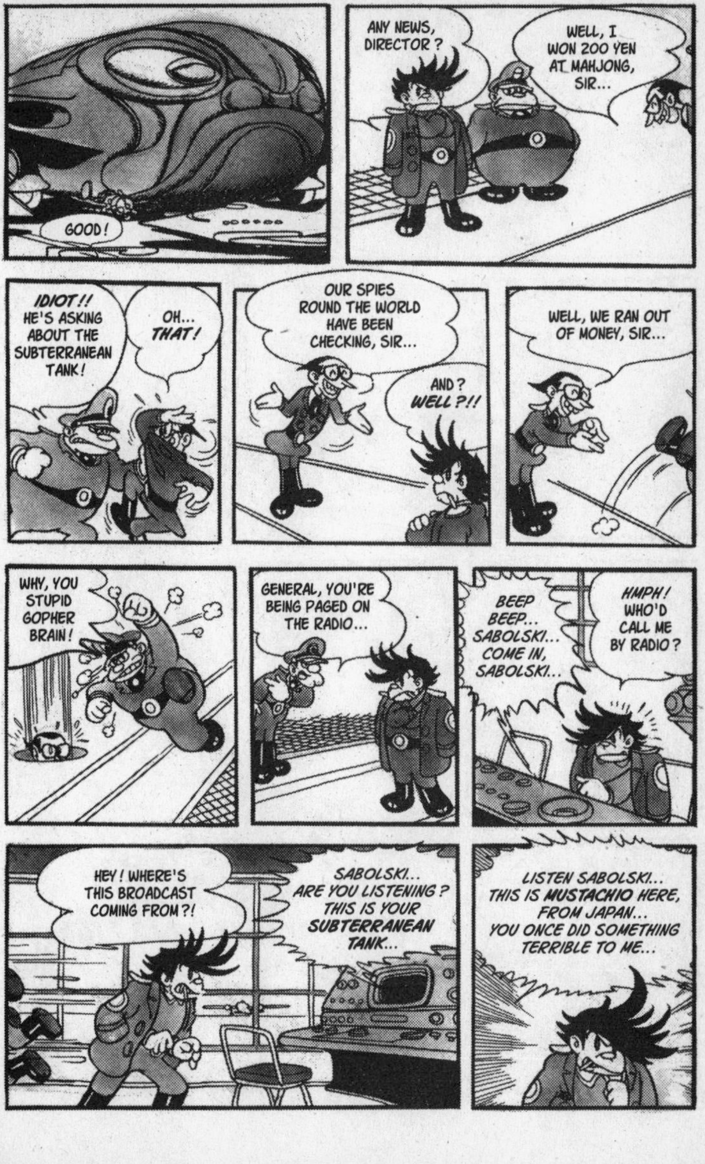
GOOD!
ANY NEWS, DIRECTOR?
WELL, I WON 200 YEN AT MAHJONG, SIR...
IDIOT!! HE'S ASKING ABOUT THE SUBTERRANEAN TANK!
OH... THAT!
OUR SPIES ROUND THE WORLD HAVE BEEN CHECKING, SIR...
AND? WELL?!!
WELL, WE RAN OUT OF MONEY, SIR...
WHY, YOU STUPID GOPHER BRAIN!
GENERAL, YOU'RE BEING PAGED ON THE RADIO...
BEEP BEEP... SABOLSKI... COME IN, SABOLSKI...
HMPH! WHO'D CALL ME BY RADIO?
HEY! WHERE'S THIS BROADCAST COMING FROM?!
SABOLSKI... ARE YOU LISTENING? THIS IS YOUR SUBTERRANEAN TANK...
LISTEN SABOLSKI... THIS IS MUSTACHIO HERE, FROM JAPAN... YOU ONCE DID SOMETHING TERRIBLE TO ME...

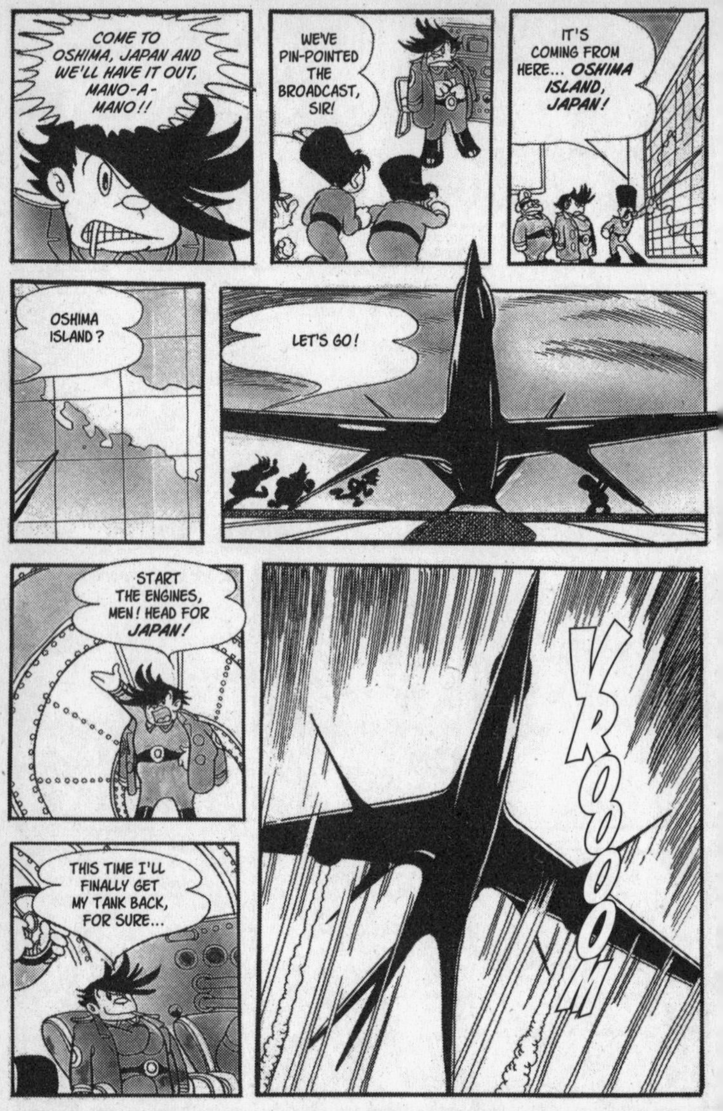
COME TO OSHIMA, JAPAN AND WE'LL HAVE IT OUT, MANO-A-MANO!!
WE'VE PIN-POINTED THE BROADCAST, SIR!
IT'S COMING FROM HERE... OSHIMA ISLAND, JAPAN!
OSHIMA ISLAND?
LET'S GO!
START THE ENGINES, MEN! HEAD FOR JAPAN!
THIS TIME I'LL FINALLY GET MY TANK BACK, FOR SURE...
VROOOOM

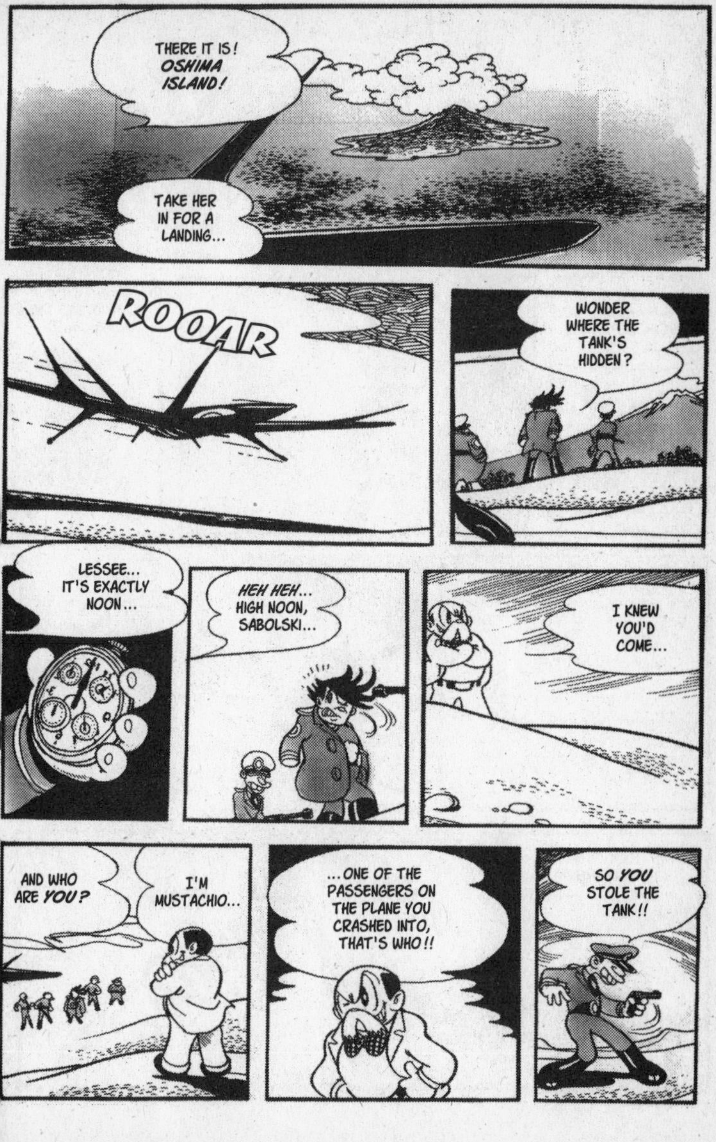
THERE IT IS! OSHIMA ISLAND!
TAKE HER IN FOR A LANDING...
ROOAR
WONDER WHERE THE TANK'S HIDDEN?
LESSEE... IT'S EXACTLY NOON...
HEH HEH... HIGH NOON, SABOLSKI...
I KNEW YOU'D COME...
AND WHO ARE YOU?
I'M MUSTACHIO...
...ONE OF THE PASSENGERS ON THE PLANE YOU CRASHED INTO, THAT'S WHO!!
SO YOU STOLE THE TANK!!

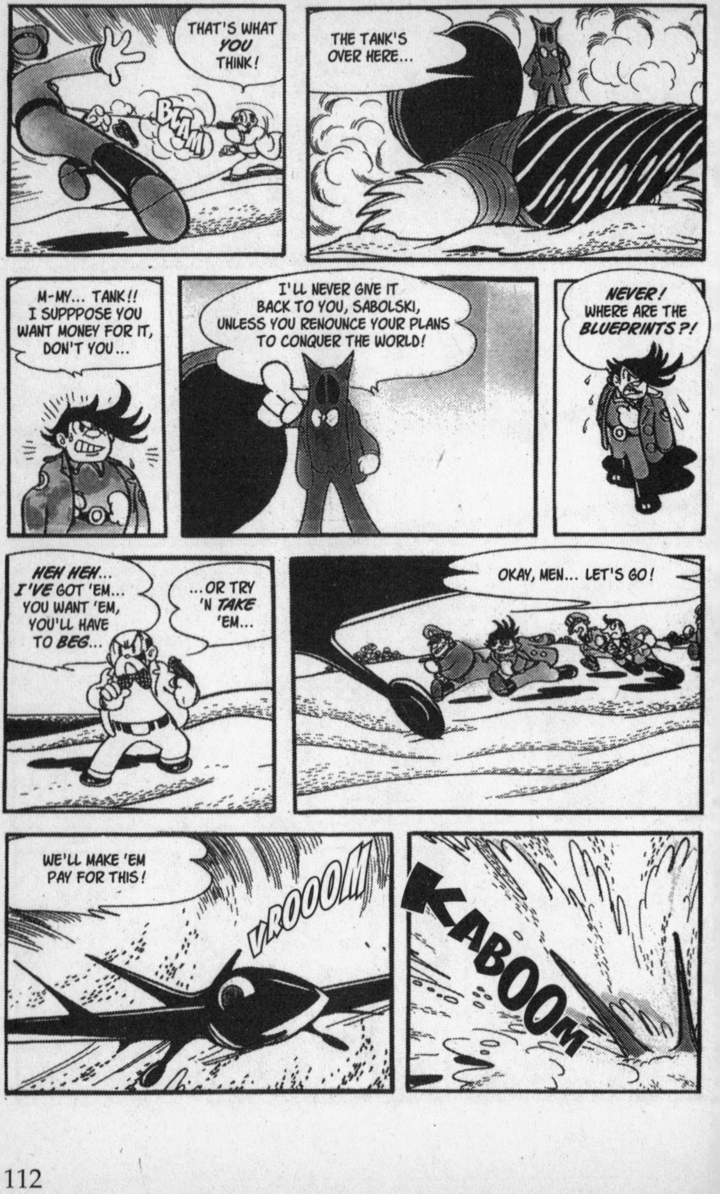
THAT'S WHAT YOU THINK!
BLAM
THE TANK'S OVER HERE...
M-MY... TANK!! I SUPPPOSE YOU WANT MONEY FOR IT, DON'T YOU...
I'LL NEVER GIVE IT BACK TO YOU, SABOLSKI, UNLESS YOU RENOUNCE YOUR PLANS TO CONQUER THE WORLD!
NEVER! WHERE ARE THE BLUEPRINTS?!
HEH HEH... I'VE GOT 'EM... YOU WANT 'EM, YOU'LL HAVE TO BEG...
...OR TRY 'N TAKE 'EM...
OKAY, MEN... LET'S GO!
WE'LL MAKE 'EM PAY FOR THIS!
VROOOM
KABOOOM

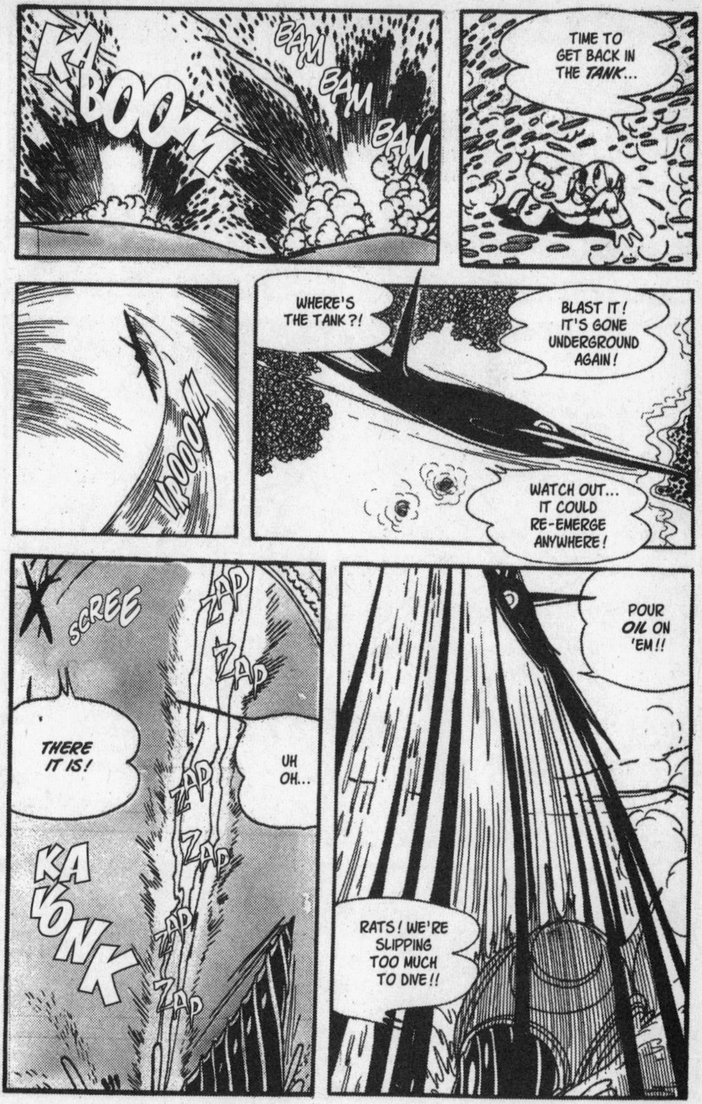
KA BOOM
BAM BAM BAM
TIME TO GET BACK IN THE *TANK*...
VROOOM
WHERE'S THE TANK?!
BLAST IT! IT'S GONE UNDERGROUND AGAIN!
WATCH OUT... IT COULD RE-EMERGE ANYWHERE!
SCREE
ZAP ZAP
THERE IT IS!
UH OH...
ZAP ZAP
KA VONK
ZAP ZAP
POUR *OIL* ON 'EM!!
RATS! WE'RE SLIPPING TOO MUCH TO DIVE!!

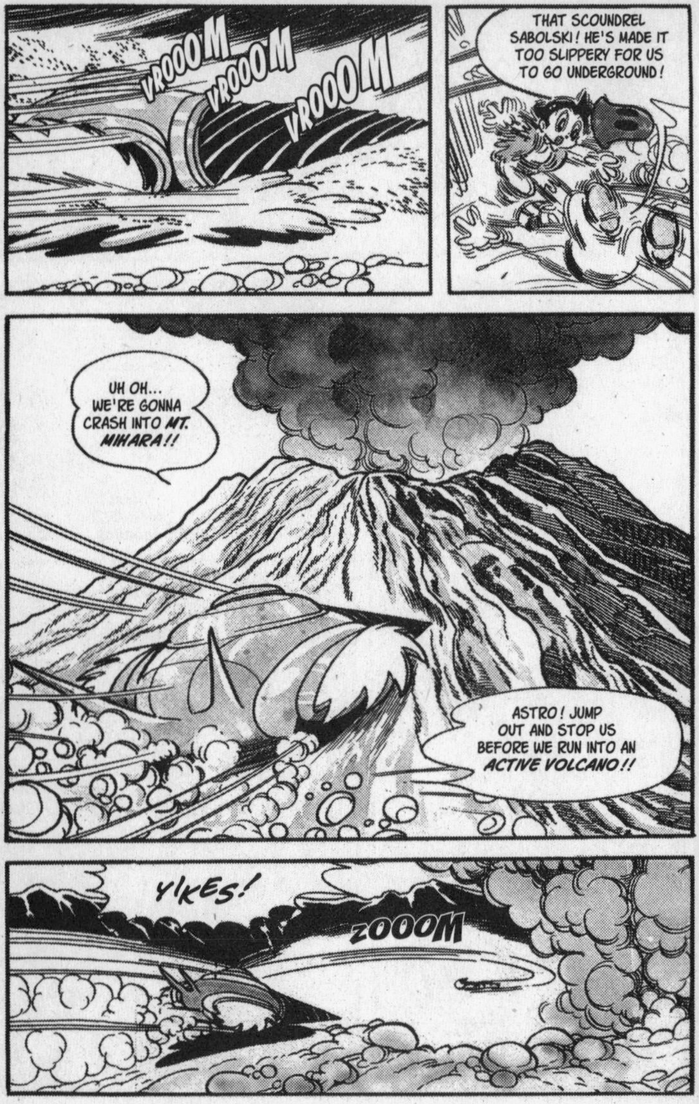
VROOOM VROOOM VROOOM
THAT SCOUNDREL SABOLSKI! HE'S MADE IT TOO SLIPPERY FOR US TO GO UNDERGROUND!
UH OH... WE'RE GONNA CRASH INTO *MT. MIHARA!!*
ASTRO! JUMP OUT AND STOP US BEFORE WE RUN INTO AN *ACTIVE VOLCANO!!*
YIKES!
ZOOOM

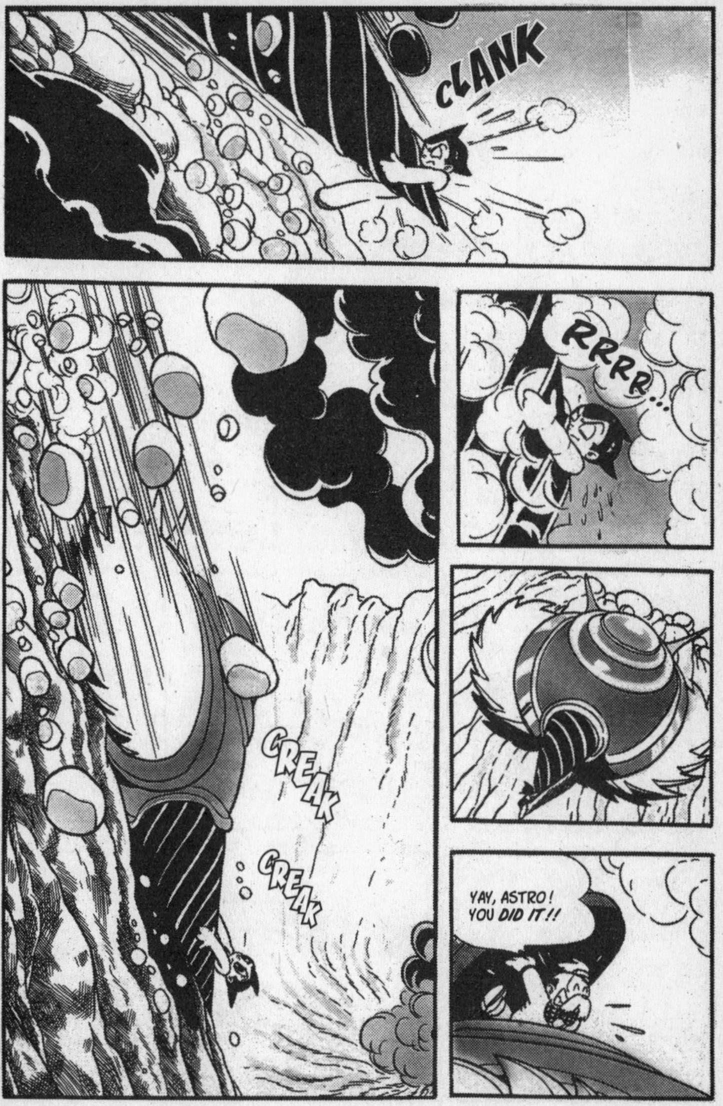
CLANK
CREAK
CREAK
RRRRR...
YAY, ASTRO! YOU DID IT!!

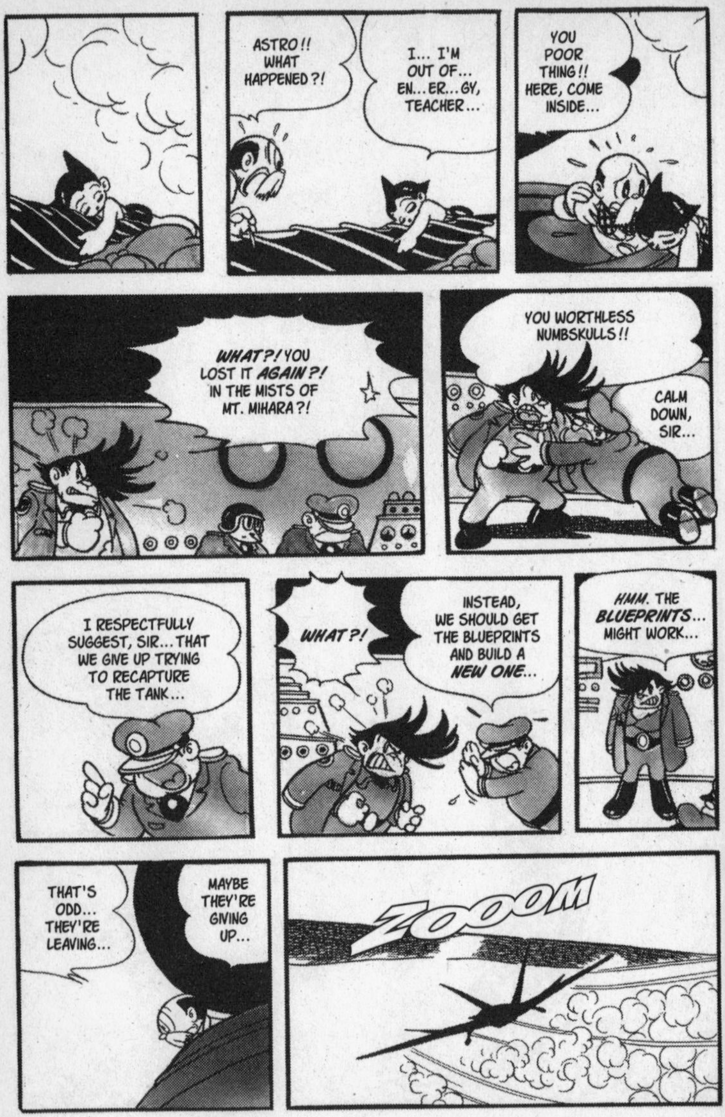
ASTRO!! WHAT HAPPENED?!
I... I'M OUT OF... EN...ER...GY, TEACHER...
YOU POOR THING!! HERE, COME INSIDE...
WHAT?! YOU LOST IT AGAIN?! IN THE MISTS OF MT. MIHARA?!
YOU WORTHLESS NUMBSKULLS!!
CALM DOWN, SIR...
I RESPECTFULLY SUGGEST, SIR... THAT WE GIVE UP TRYING TO RECAPTURE THE TANK...
WHAT?!
INSTEAD, WE SHOULD GET THE BLUEPRINTS AND BUILD A NEW ONE...
HMM. THE BLUEPRINTS... MIGHT WORK...
THAT'S ODD... THEY'RE LEAVING...
MAYBE THEY'RE GIVING UP...
ZOOOM

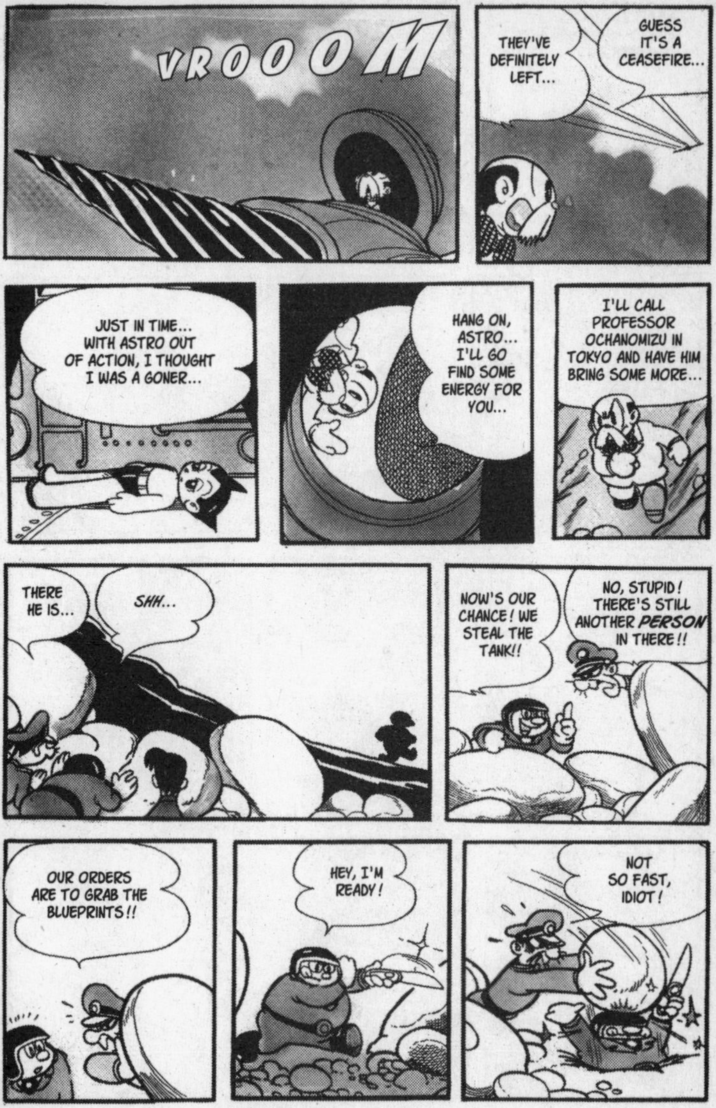
VROOOOM
THEY'VE DEFINITELY LEFT...
GUESS IT'S A CEASEFIRE...
JUST IN TIME... WITH ASTRO OUT OF ACTION, I THOUGHT I WAS A GONER...
HANG ON, ASTRO... I'LL GO FIND SOME ENERGY FOR YOU...
I'LL CALL PROFESSOR OCHANOMIZU IN TOKYO AND HAVE HIM BRING SOME MORE...
THERE HE IS...
SHH...
NOW'S OUR CHANCE! WE STEAL THE TANK!!
NO, STUPID! THERE'S STILL ANOTHER PERSON IN THERE!!
OUR ORDERS ARE TO GRAB THE BLUEPRINTS!!
HEY, I'M READY!
NOT SO FAST, IDIOT!

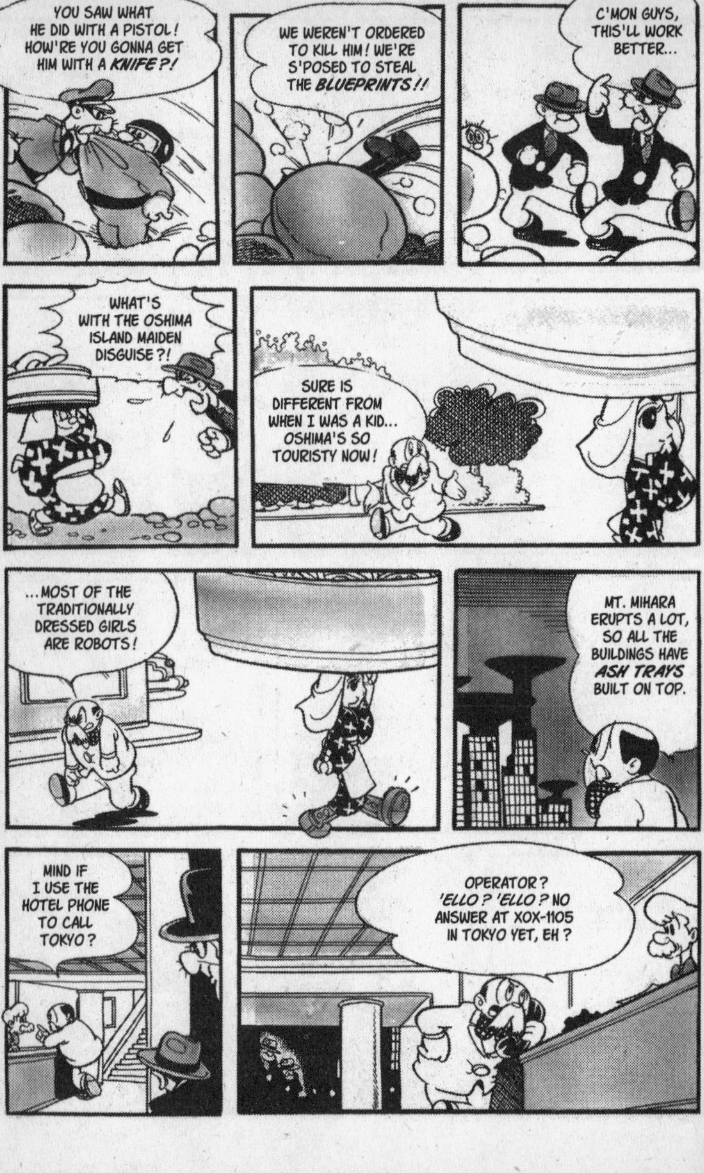
YOU SAW WHAT HE DID WITH A PISTOL! HOW'RE YOU GONNA GET HIM WITH A KNIFE?!
WE WEREN'T ORDERED TO KILL HIM! WE'RE S'POSED TO STEAL THE BLUEPRINTS!!
C'MON GUYS, THIS'LL WORK BETTER...
WHAT'S WITH THE OSHIMA ISLAND MAIDEN DISGUISE?!
SURE IS DIFFERENT FROM WHEN I WAS A KID... OSHIMA'S SO TOURISTY NOW!
...MOST OF THE TRADITIONALLY DRESSED GIRLS ARE ROBOTS!
MT. MIHARA ERUPTS A LOT, SO ALL THE BUILDINGS HAVE ASH TRAYS BUILT ON TOP.
MIND IF I USE THE HOTEL PHONE TO CALL TOKYO?
OPERATOR? 'ELLO? 'ELLO? NO ANSWER AT XOX-1105 IN TOKYO YET, EH?

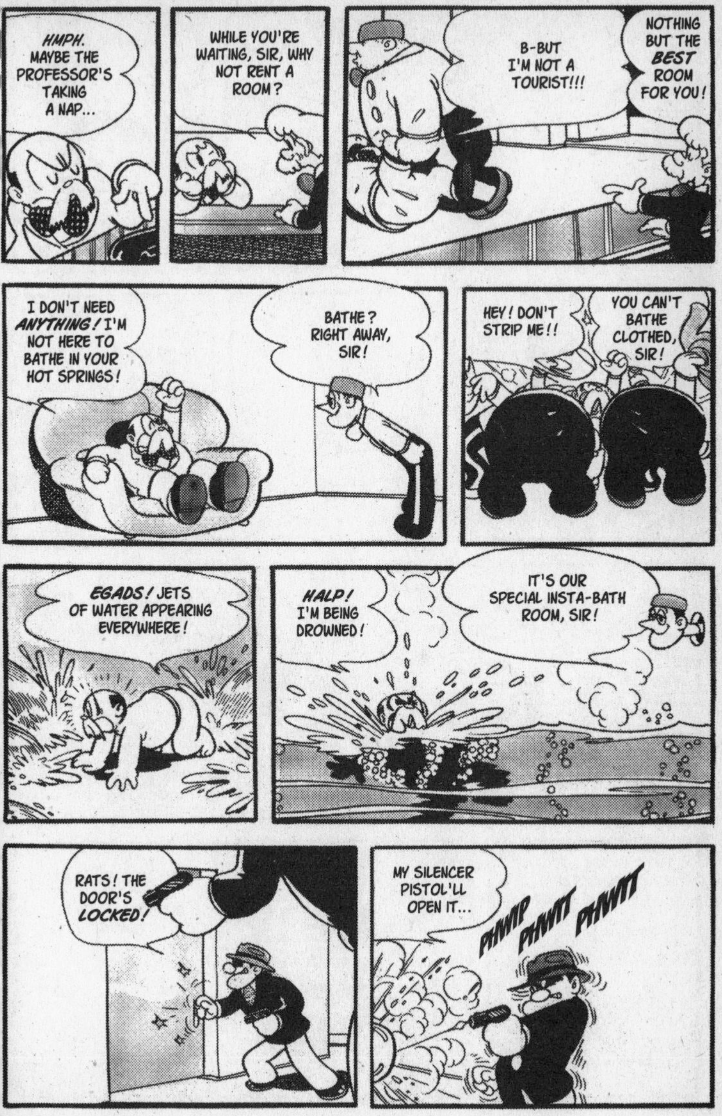
HMPH. MAYBE THE PROFESSOR'S TAKING A NAP...
WHILE YOU'RE WAITING, SIR, WHY NOT RENT A ROOM?
B-BUT I'M NOT A TOURIST!!!
NOTHING BUT THE BEST ROOM FOR YOU!
I DON'T NEED ANYTHING! I'M NOT HERE TO BATHE IN YOUR HOT SPRINGS!
BATHE? RIGHT AWAY, SIR!
HEY! DON'T STRIP ME!!
YOU CAN'T BATHE CLOTHED, SIR!
EGADS! JETS OF WATER APPEARING EVERYWHERE!
HALP! I'M BEING DROWNED!
IT'S OUR SPECIAL INSTA-BATH ROOM, SIR!
RATS! THE DOOR'S LOCKED!
MY SILENCER PISTOL'LL OPEN IT...
PHWIP
PHWIT
PHWIT

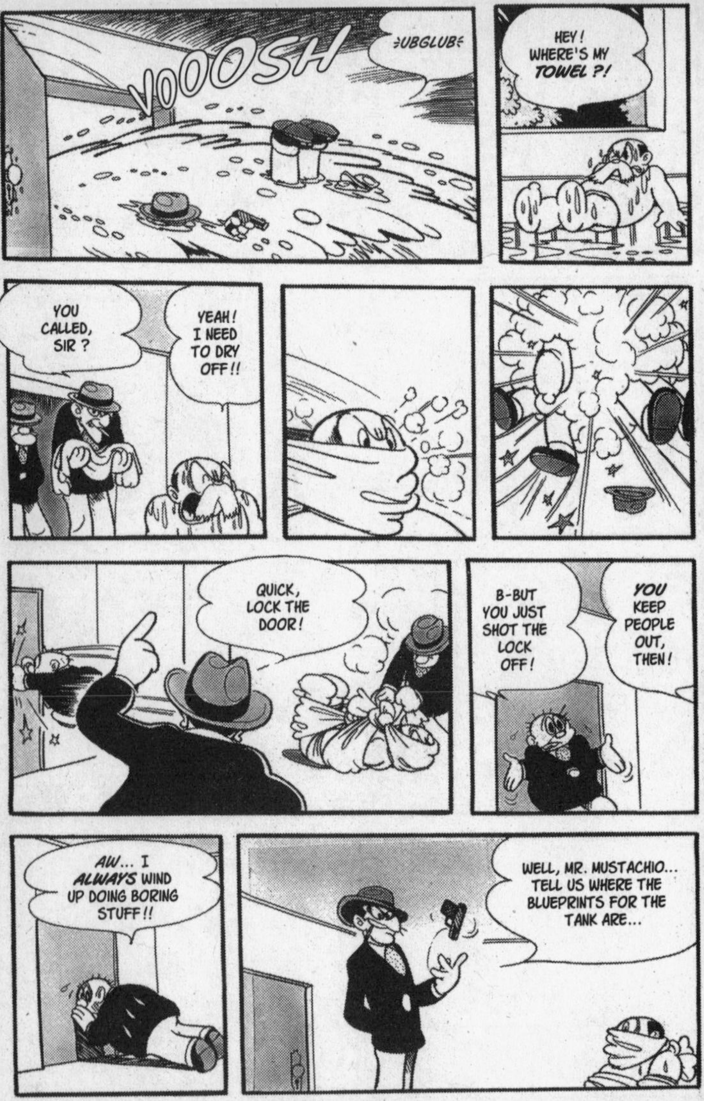
VOOOSH
≶UBGLUB≶
HEY! WHERE'S MY TOWEL ?!
YOU CALLED, SIR ?
YEAH! I NEED TO DRY OFF!!
QUICK, LOCK THE DOOR!
B-BUT YOU JUST SHOT THE LOCK OFF!
YOU KEEP PEOPLE OUT, THEN!
AW... I ALWAYS WIND UP DOING BORING STUFF!!
WELL, MR. MUSTACHIO... TELL US WHERE THE BLUEPRINTS FOR THE TANK ARE...

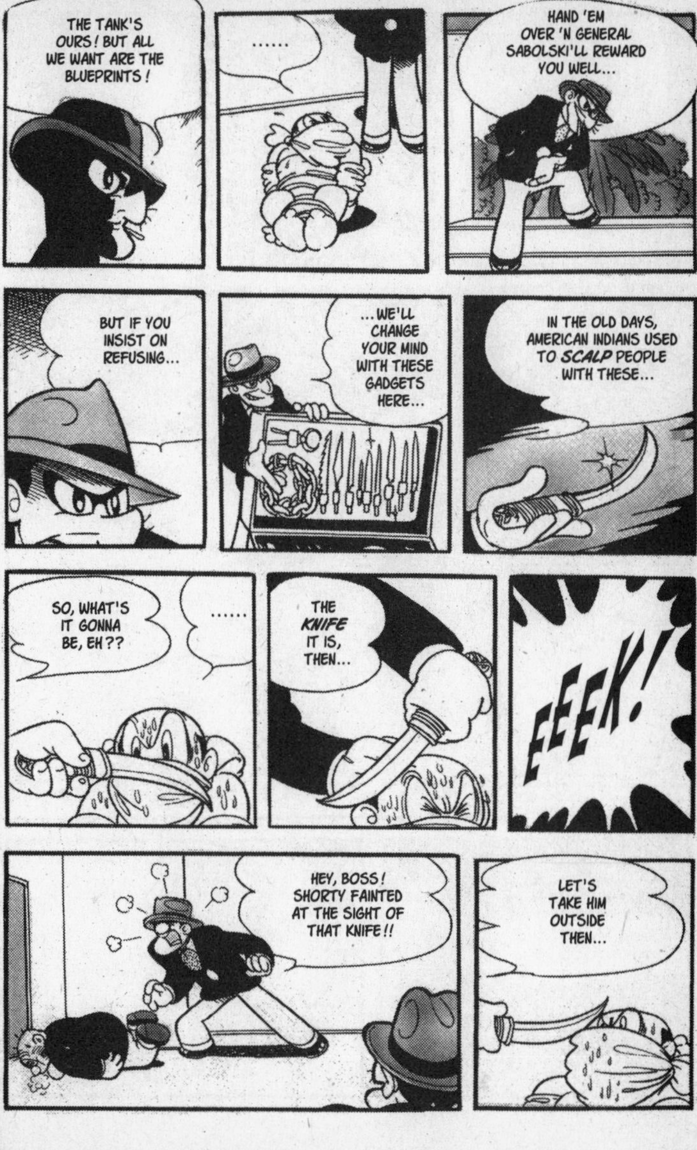
THE TANK'S OURS! BUT ALL WE WANT ARE THE BLUEPRINTS!
......
HAND 'EM OVER 'N GENERAL SABOLSKI'LL REWARD YOU WELL...
BUT IF YOU INSIST ON REFUSING...
...WE'LL CHANGE YOUR MIND WITH THESE GADGETS HERE...
IN THE OLD DAYS, AMERICAN INDIANS USED TO SCALP PEOPLE WITH THESE...
SO, WHAT'S IT GONNA BE, EH??
......
THE KNIFE IT IS, THEN...
EEEK!
HEY, BOSS! SHORTY FAINTED AT THE SIGHT OF THAT KNIFE!!
LET'S TAKE HIM OUTSIDE THEN...

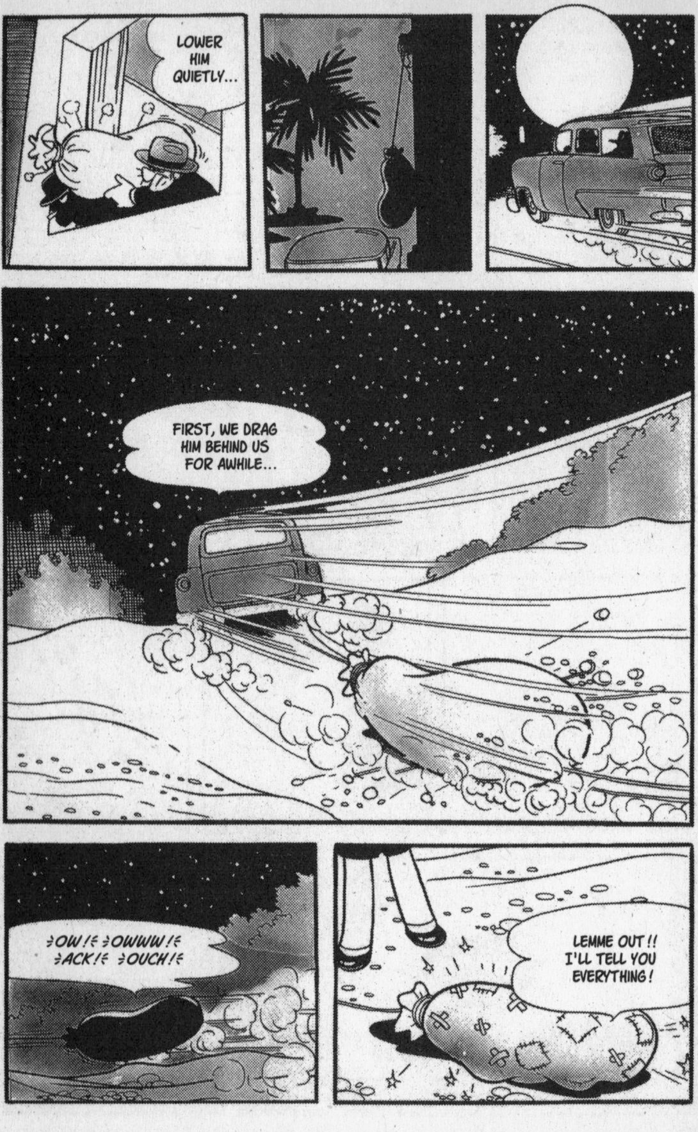
LOWER HIM QUIETLY...
FIRST, WE DRAG HIM BEHIND US FOR AWHILE...
OW! OWWW! ACK! OUCH!
LEMME OUT!! I'LL TELL YOU EVERYTHING!

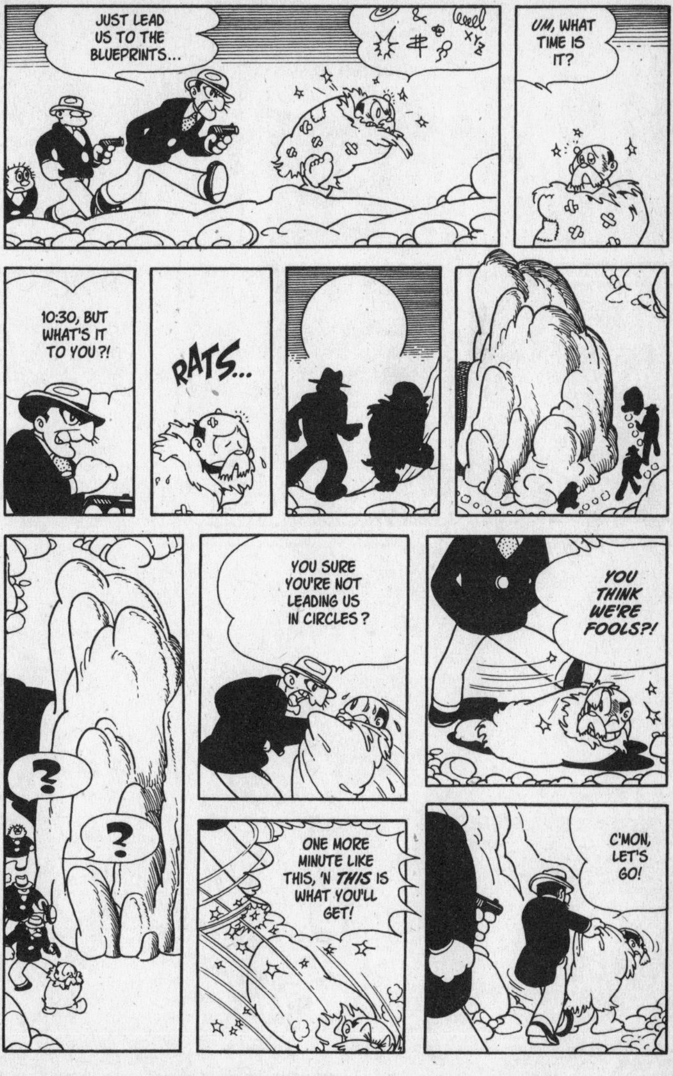
JUST LEAD US TO THE BLUEPRINTS...
& XYZ
UM, WHAT TIME IS IT?
10:30, BUT WHAT'S IT TO YOU?!
RATS...
?
?
YOU SURE YOU'RE NOT LEADING US IN CIRCLES?
YOU THINK WE'RE FOOLS?!
ONE MORE MINUTE LIKE THIS, 'N *THIS* IS WHAT YOU'LL GET!
C'MON, LET'S GO!

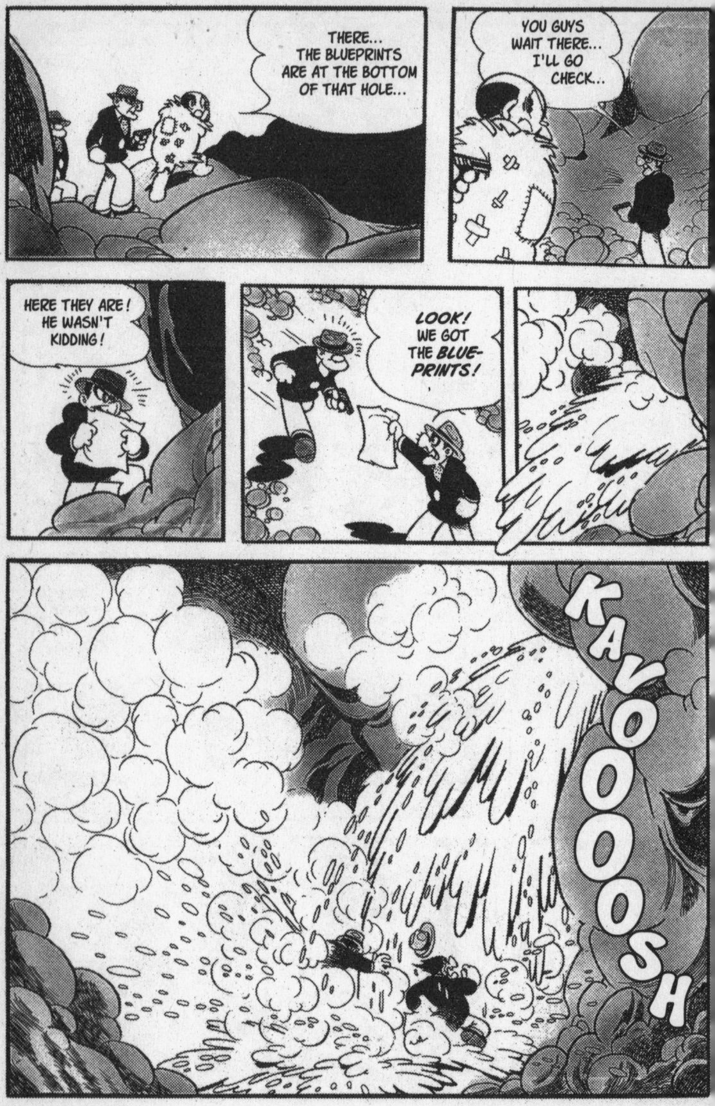
THERE... THE BLUEPRINTS ARE AT THE BOTTOM OF THAT HOLE...
YOU GUYS WAIT THERE... I'LL GO CHECK...
HERE THEY ARE! HE WASN'T KIDDING!
LOOK! WE GOT THE BLUE-PRINTS!
KAVOOOOOSH

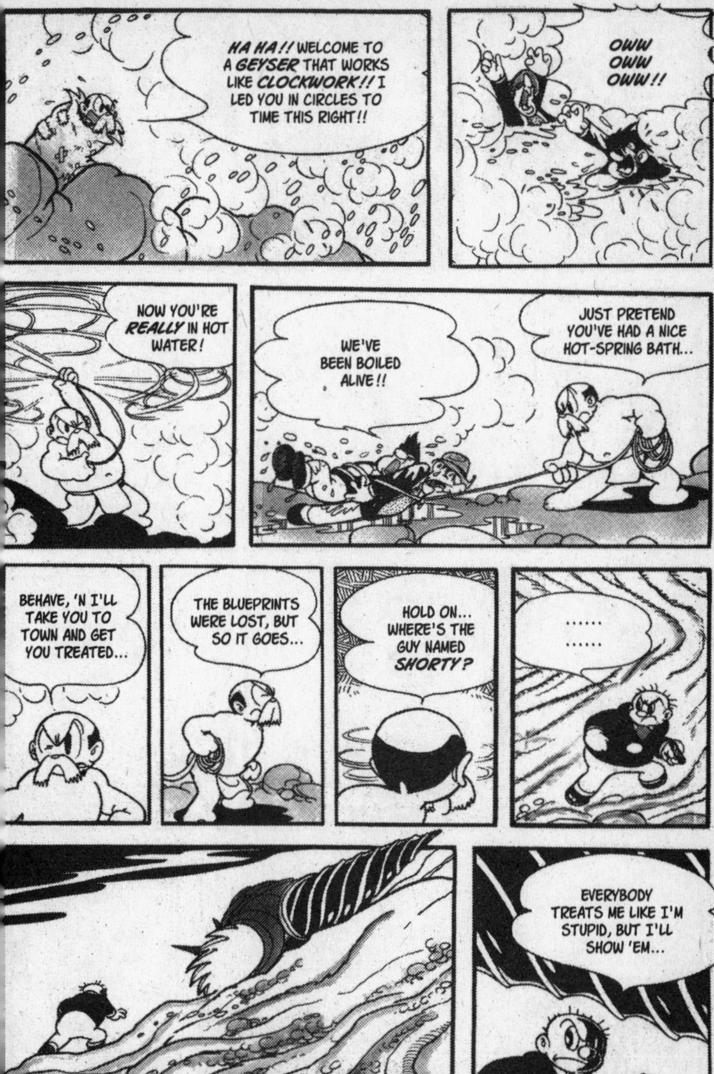
HA HA!! WELCOME TO A GEYSER THAT WORKS LIKE CLOCKWORK!! I LED YOU IN CIRCLES TO TIME THIS RIGHT!!
OWW OWW OWW!!
NOW YOU'RE REALLY IN HOT WATER!
WE'VE BEEN BOILED ALIVE!!
JUST PRETEND YOU'VE HAD A NICE HOT-SPRING BATH...
BEHAVE, 'N I'LL TAKE YOU TO TOWN AND GET YOU TREATED...
THE BLUEPRINTS WERE LOST, BUT SO IT GOES...
HOLD ON... WHERE'S THE GUY NAMED SHORTY?
....
EVERYBODY TREATS ME LIKE I'M STUPID, BUT I'LL SHOW 'EM...

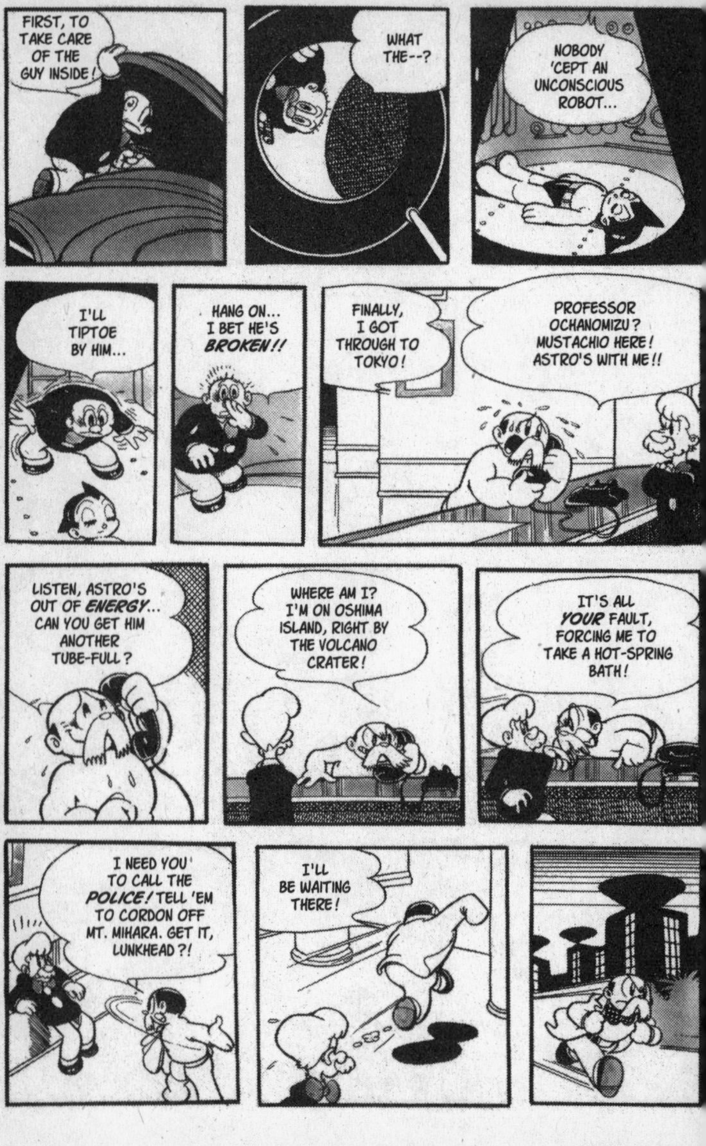
FIRST, TO TAKE CARE OF THE GUY INSIDE!
WHAT THE--?
NOBODY 'CEPT AN UNCONSCIOUS ROBOT...
I'LL TIPTOE BY HIM...
HANG ON... I BET HE'S BROKEN!!
FINALLY, I GOT THROUGH TO TOKYO!
PROFESSOR OCHANOMIZU? MUSTACHIO HERE! ASTRO'S WITH ME!!
LISTEN, ASTRO'S OUT OF ENERGY... CAN YOU GET HIM ANOTHER TUBE-FULL?
WHERE AM I? I'M ON OSHIMA ISLAND, RIGHT BY THE VOLCANO CRATER!
IT'S ALL YOUR FAULT, FORCING ME TO TAKE A HOT-SPRING BATH!
I NEED YOU TO CALL THE POLICE! TELL 'EM TO CORDON OFF MT. MIHARA. GET IT, LUNKHEAD?!
I'LL BE WAITING THERE!

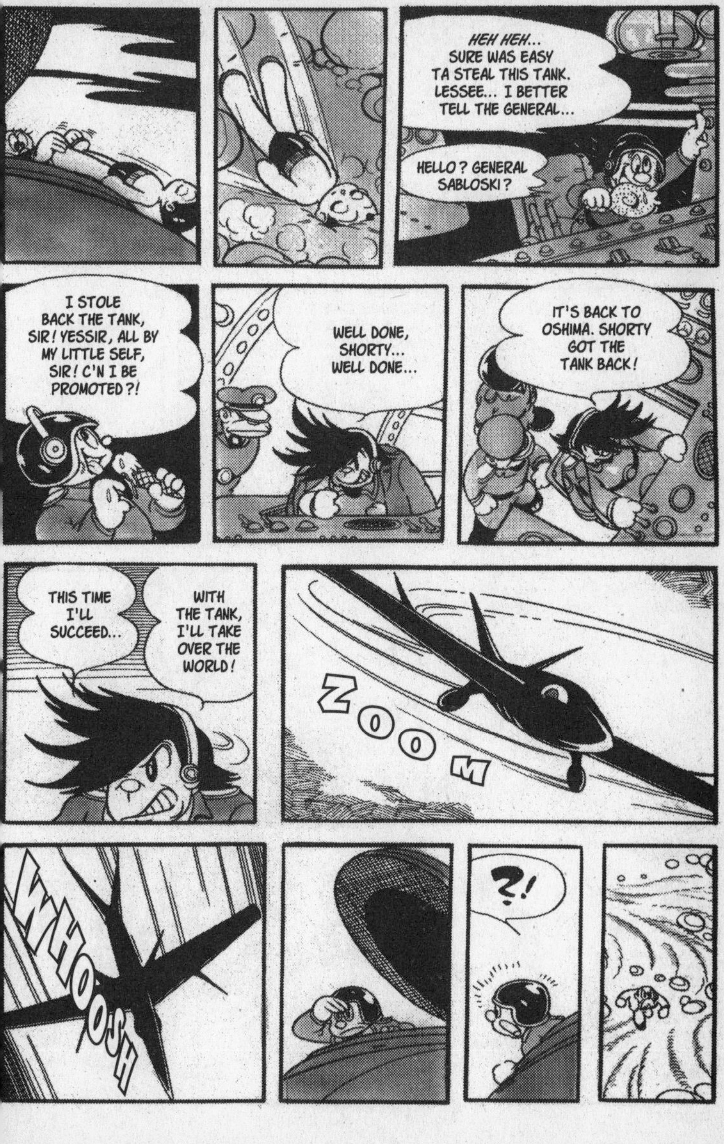
HEH HEH... SURE WAS EASY TA STEAL THIS TANK. LESSEE... I BETTER TELL THE GENERAL...
HELLO? GENERAL SABLOSKI?
I STOLE BACK THE TANK, SIR! YESSIR, ALL BY MY LITTLE SELF, SIR! C'N I BE PROMOTED?!
WELL DONE, SHORTY... WELL DONE...
IT'S BACK TO OSHIMA. SHORTY GOT THE TANK BACK!
THIS TIME I'LL SUCCEED...
WITH THE TANK, I'LL TAKE OVER THE WORLD!
ZOOM
WHOOSH
?!

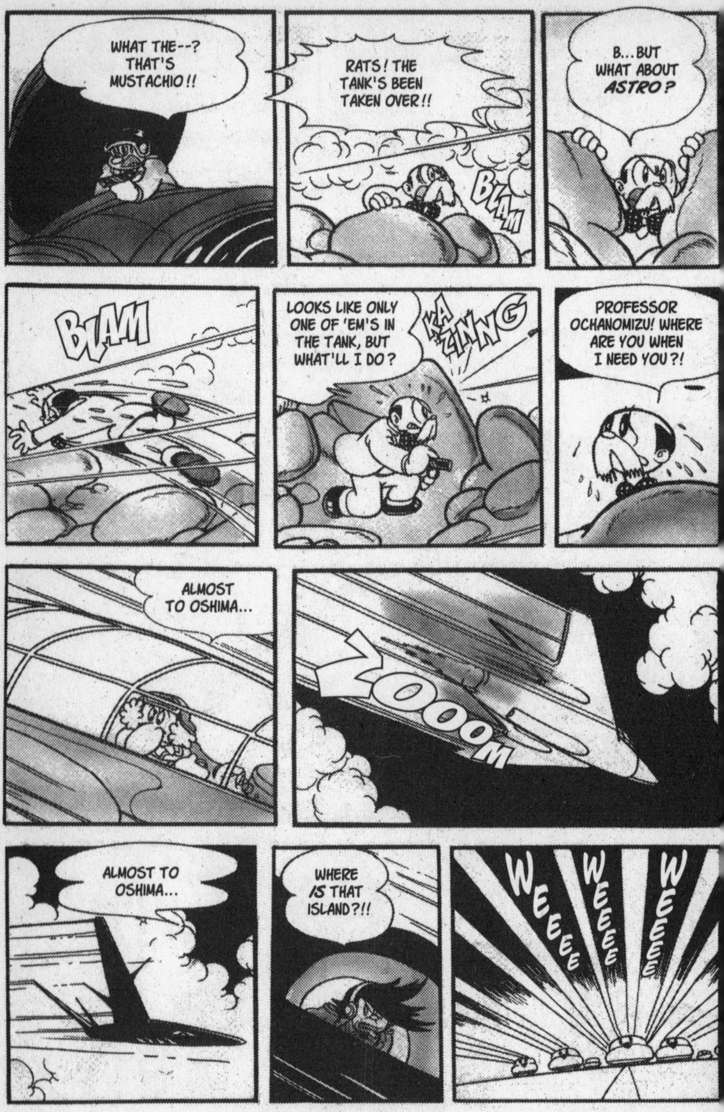

WHAT THE--? THAT'S MUSTACHIO!!
RATS! THE TANK'S BEEN TAKEN OVER!!
BLAM
B...BUT WHAT ABOUT *ASTRO?*
BLAM
LOOKS LIKE ONLY ONE OF 'EM'S IN THE TANK, BUT WHAT'LL I DO?
KAZINNG
PROFESSOR OCHANOMIZU! WHERE ARE YOU WHEN I NEED YOU?!
ALMOST TO OSHIMA...
ZOOOOM
ALMOST TO OSHIMA...
WHERE *IS* THAT ISLAND?!!
WEEEEE
WEEEEE
WEEEEE

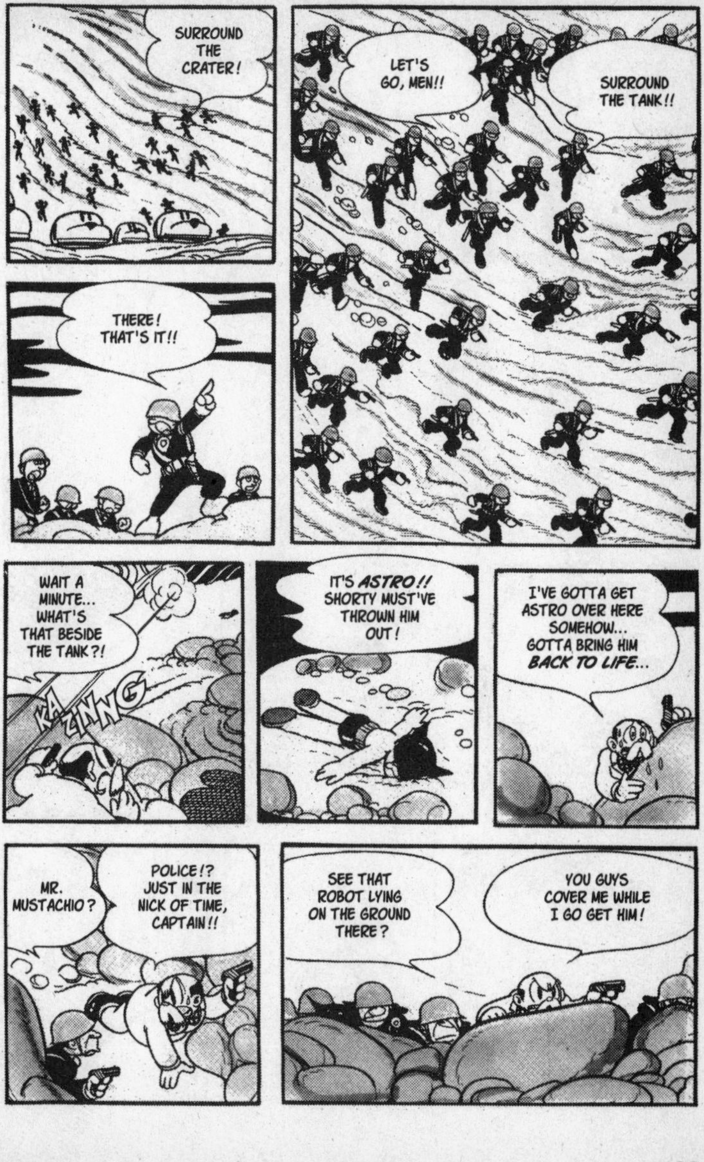
SURROUND THE CRATER!
THERE! THAT'S IT!!
LET'S GO, MEN!!
SURROUND THE TANK!!
WAIT A MINUTE... WHAT'S THAT BESIDE THE TANK?!
KAZINNG
IT'S ASTRO!! SHORTY MUST'VE THROWN HIM OUT!
I'VE GOTTA GET ASTRO OVER HERE SOMEHOW... GOTTA BRING HIM BACK TO LIFE...
MR. MUSTACHIO?
POLICE!? JUST IN THE NICK OF TIME, CAPTAIN!!
SEE THAT ROBOT LYING ON THE GROUND THERE?
YOU GUYS COVER ME WHILE I GO GET HIM!

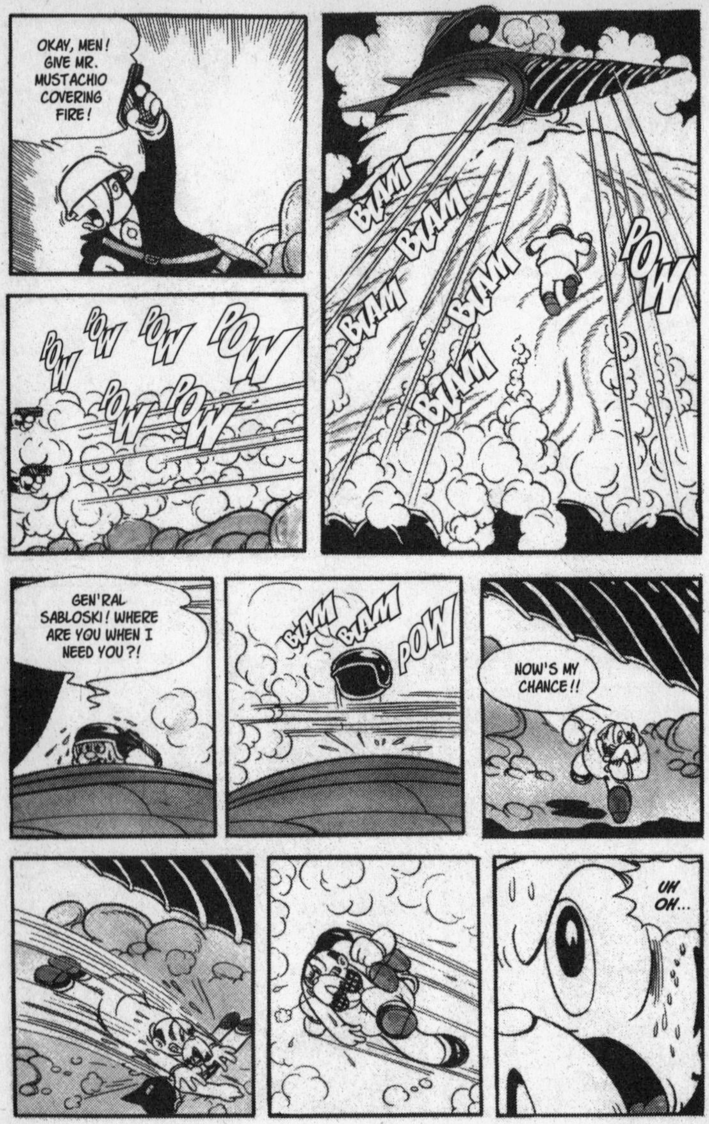
OKAY, MEN! GIVE MR. MUSTACHIO COVERING FIRE!
POW
POW
POW
POW
POW
POW
BLAM
BLAM
BLAM
BLAM
BLAM
BLAM
POW
GEN'RAL SABLOSKI! WHERE ARE YOU WHEN I NEED YOU?!
BLAM
BLAM
POW
NOW'S MY CHANCE!!
UH OH...

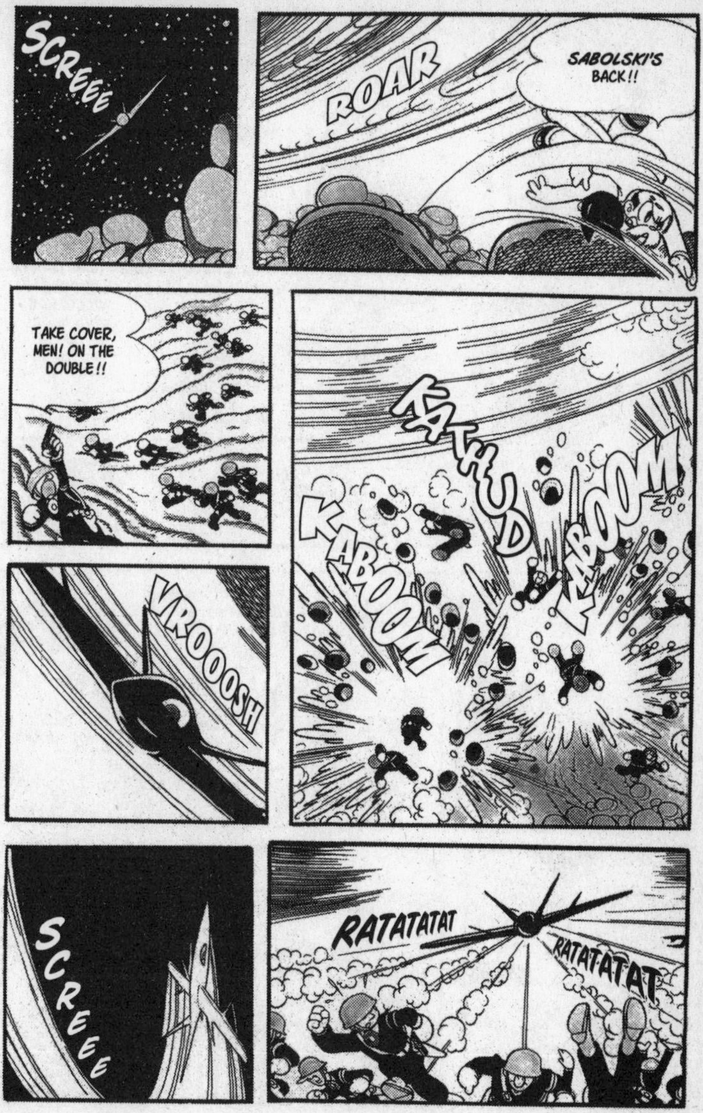
SCREEE
ROAR
SABOLSKI'S BACK!!
TAKE COVER, MEN! ON THE DOUBLE!!
KATHUD
KABOOM
KABOOM
VROOOOSH
SCREEE
RATATATAT
RATATATAT

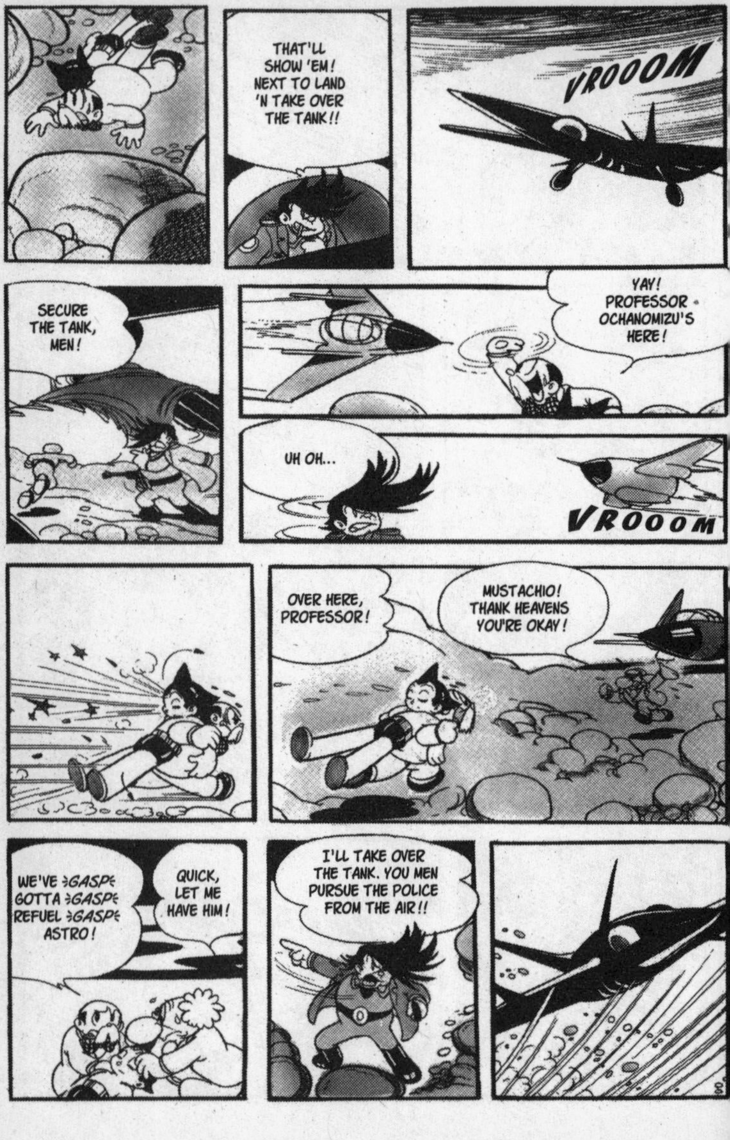
THAT'LL SHOW 'EM! NEXT TO LAND 'N TAKE OVER THE TANK!!
VROOOM
SECURE THE TANK, MEN!
YAY! PROFESSOR OCHANOMIZU'S HERE!
UH OH...
VROOOM
OVER HERE, PROFESSOR!
MUSTACHIO! THANK HEAVENS YOU'RE OKAY!
WE'VE ≥GASP≤ GOTTA ≥GASP≤ REFUEL ≥GASP≤ ASTRO!
QUICK, LET ME HAVE HIM!
I'LL TAKE OVER THE TANK. YOU MEN PURSUE THE POLICE FROM THE AIR!!

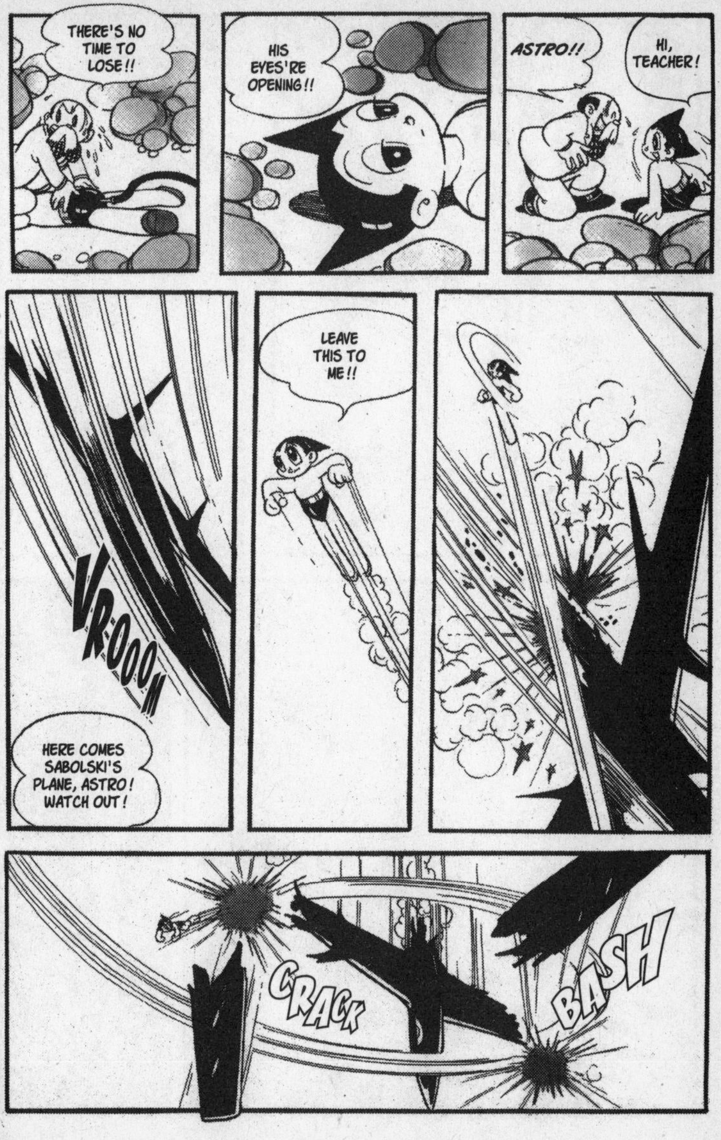

THERE'S NO TIME TO LOSE!!
HIS EYES'RE OPENING!!
ASTRO!!
HI, TEACHER!
VROOOM
HERE COMES SABOLSKI'S PLANE, ASTRO! WATCH OUT!
LEAVE THIS TO ME!!
CRACK
BASH

 KAAVOOOOMP

 WHAT THE--?!! OH MY GOSH...

 I'LL HAVE TO GO UNDERGROUND IN THE TANK!!

 NOT SO FAST, SABOLSKI!

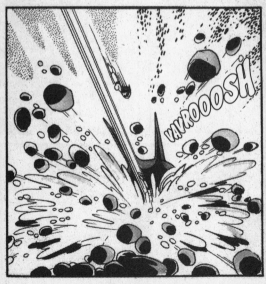 KAVROOOSH

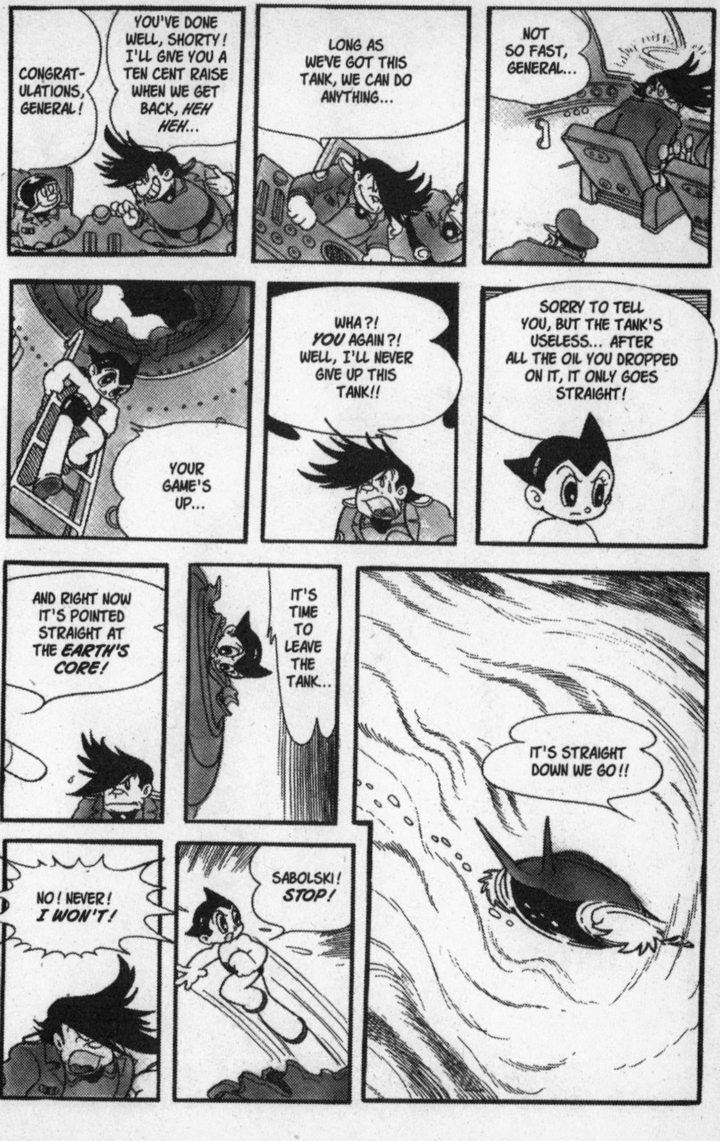
CONGRAT-ULATIONS, GENERAL!
YOU'VE DONE WELL, SHORTY! I'LL GIVE YOU A TEN CENT RAISE WHEN WE GET BACK, *HEH HEH*...
LONG AS WE'VE GOT THIS TANK, WE CAN DO ANYTHING...
NOT SO FAST, GENERAL...
YOUR GAME'S UP...
WHA?! *YOU* AGAIN?! WELL, I'LL NEVER GIVE UP THIS TANK!!
SORRY TO TELL YOU, BUT THE TANK'S USELESS... AFTER ALL THE OIL YOU DROPPED ON IT, IT ONLY GOES STRAIGHT!
AND RIGHT NOW IT'S POINTED STRAIGHT AT THE *EARTH'S CORE!*
IT'S TIME TO LEAVE THE TANK...
IT'S STRAIGHT DOWN WE GO!!
NO! NEVER! *I WON'T!*
SABOLSKI! *STOP!*

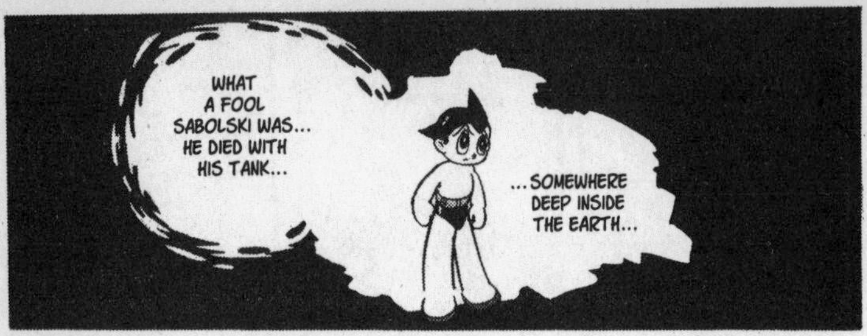
WHAT A FOOL SABOLSKI WAS... HE DIED WITH HIS TANK...
...SOMEWHERE DEEP INSIDE THE EARTH...

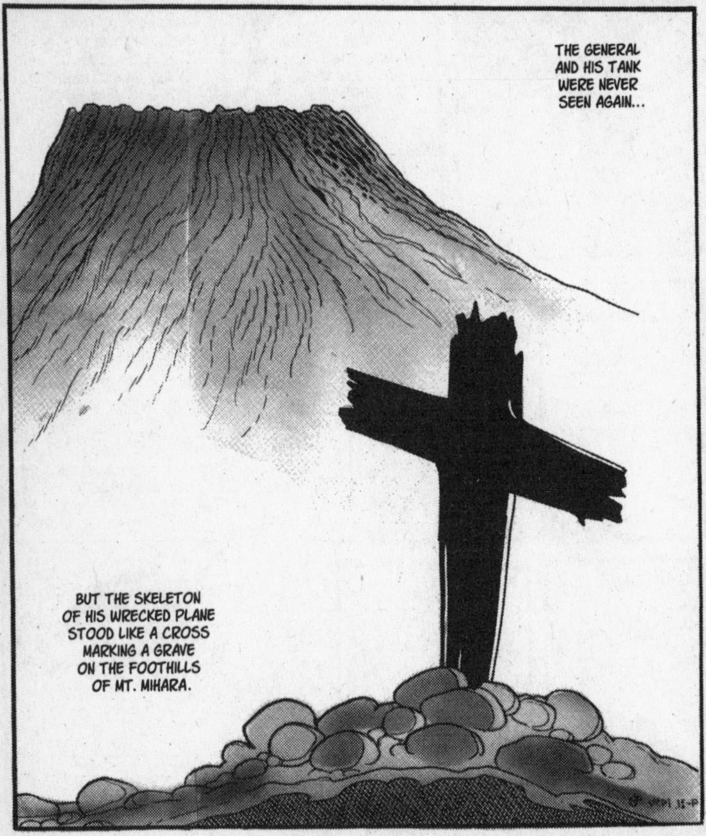
THE GENERAL AND HIS TANK WERE NEVER SEEN AGAIN...
BUT THE SKELETON OF HIS WRECKED PLANE STOOD LIKE A CROSS MARKING A GRAVE ON THE FOOTHILLS OF MT. MIHARA.

THE MAN
WHO RETURNED
FROM MARS

First serialized from January to March 1968
in *Shonen* magazine.

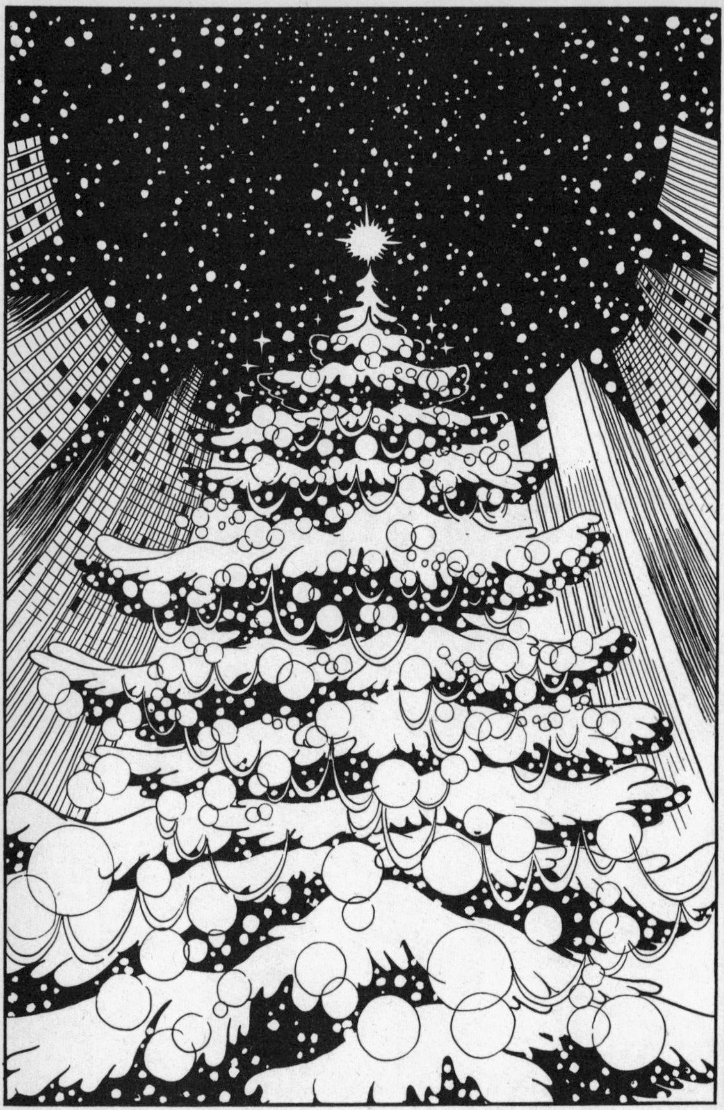

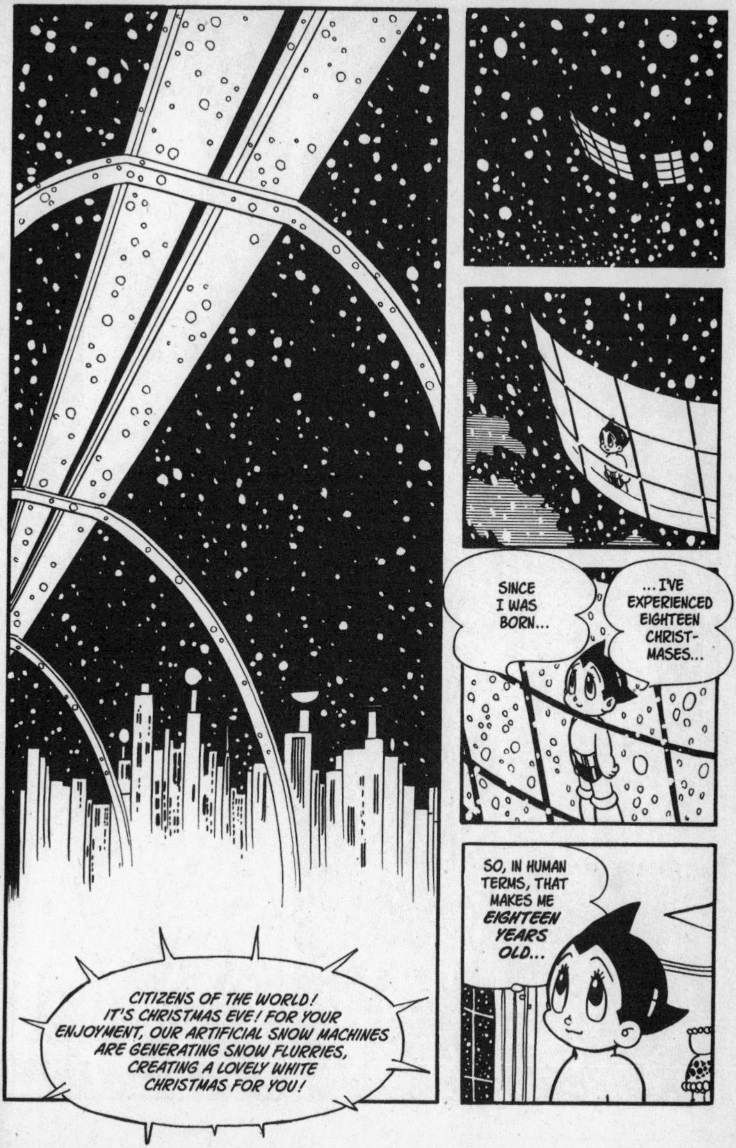

CITIZENS OF THE WORLD! IT'S CHRISTMAS EVE! FOR YOUR ENJOYMENT, OUR ARTIFICIAL SNOW MACHINES ARE GENERATING SNOW FLURRIES, CREATING A LOVELY WHITE CHRISTMAS FOR YOU!
SINCE I WAS BORN...
...I'VE EXPERIENCED EIGHTEEN CHRIST-MASES...
SO, IN HUMAN TERMS, THAT MAKES ME *EIGHTEEN YEARS OLD...*

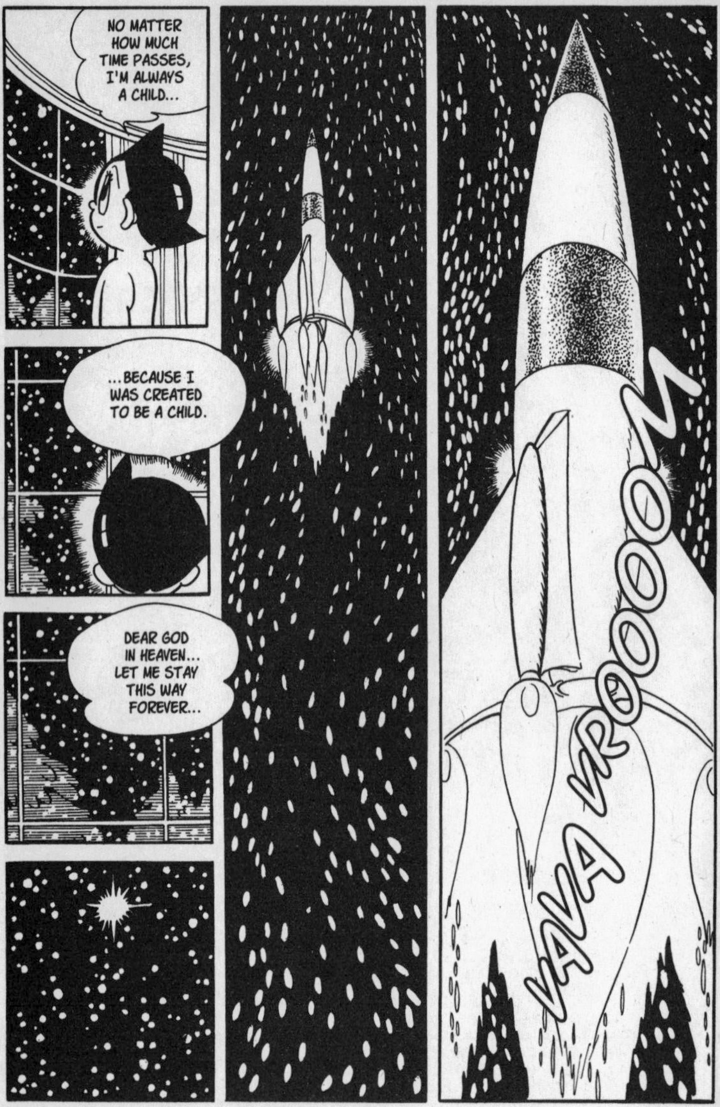
NO MATTER HOW MUCH TIME PASSES, I'M ALWAYS A CHILD...
...BECAUSE I WAS CREATED TO BE A CHILD.
DEAR GOD IN HEAVEN... LET ME STAY THIS WAY FOREVER...
VAVA VROOOOM

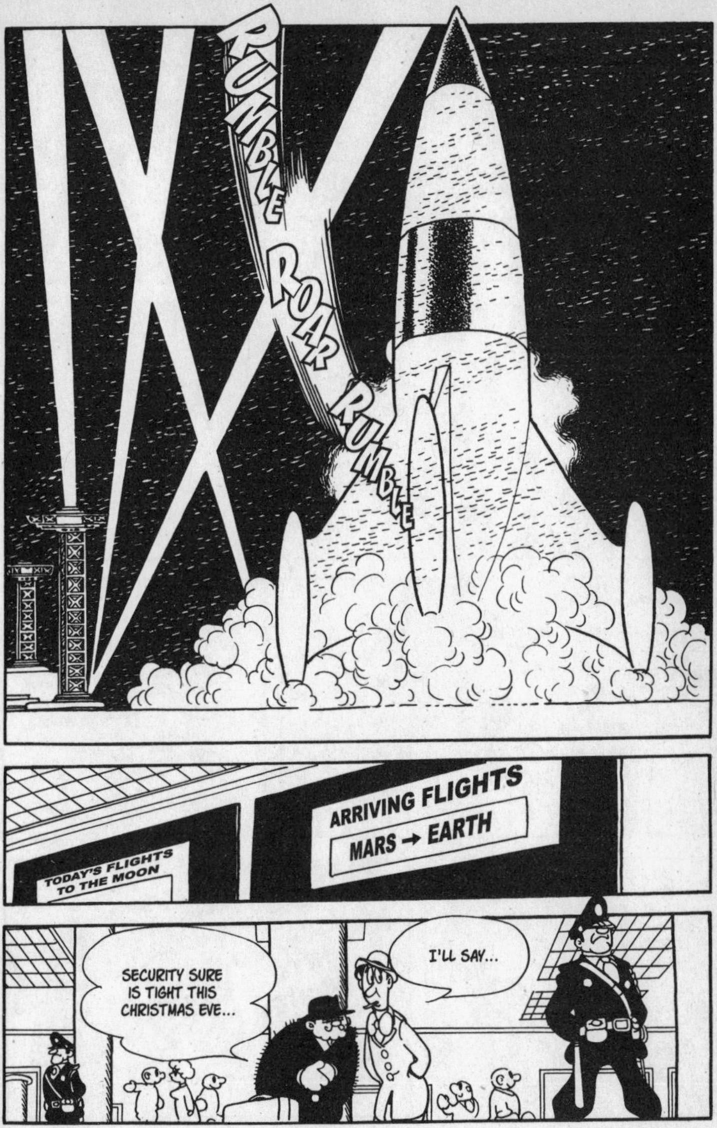
RUMBLE
ROAR
RUMBLE
ARRIVING FLIGHTS
MARS → EARTH
TODAY'S FLIGHTS TO THE MOON
SECURITY SURE IS TIGHT THIS CHRISTMAS EVE...
I'LL SAY...

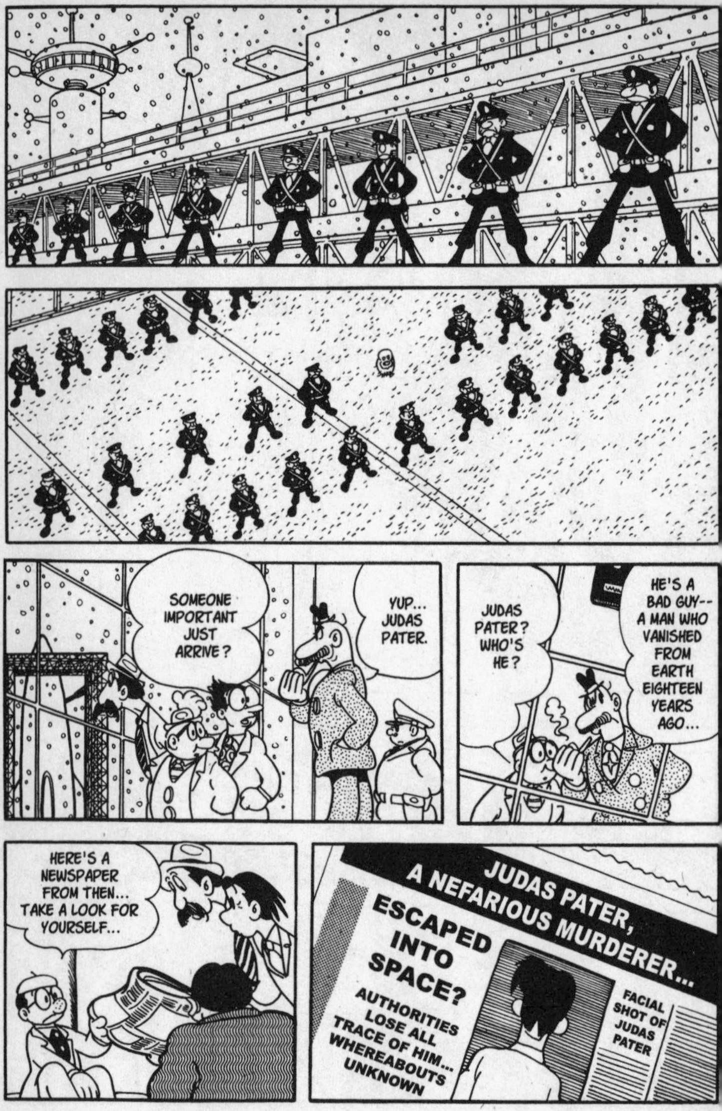
SOMEONE IMPORTANT JUST ARRIVE?
YUP... JUDAS PATER.
JUDAS PATER? WHO'S HE?
HE'S A BAD GUY-- A MAN WHO VANISHED FROM EARTH EIGHTEEN YEARS AGO...
HERE'S A NEWSPAPER FROM THEN... TAKE A LOOK FOR YOURSELF...
JUDAS PATER, A NEFARIOUS MURDERER...
ESCAPED INTO SPACE?
AUTHORITIES LOSE ALL TRACE OF HIM... WHEREABOUTS UNKNOWN
FACIAL SHOT OF JUDAS PATER

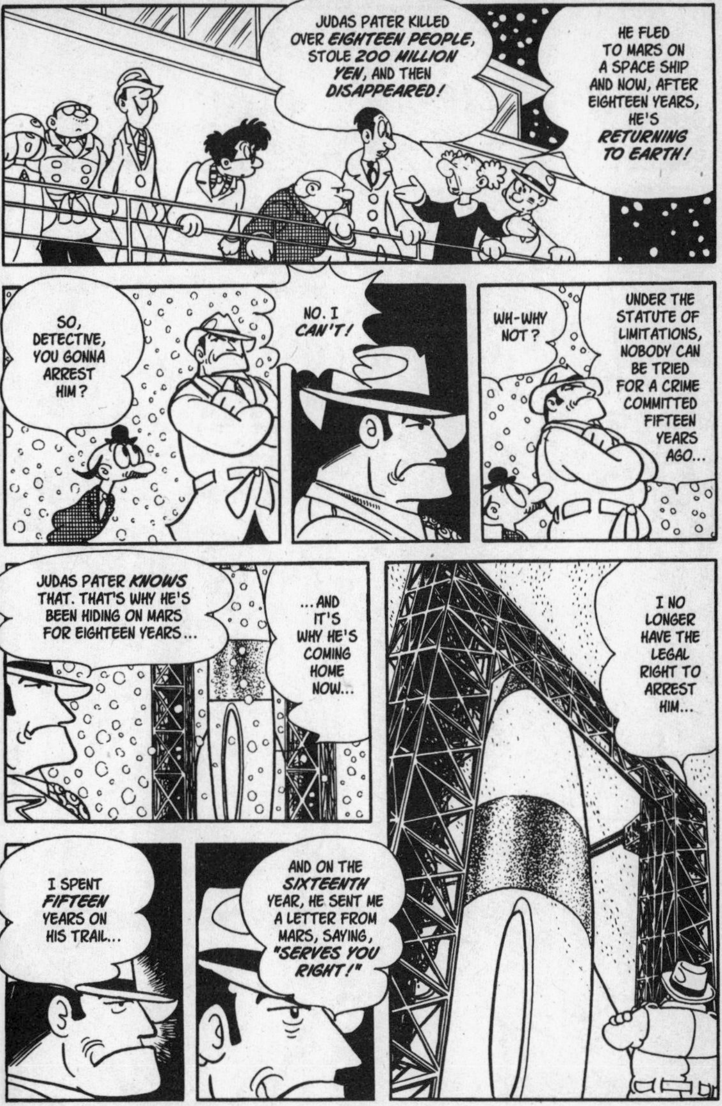

JUDAS PATER KILLED OVER EIGHTEEN PEOPLE, STOLE 200 MILLION YEN, AND THEN DISAPPEARED!
HE FLED TO MARS ON A SPACE SHIP AND NOW, AFTER EIGHTEEN YEARS, HE'S RETURNING TO EARTH!
SO, DETECTIVE, YOU GONNA ARREST HIM?
NO. I CAN'T!
WH-WHY NOT?
UNDER THE STATUTE OF LIMITATIONS, NOBODY CAN BE TRIED FOR A CRIME COMMITTED FIFTEEN YEARS AGO...
JUDAS PATER KNOWS THAT. THAT'S WHY HE'S BEEN HIDING ON MARS FOR EIGHTEEN YEARS...
...AND IT'S WHY HE'S COMING HOME NOW...
I SPENT FIFTEEN YEARS ON HIS TRAIL...
AND ON THE SIXTEENTH YEAR, HE SENT ME A LETTER FROM MARS, SAYING, "SERVES YOU RIGHT!"
I NO LONGER HAVE THE LEGAL RIGHT TO ARREST HIM...

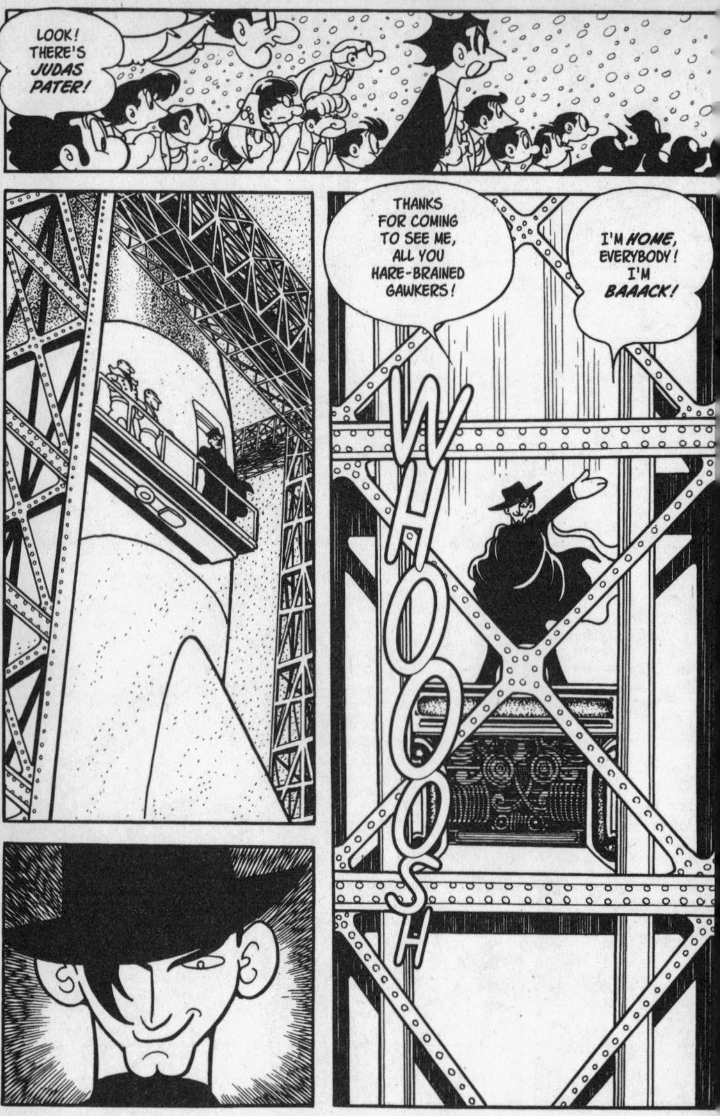
LOOK! THERE'S JUDAS PATER!
THANKS FOR COMING TO SEE ME, ALL YOU HARE-BRAINED GAWKERS!
I'M HOME, EVERYBODY! I'M BAAACK!
WHOOOOSH

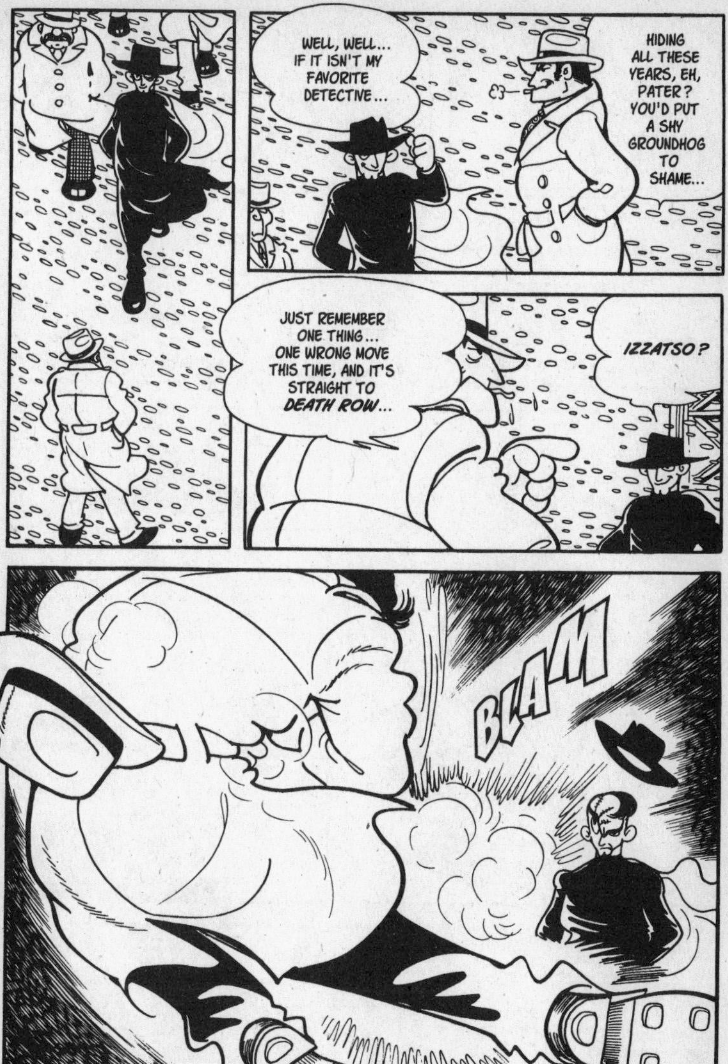

WELL, WELL... IF IT ISN'T MY FAVORITE DETECTIVE...
HIDING ALL THESE YEARS, EH, PATER? YOU'D PUT A SHY GROUNDHOG TO SHAME...
JUST REMEMBER ONE THING... ONE WRONG MOVE THIS TIME, AND IT'S STRAIGHT TO *DEATH ROW*...
IZZATSO?
BLA-M

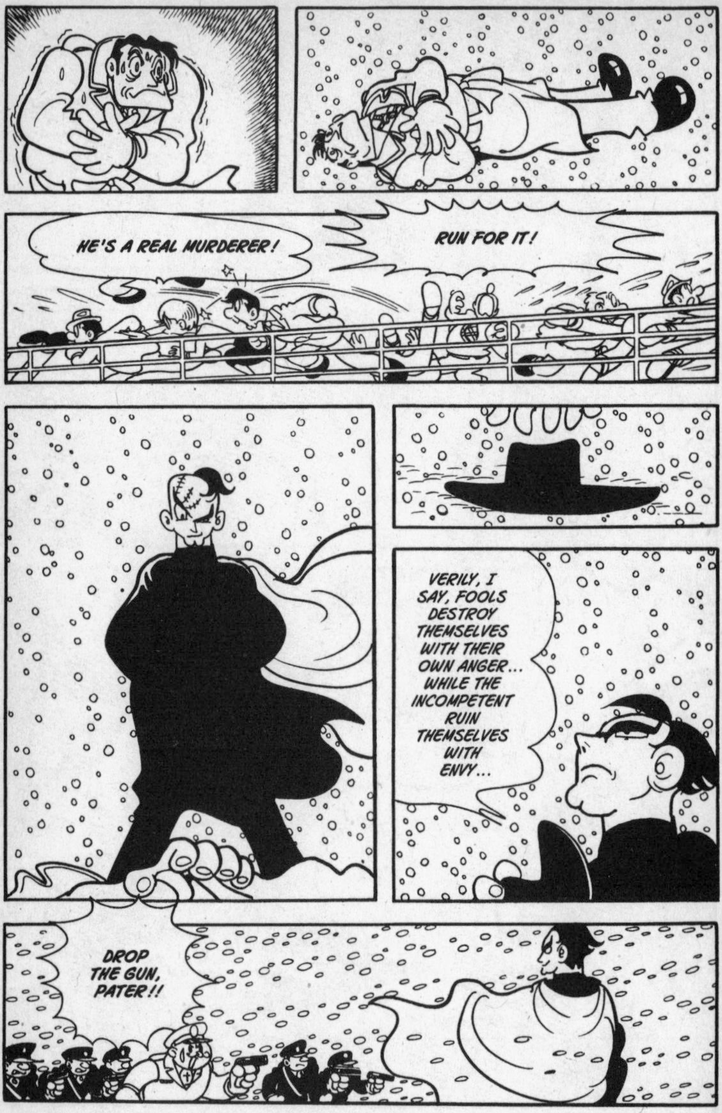
HE'S A REAL MURDERER!
RUN FOR IT!
VERILY, I SAY, FOOLS DESTROY THEMSELVES WITH THEIR OWN ANGER... WHILE THE INCOMPETENT RUIN THEMSELVES WITH ENVY...
DROP THE GUN, PATER!!

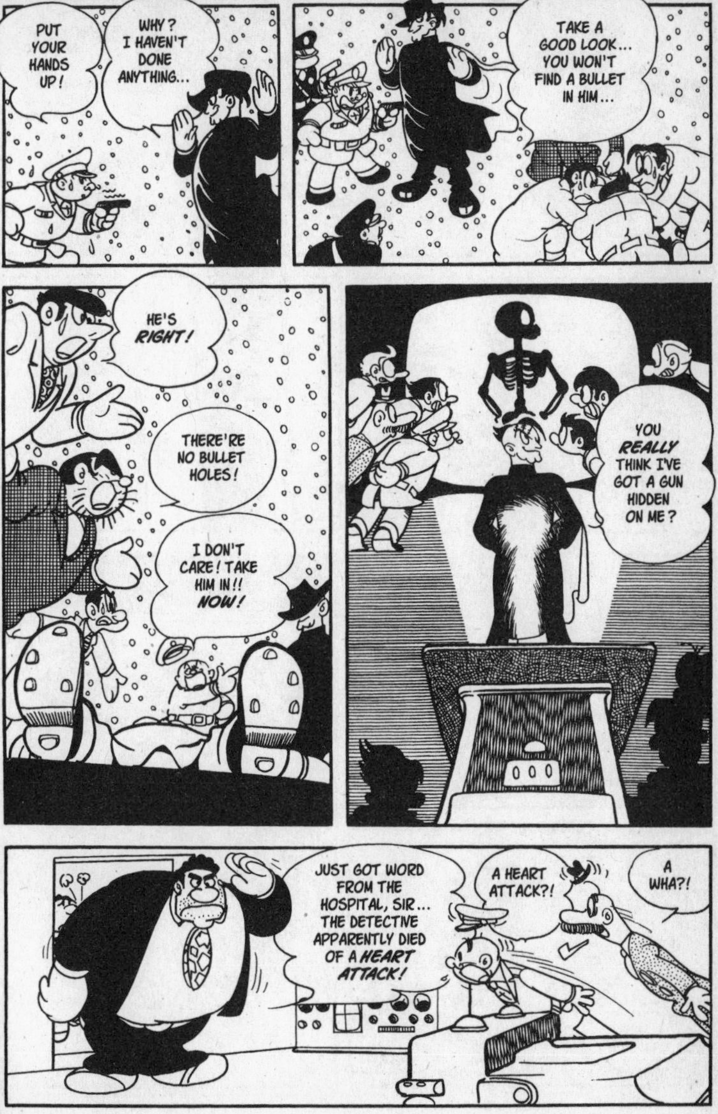
PUT YOUR HANDS UP!
WHY? I HAVEN'T DONE ANYTHING...
TAKE A GOOD LOOK... YOU WON'T FIND A BULLET IN HIM...
HE'S RIGHT!
THERE'RE NO BULLET HOLES!
I DON'T CARE! TAKE HIM IN!! NOW!
YOU REALLY THINK I'VE GOT A GUN HIDDEN ON ME?
JUST GOT WORD FROM THE HOSPITAL, SIR... THE DETECTIVE APPARENTLY DIED OF A HEART ATTACK!
A HEART ATTACK?!
A WHA?!

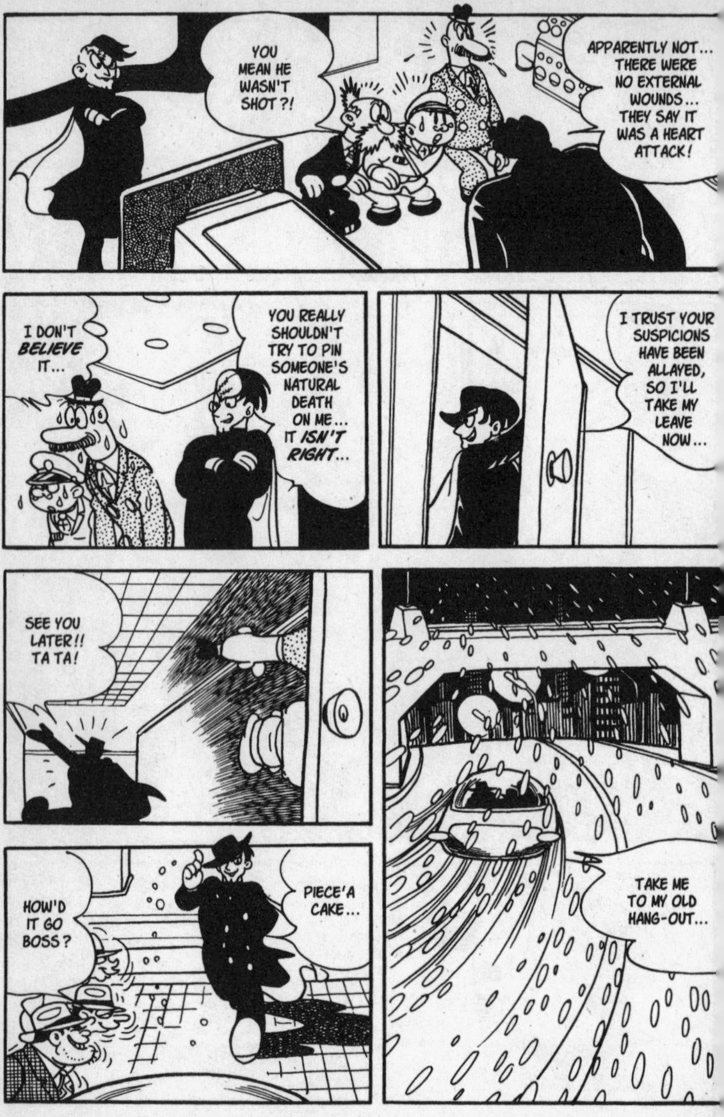
YOU MEAN HE WASN'T SHOT?!
APPARENTLY NOT... THERE WERE NO EXTERNAL WOUNDS... THEY SAY IT WAS A HEART ATTACK!
I DON'T *BELIEVE* IT...
YOU REALLY SHOULDN'T TRY TO PIN SOMEONE'S NATURAL DEATH ON ME... IT *ISN'T RIGHT*...
I TRUST YOUR SUSPICIONS HAVE BEEN ALLAYED, SO I'LL TAKE MY LEAVE NOW...
SEE YOU LATER!! TA TA!
HOW'D IT GO BOSS?
PIECE'A CAKE...
TAKE ME TO MY OLD HANG-OUT...

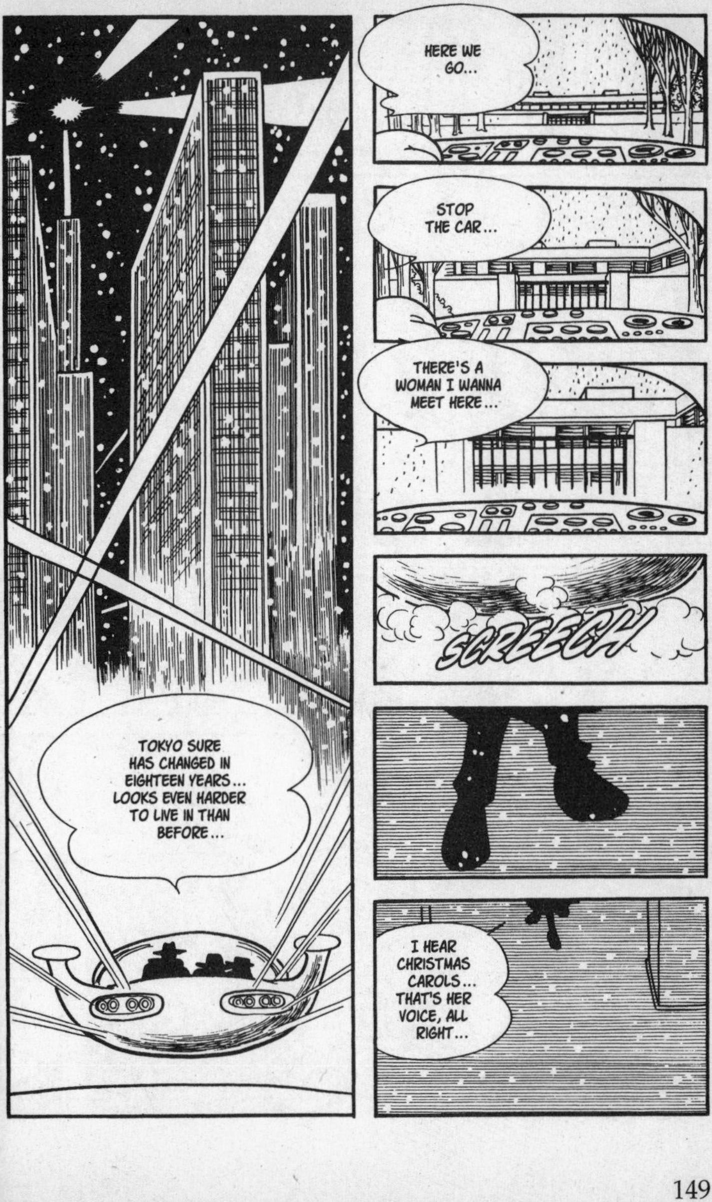
TOKYO SURE HAS CHANGED IN EIGHTEEN YEARS... LOOKS EVEN HARDER TO LIVE IN THAN BEFORE...
HERE WE GO...
STOP THE CAR...
THERE'S A WOMAN I WANNA MEET HERE...
SCREECH
I HEAR CHRISTMAS CAROLS... THAT'S HER VOICE, ALL RIGHT...

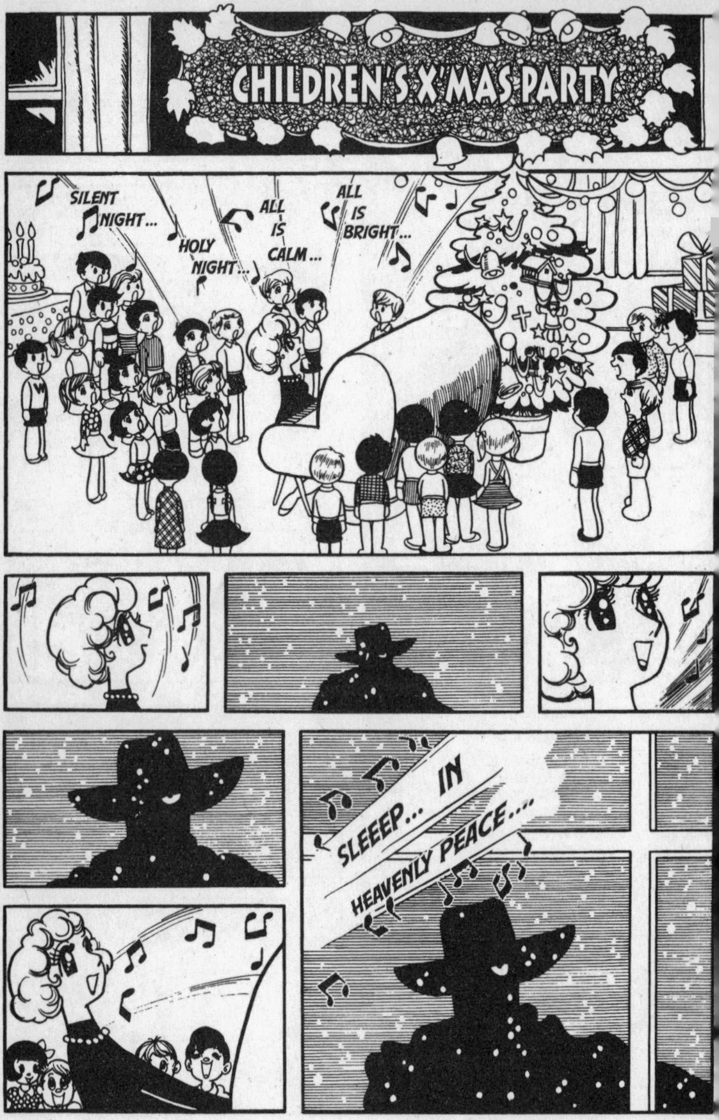
CHILDREN'S X'MAS PARTY
SILENT NIGHT...
HOLY NIGHT...
ALL IS CALM...
ALL IS BRIGHT...
SLEEEP... IN
HEAVENLY PEACE....

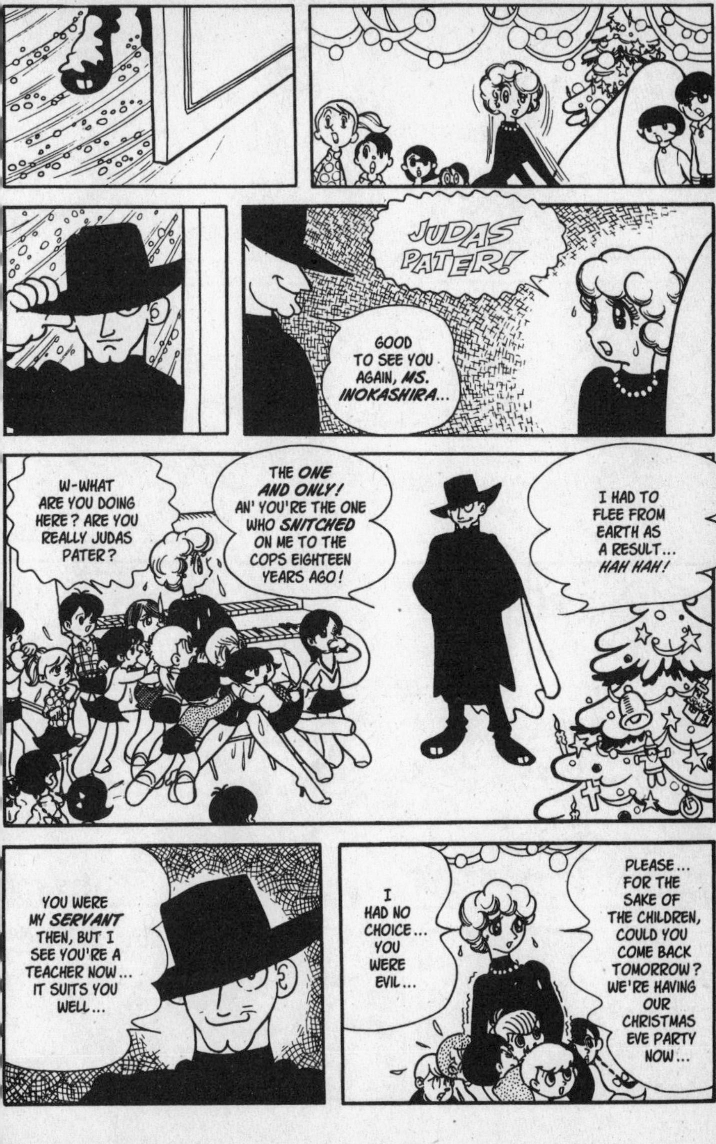
JUDAS PATER!
GOOD TO SEE YOU AGAIN, MS. INOKASHIRA...
W-WHAT ARE YOU DOING HERE? ARE YOU REALLY JUDAS PATER?
THE ONE AND ONLY! AN' YOU'RE THE ONE WHO SNITCHED ON ME TO THE COPS EIGHTEEN YEARS AGO!
I HAD TO FLEE FROM EARTH AS A RESULT... HAH HAH!
YOU WERE MY SERVANT THEN, BUT I SEE YOU'RE A TEACHER NOW... IT SUITS YOU WELL...
I HAD NO CHOICE... YOU WERE EVIL...
PLEASE... FOR THE SAKE OF THE CHILDREN, COULD YOU COME BACK TOMORROW? WE'RE HAVING OUR CHRISTMAS EVE PARTY NOW...

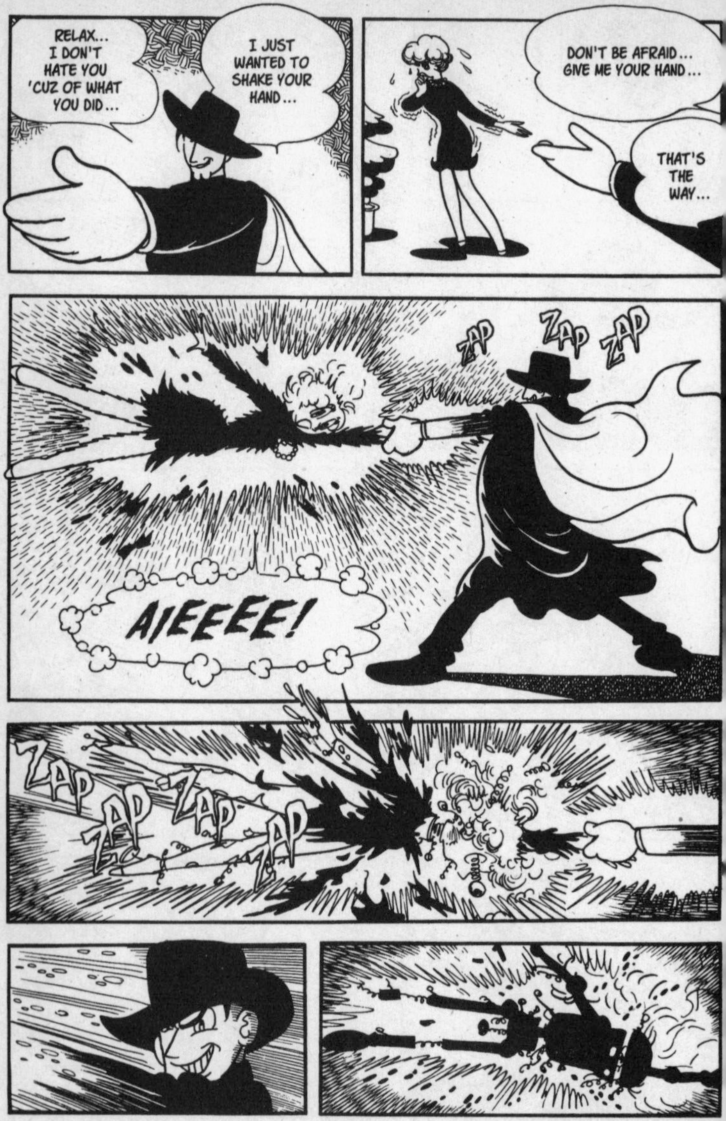

RELAX... I DON'T HATE YOU 'CUZ OF WHAT YOU DID...
I JUST WANTED TO SHAKE YOUR HAND...
DON'T BE AFRAID... GIVE ME YOUR HAND...
THAT'S THE WAY...
ZAP ZAP ZAP
AIEEEE!
ZAP ZAP ZAP ZAP ZAP

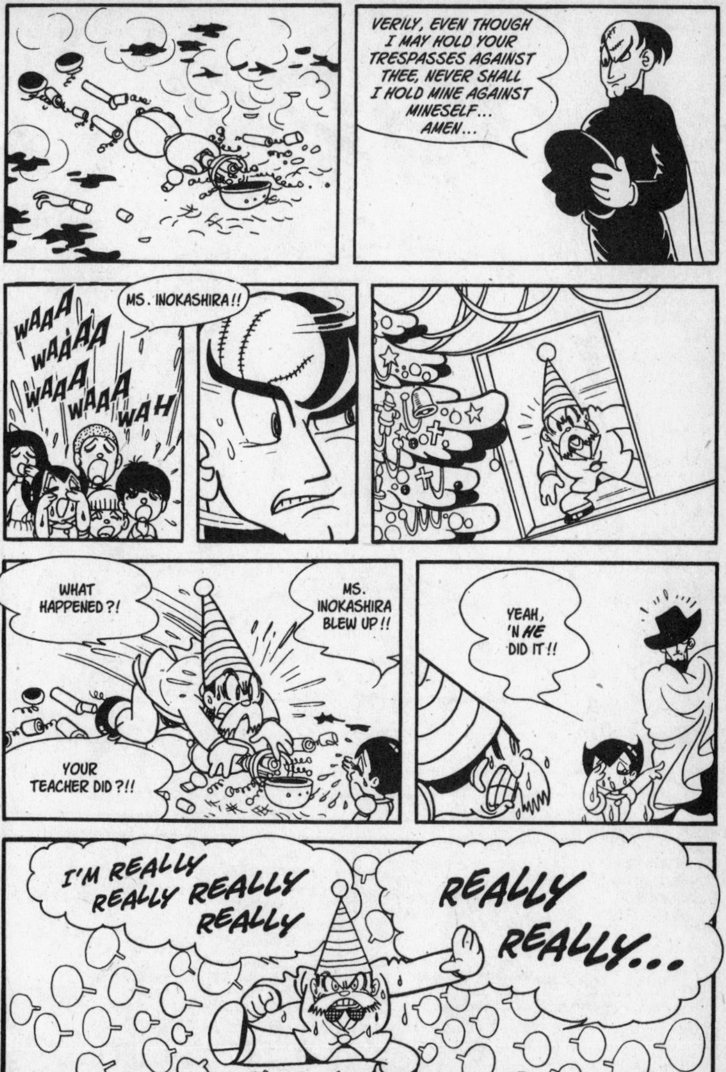
VERILY, EVEN THOUGH I MAY HOLD YOUR TRESPASSES AGAINST THEE, NEVER SHALL I HOLD MINE AGAINST MINESELF... AMEN...
WAAA WAAAA WAAA WAAA WAH
MS. INOKASHIRA!!
WHAT HAPPENED?!
MS. INOKASHIRA BLEW UP!!
YOUR TEACHER DID?!!
YEAH, 'N HE DID IT!!
I'M REALLY REALLY REALLY REALLY
REALLY REALLY...

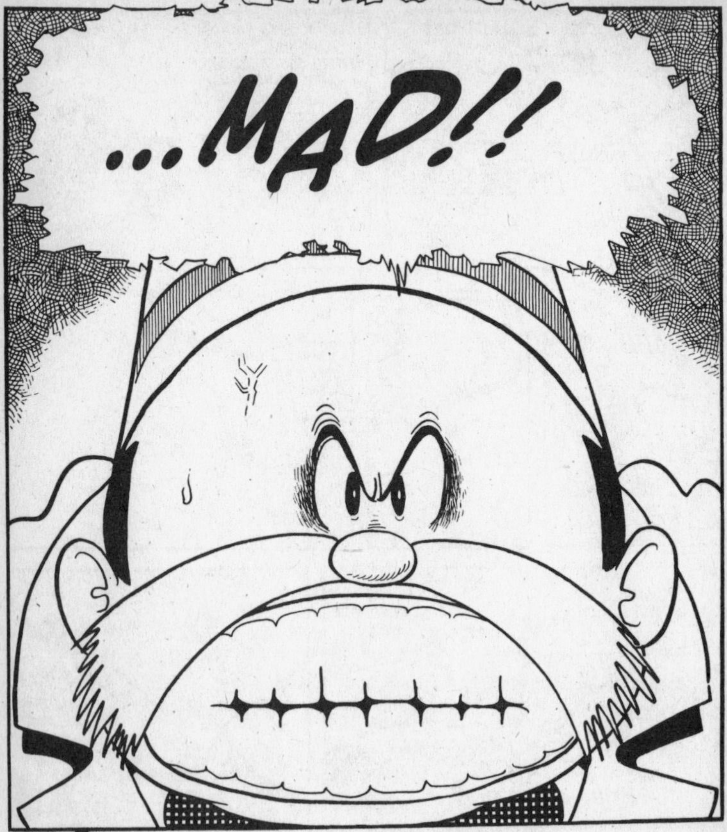
...MAD!!

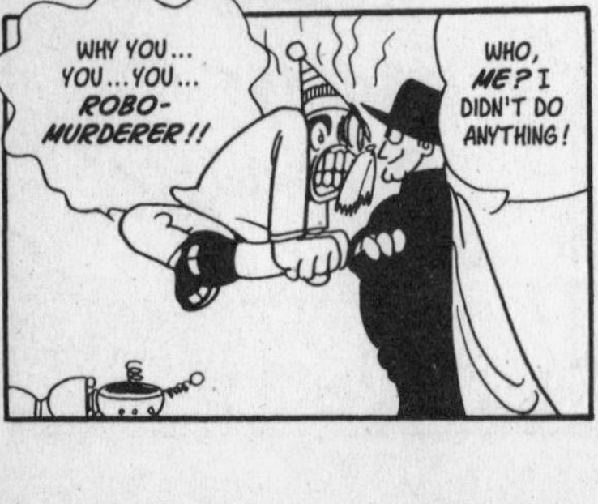
WHY YOU... YOU...YOU... ROBO-MURDERER!!
WHO, ME? I DIDN'T DO ANYTHING!

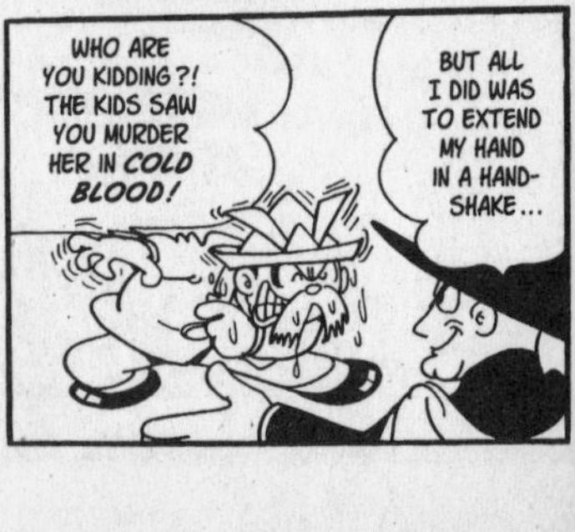
WHO ARE YOU KIDDING?! THE KIDS SAW YOU MURDER HER IN COLD BLOOD!
BUT ALL I DID WAS TO EXTEND MY HAND IN A HAND-SHAKE...

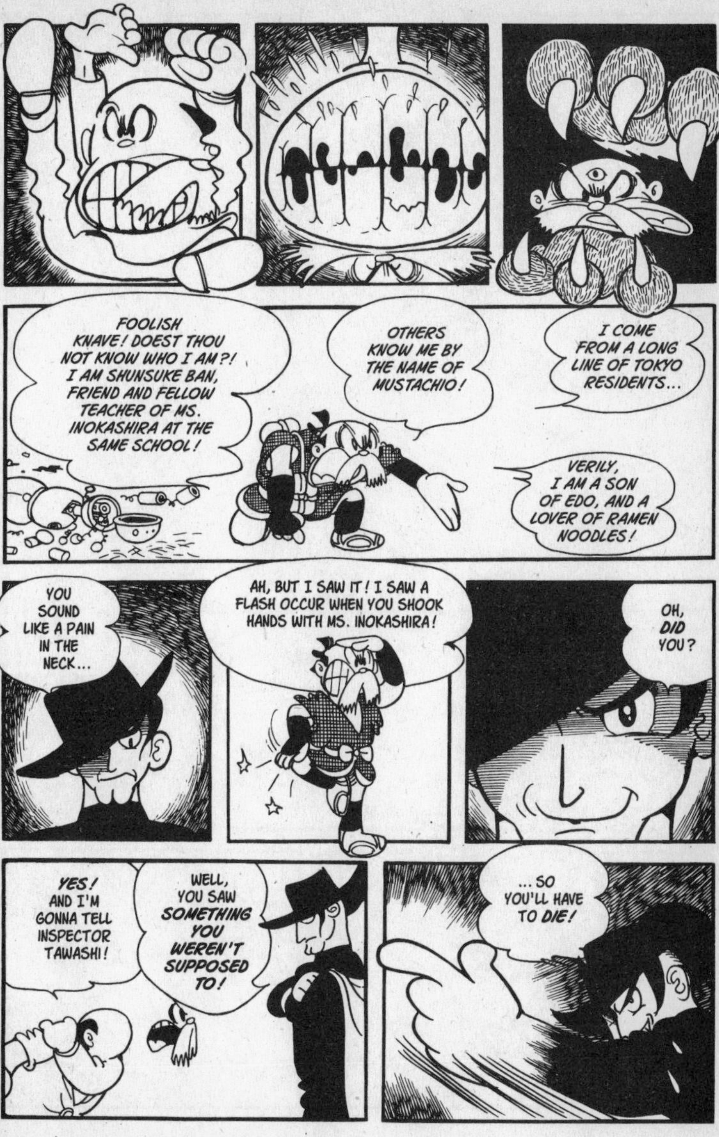
FOOLISH KNAVE! DOEST THOU NOT KNOW WHO I AM?! I AM SHUNSUKE BAN, FRIEND AND FELLOW TEACHER OF MS. INOKASHIRA AT THE SAME SCHOOL!
OTHERS KNOW ME BY THE NAME OF MUSTACHIO!
I COME FROM A LONG LINE OF TOKYO RESIDENTS...
VERILY, I AM A SON OF EDO, AND A LOVER OF RAMEN NOODLES!
YOU SOUND LIKE A PAIN IN THE NECK...
AH, BUT I SAW IT! I SAW A FLASH OCCUR WHEN YOU SHOOK HANDS WITH MS. INOKASHIRA!
OH, DID YOU?
YES! AND I'M GONNA TELL INSPECTOR TAWASHI!
WELL, YOU SAW SOMETHING YOU WEREN'T SUPPOSED TO!
...SO YOU'LL HAVE TO DIE!

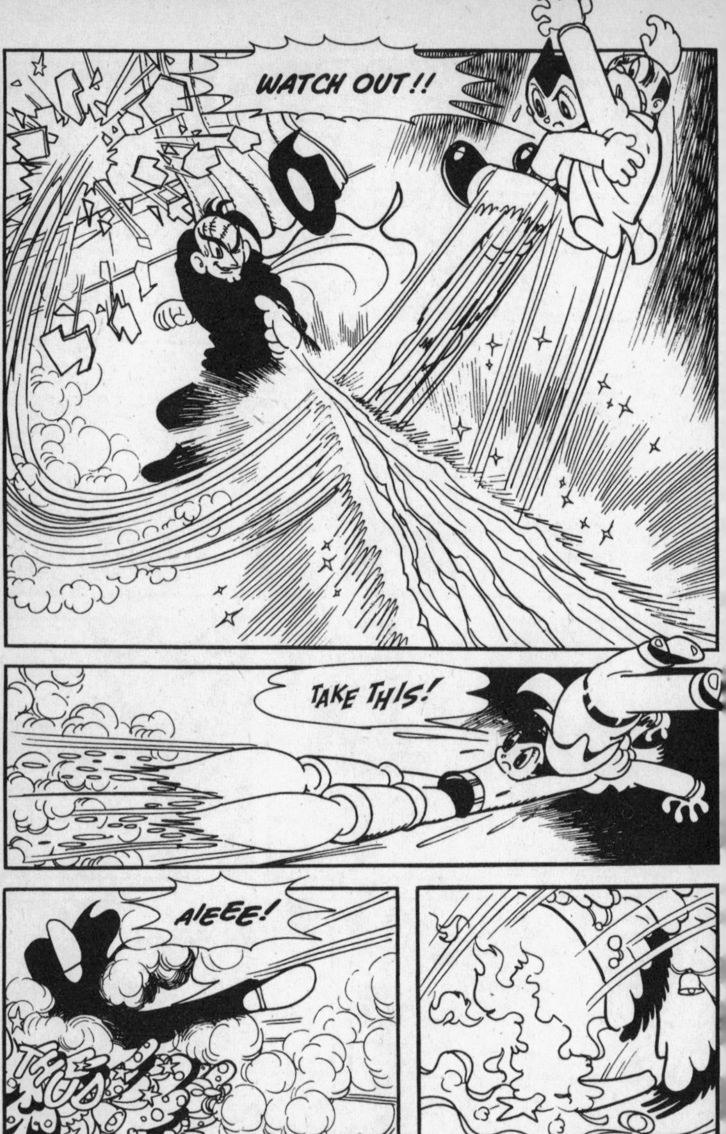
WATCH OUT!!
TAKE THIS!
AIEEE!
THUD

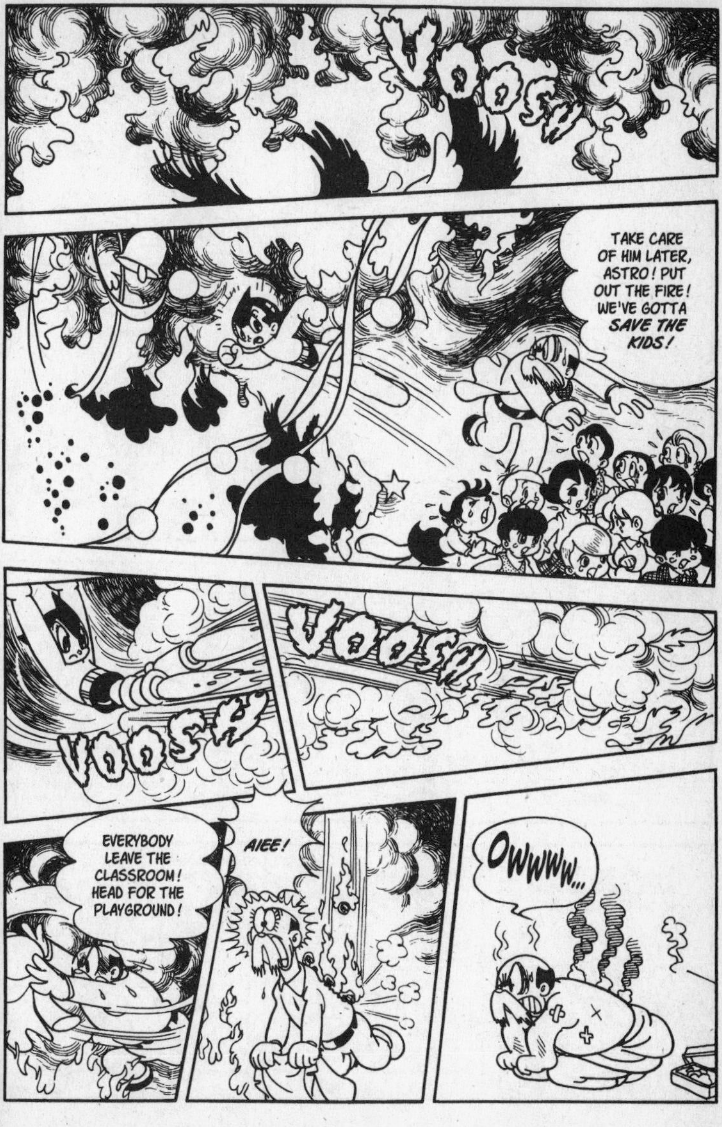
VOOSH
TAKE CARE OF HIM LATER, ASTRO! PUT OUT THE FIRE! WE'VE GOTTA SAVE THE KIDS!
VOOSH
VOOSH
EVERYBODY LEAVE THE CLASSROOM! HEAD FOR THE PLAYGROUND!
AIEE!
OWWWW...

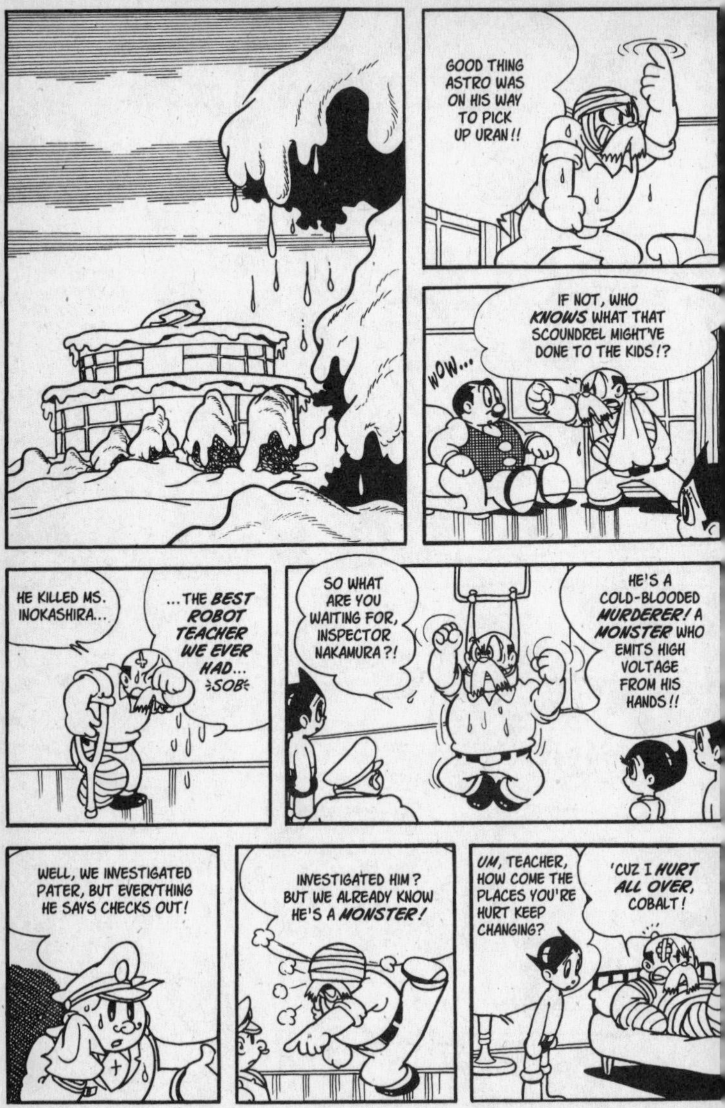
GOOD THING ASTRO WAS ON HIS WAY TO PICK UP URAN!!
IF NOT, WHO KNOWS WHAT THAT SCOUNDREL MIGHT'VE DONE TO THE KIDS!?
WOW...
HE KILLED MS. INOKASHIRA...
...THE BEST ROBOT TEACHER WE EVER HAD...
SOB
SO WHAT ARE YOU WAITING FOR, INSPECTOR NAKAMURA?!
HE'S A COLD-BLOODED MURDERER! A MONSTER WHO EMITS HIGH VOLTAGE FROM HIS HANDS!!
WELL, WE INVESTIGATED PATER, BUT EVERYTHING HE SAYS CHECKS OUT!
INVESTIGATED HIM? BUT WE ALREADY KNOW HE'S A MONSTER!
UM, TEACHER, HOW COME THE PLACES YOU'RE HURT KEEP CHANGING?
'CUZ I HURT ALL OVER, COBALT!

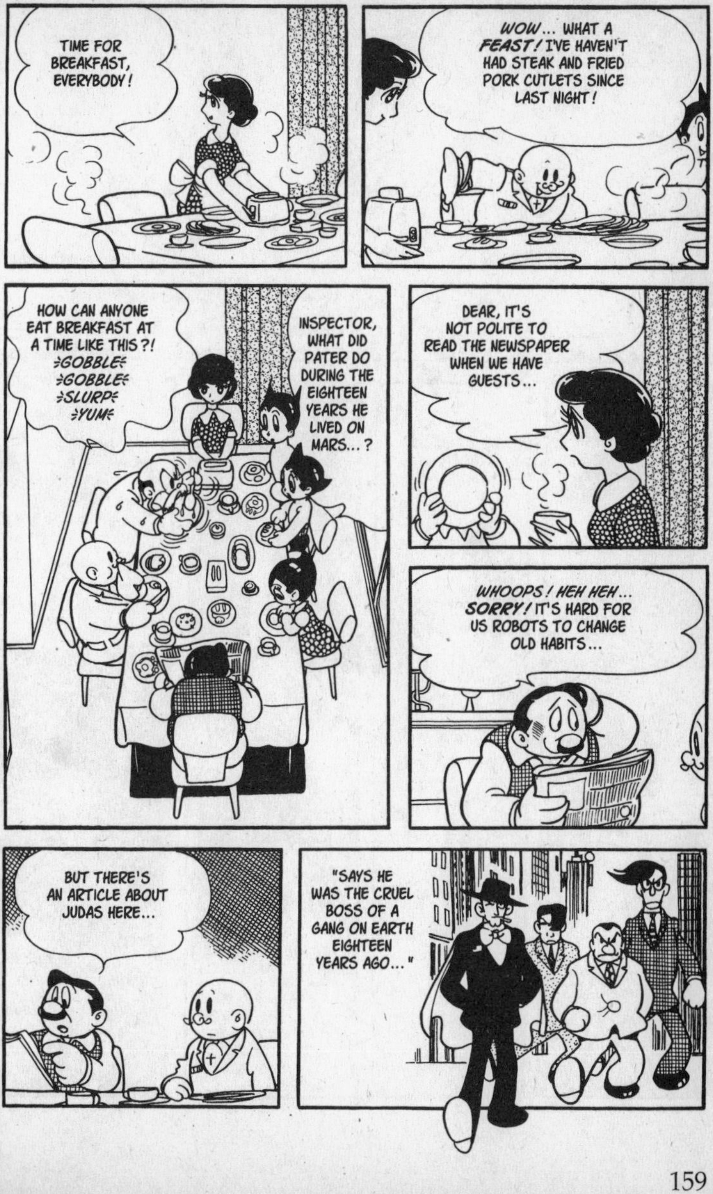
TIME FOR BREAKFAST, EVERYBODY!
WOW... WHAT A FEAST! I'VE HAVEN'T HAD STEAK AND FRIED PORK CUTLETS SINCE LAST NIGHT!
HOW CAN ANYONE EAT BREAKFAST AT A TIME LIKE THIS?! GOBBLE GOBBLE SLURP YUM
INSPECTOR, WHAT DID PATER DO DURING THE EIGHTEEN YEARS HE LIVED ON MARS...?
DEAR, IT'S NOT POLITE TO READ THE NEWSPAPER WHEN WE HAVE GUESTS...
WHOOPS! HEH HEH... SORRY! IT'S HARD FOR US ROBOTS TO CHANGE OLD HABITS...
BUT THERE'S AN ARTICLE ABOUT JUDAS HERE...
"SAYS HE WAS THE CRUEL BOSS OF A GANG ON EARTH EIGHTEEN YEARS AGO..."

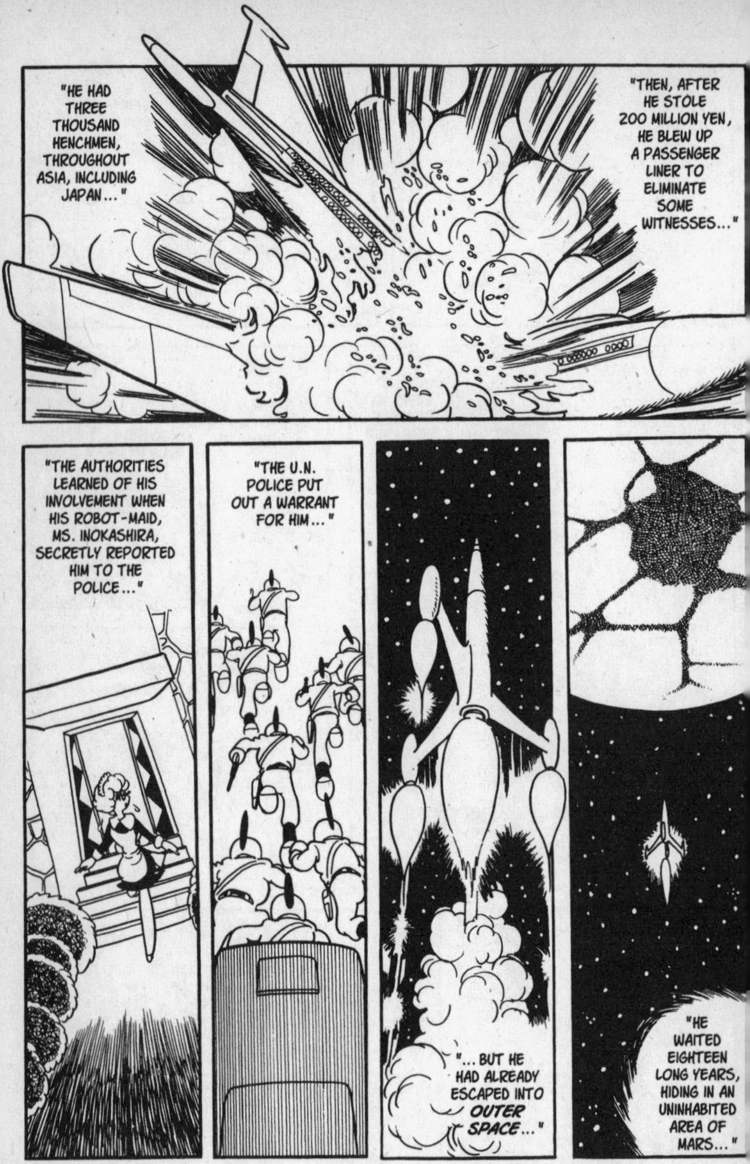
"HE HAD THREE THOUSAND HENCHMEN, THROUGHOUT ASIA, INCLUDING JAPAN..."
"THEN, AFTER HE STOLE 200 MILLION YEN, HE BLEW UP A PASSENGER LINER TO ELIMINATE SOME WITNESSES..."
"THE AUTHORITIES LEARNED OF HIS INVOLVEMENT WHEN HIS ROBOT-MAID, MS. INOKASHIRA, SECRETLY REPORTED HIM TO THE POLICE..."
"THE U.N. POLICE PUT OUT A WARRANT FOR HIM..."
"... BUT HE HAD ALREADY ESCAPED INTO *OUTER SPACE*..."
"HE WAITED EIGHTEEN LONG YEARS, HIDING IN AN UNINHABITED AREA OF MARS..."

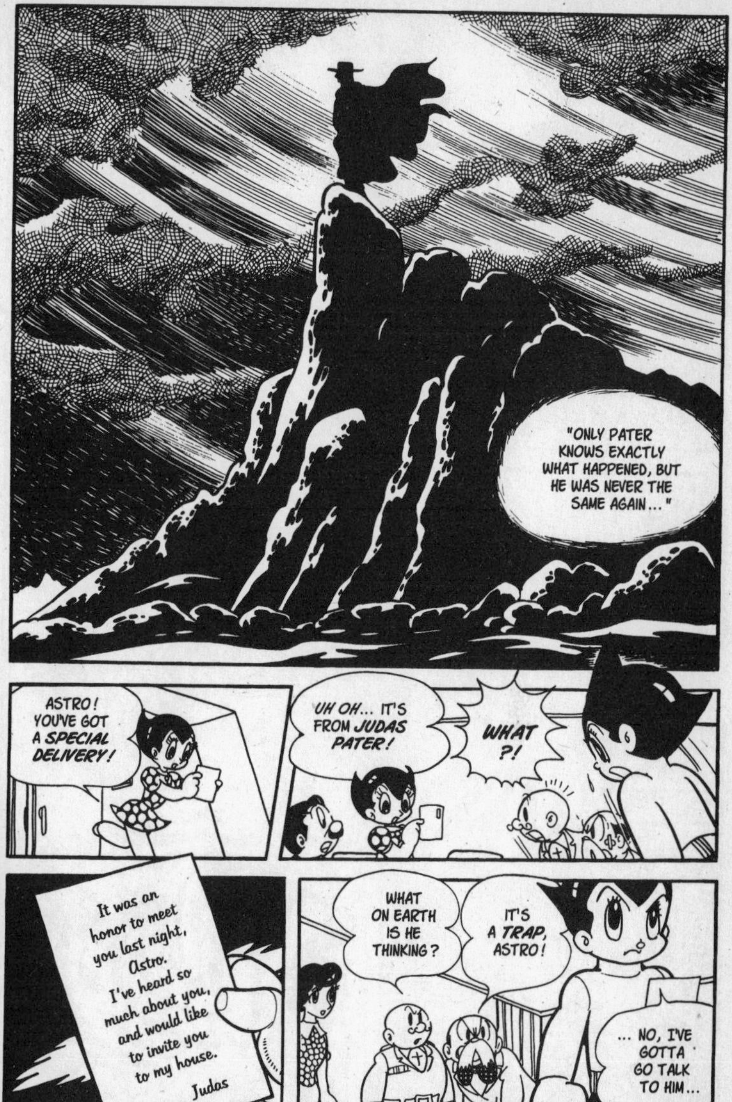

"ONLY PATER KNOWS EXACTLY WHAT HAPPENED, BUT HE WAS NEVER THE SAME AGAIN..."
ASTRO! YOU'VE GOT A SPECIAL DELIVERY!
UH OH... IT'S FROM JUDAS PATER!
WHAT ?!
It was an honor to meet you last night, Astro. I've heard so much about you, and would like to invite you to my house. Judas
WHAT ON EARTH IS HE THINKING?
IT'S A TRAP, ASTRO!
... NO, I'VE GOTTA GO TALK TO HIM...

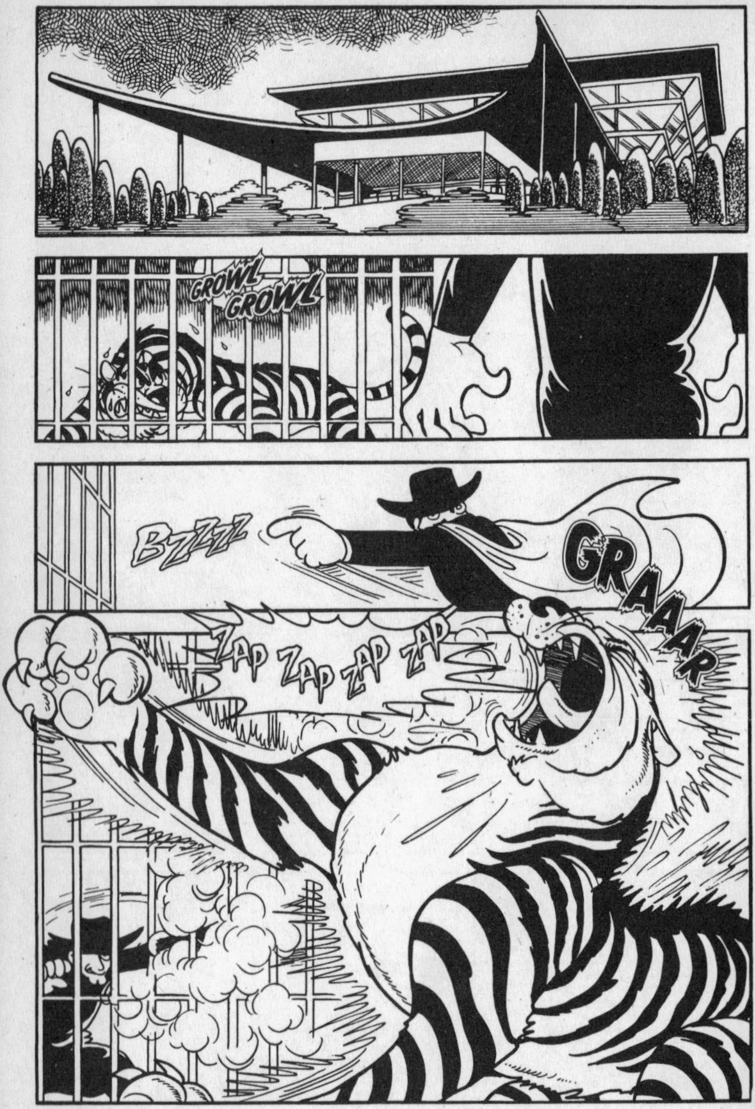

GROWL
GROWL
BZZZZ
GRAAAAR
ZAP ZAP ZAP ZAP

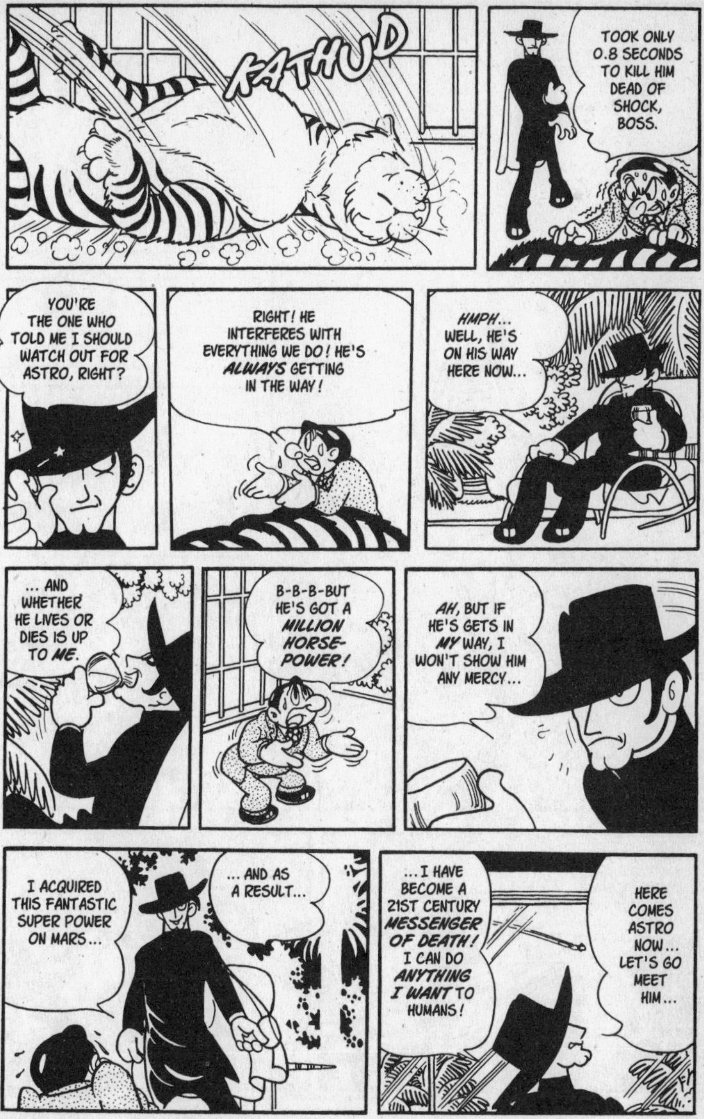
KATHUD
TOOK ONLY 0.8 SECONDS TO KILL HIM DEAD OF SHOCK, BOSS.
YOU'RE THE ONE WHO TOLD ME I SHOULD WATCH OUT FOR ASTRO, RIGHT?
RIGHT! HE INTERFERES WITH EVERYTHING WE DO! HE'S ALWAYS GETTING IN THE WAY!
HMPH... WELL, HE'S ON HIS WAY HERE NOW...
... AND WHETHER HE LIVES OR DIES IS UP TO ME.
B-B-B-BUT HE'S GOT A MILLION HORSE-POWER!
AH, BUT IF HE'S GETS IN MY WAY, I WON'T SHOW HIM ANY MERCY...
I ACQUIRED THIS FANTASTIC SUPER POWER ON MARS...
... AND AS A RESULT...
...I HAVE BECOME A 21ST CENTURY MESSENGER OF DEATH! I CAN DO ANYTHING I WANT TO HUMANS!
HERE COMES ASTRO NOW... LET'S GO MEET HIM...

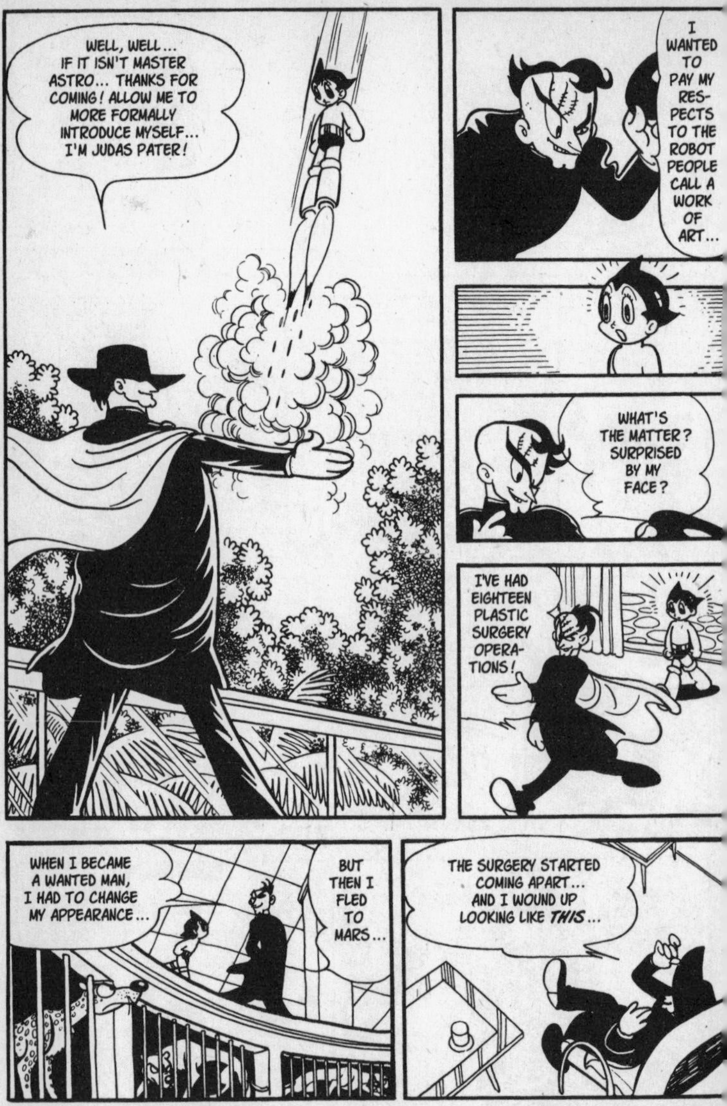
WELL, WELL... IF IT ISN'T MASTER ASTRO... THANKS FOR COMING! ALLOW ME TO MORE FORMALLY INTRODUCE MYSELF... I'M JUDAS PATER!
I WANTED TO PAY MY RESPECTS TO THE ROBOT PEOPLE CALL A WORK OF ART...
WHAT'S THE MATTER? SURPRISED BY MY FACE?
I'VE HAD EIGHTEEN PLASTIC SURGERY OPERATIONS!
WHEN I BECAME A WANTED MAN, I HAD TO CHANGE MY APPEARANCE...
BUT THEN I FLED TO MARS...
THE SURGERY STARTED COMING APART... AND I WOUND UP LOOKING LIKE *THIS*...

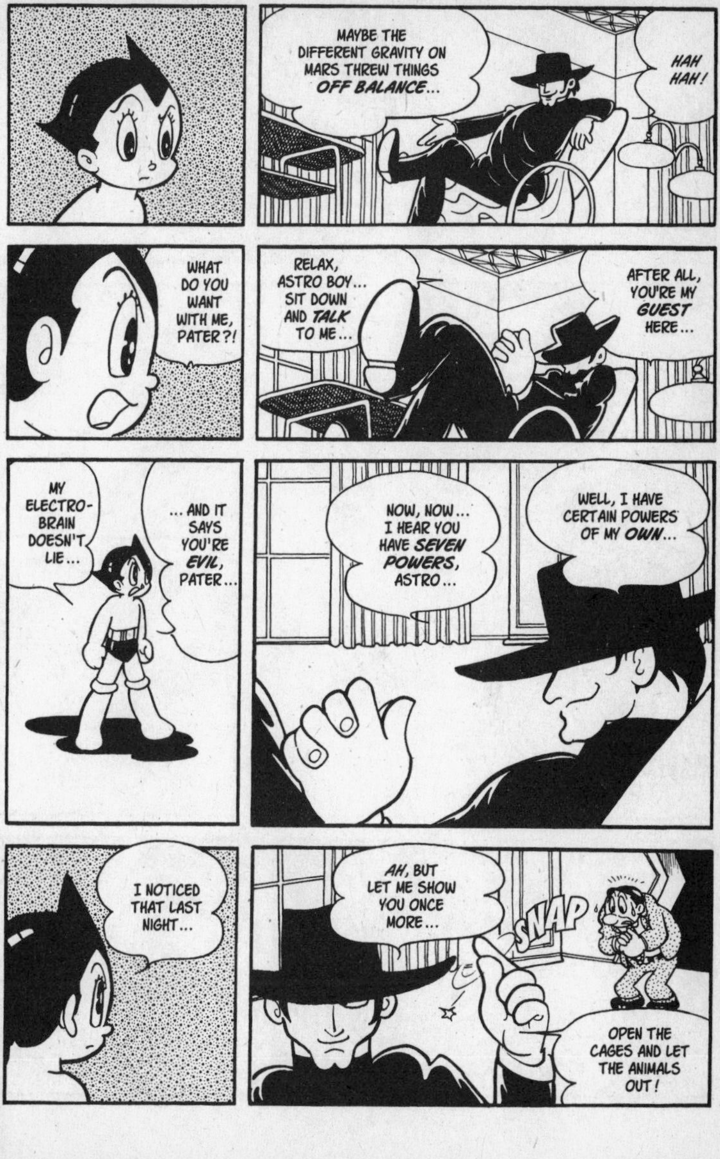
MAYBE THE DIFFERENT GRAVITY ON MARS THREW THINGS *OFF BALANCE*...
HAH HAH!
WHAT DO YOU WANT WITH ME, PATER?!
RELAX, ASTRO BOY... SIT DOWN AND *TALK* TO ME...
AFTER ALL, YOU'RE MY *GUEST* HERE...
MY ELECTRO-BRAIN DOESN'T LIE...
... AND IT SAYS YOU'RE *EVIL*, PATER...
NOW, NOW... I HEAR YOU HAVE *SEVEN POWERS*, ASTRO...
WELL, I HAVE CERTAIN POWERS OF MY *OWN*...
I NOTICED THAT LAST NIGHT...
AH, BUT LET ME SHOW YOU ONCE MORE...
SNAP
OPEN THE CAGES AND LET THE ANIMALS OUT!

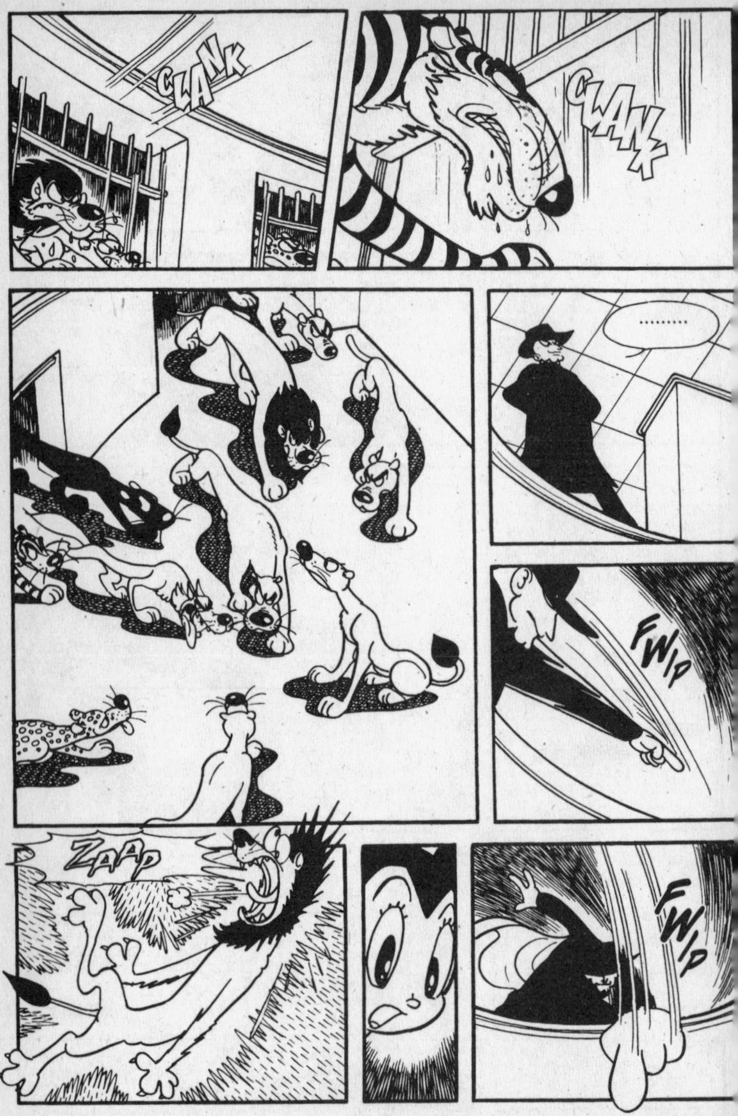
CLANK
CLANK
....
FWIP
ZAAP
FWIP

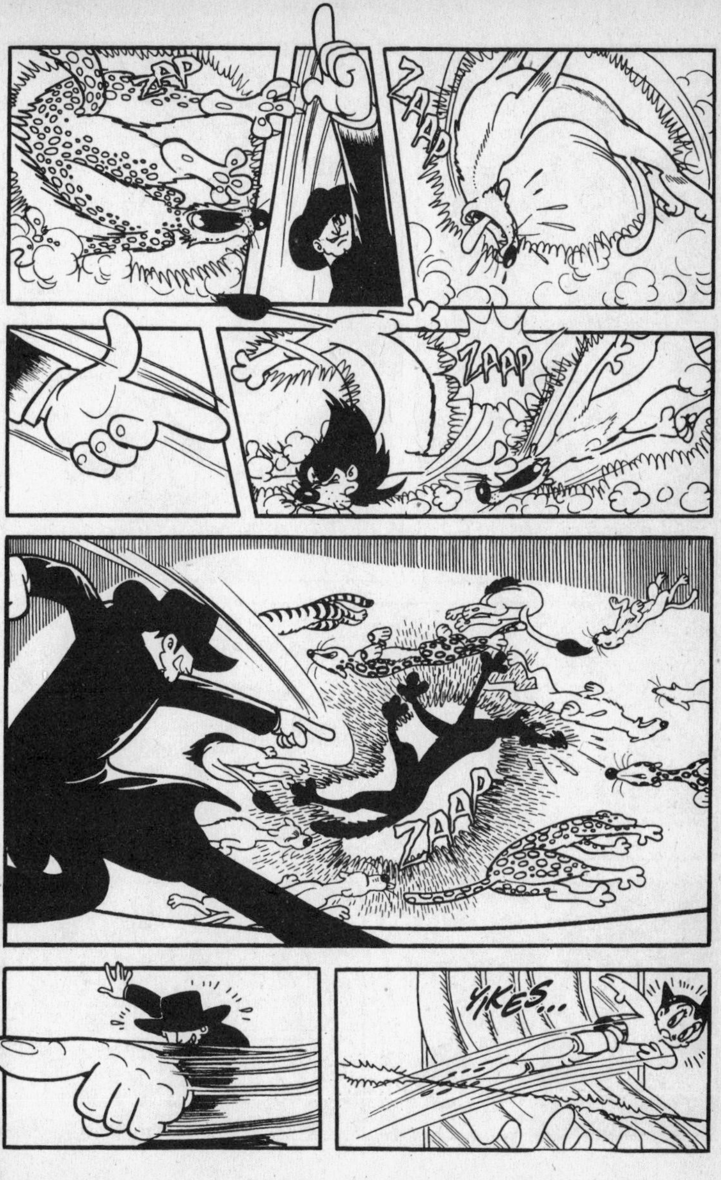
ZAP
ZAAP
ZAAP
ZAAP
YIKES...

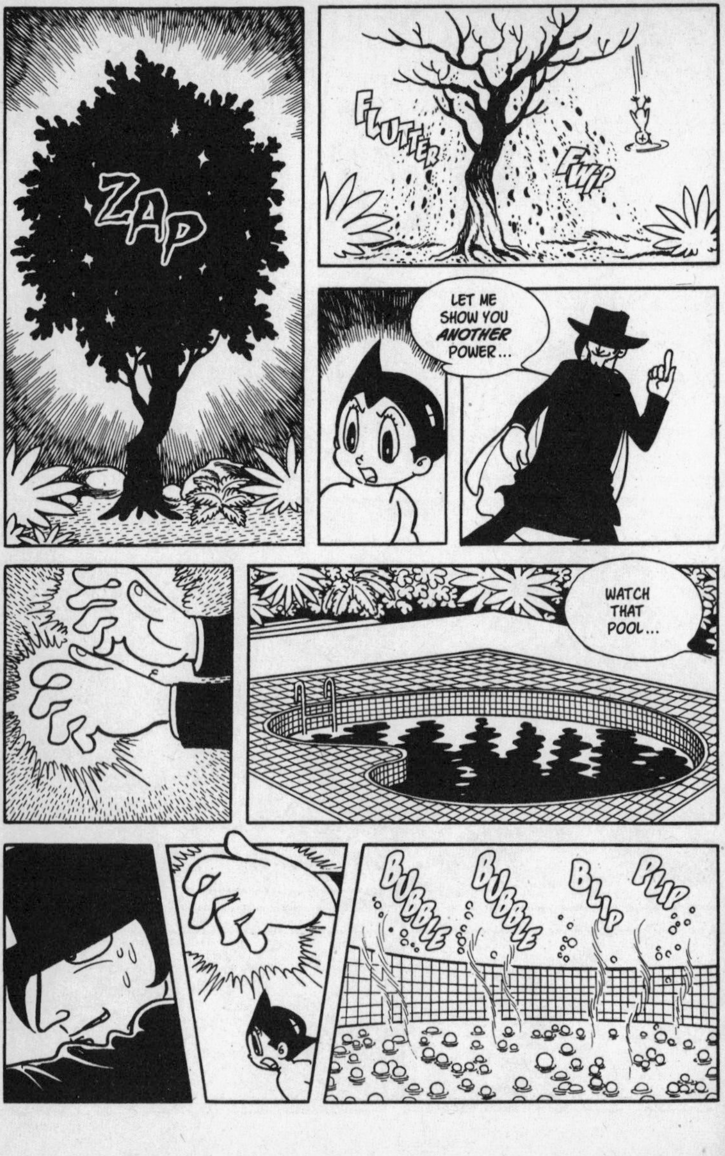
ZAP
FLUTTER
FWIP
LET ME SHOW YOU ANOTHER POWER...
WATCH THAT POOL...
BUBBLE
BUBBLE
BLIP
PLIP

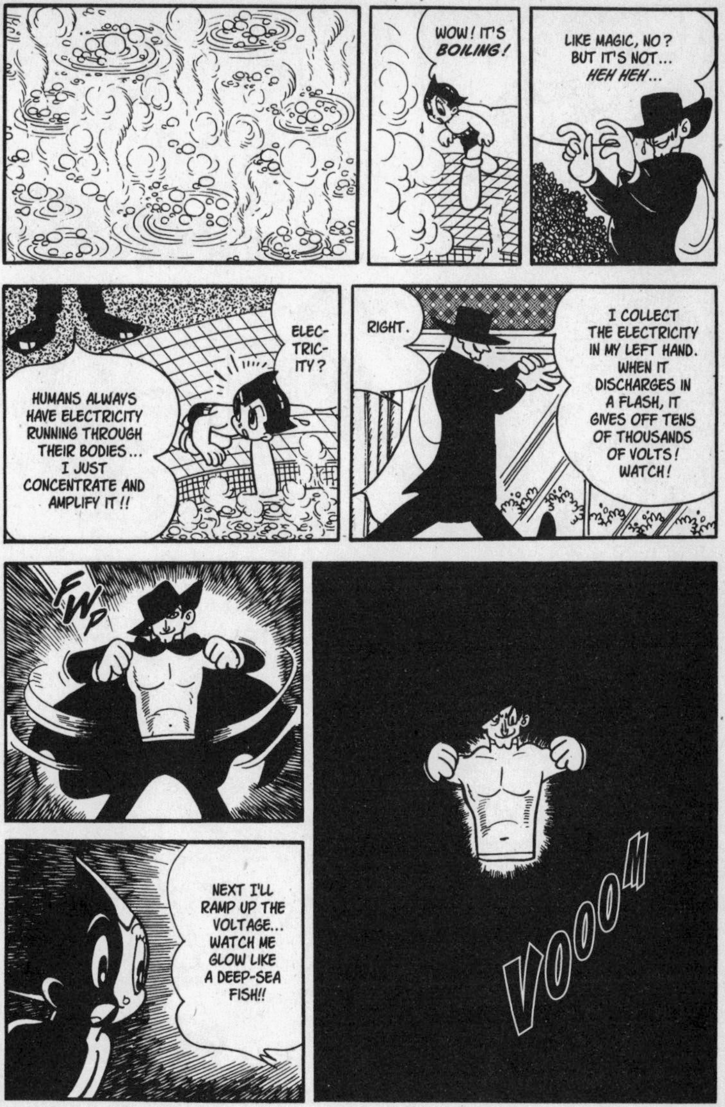
WOW! IT'S *BOILING!*
LIKE MAGIC, NO? BUT IT'S NOT... *HEH HEH...*
ELEC-TRIC-ITY?
HUMANS ALWAYS HAVE ELECTRICITY RUNNING THROUGH THEIR BODIES... I JUST CONCENTRATE AND AMPLIFY IT!!
RIGHT.
I COLLECT THE ELECTRICITY IN MY LEFT HAND. WHEN IT DISCHARGES IN A FLASH, IT GIVES OFF TENS OF THOUSANDS OF VOLTS! WATCH!
FWP
NEXT I'LL RAMP UP THE VOLTAGE... WATCH ME GLOW LIKE A DEEP-SEA FISH!!
VOOOM

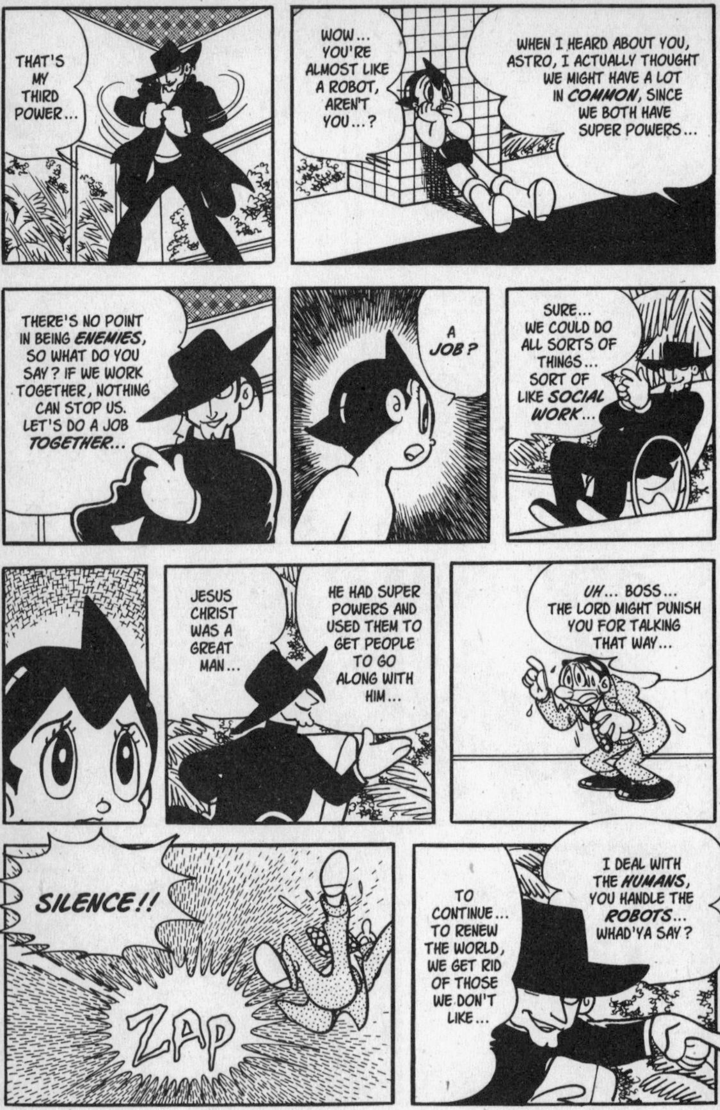
THAT'S MY THIRD POWER...
WOW... YOU'RE ALMOST LIKE A ROBOT, AREN'T YOU...?
WHEN I HEARD ABOUT YOU, ASTRO, I ACTUALLY THOUGHT WE MIGHT HAVE A LOT IN COMMON, SINCE WE BOTH HAVE SUPER POWERS...
THERE'S NO POINT IN BEING ENEMIES, SO WHAT DO YOU SAY? IF WE WORK TOGETHER, NOTHING CAN STOP US. LET'S DO A JOB TOGETHER...
A JOB?
SURE... WE COULD DO ALL SORTS OF THINGS... SORT OF LIKE SOCIAL WORK...
JESUS CHRIST WAS A GREAT MAN...
HE HAD SUPER POWERS AND USED THEM TO GET PEOPLE TO GO ALONG WITH HIM...
UH... BOSS... THE LORD MIGHT PUNISH YOU FOR TALKING THAT WAY...
SILENCE!!
ZAP
TO CONTINUE... TO RENEW THE WORLD, WE GET RID OF THOSE WE DON'T LIKE...
I DEAL WITH THE HUMANS, YOU HANDLE THE ROBOTS... WHAD'YA SAY?

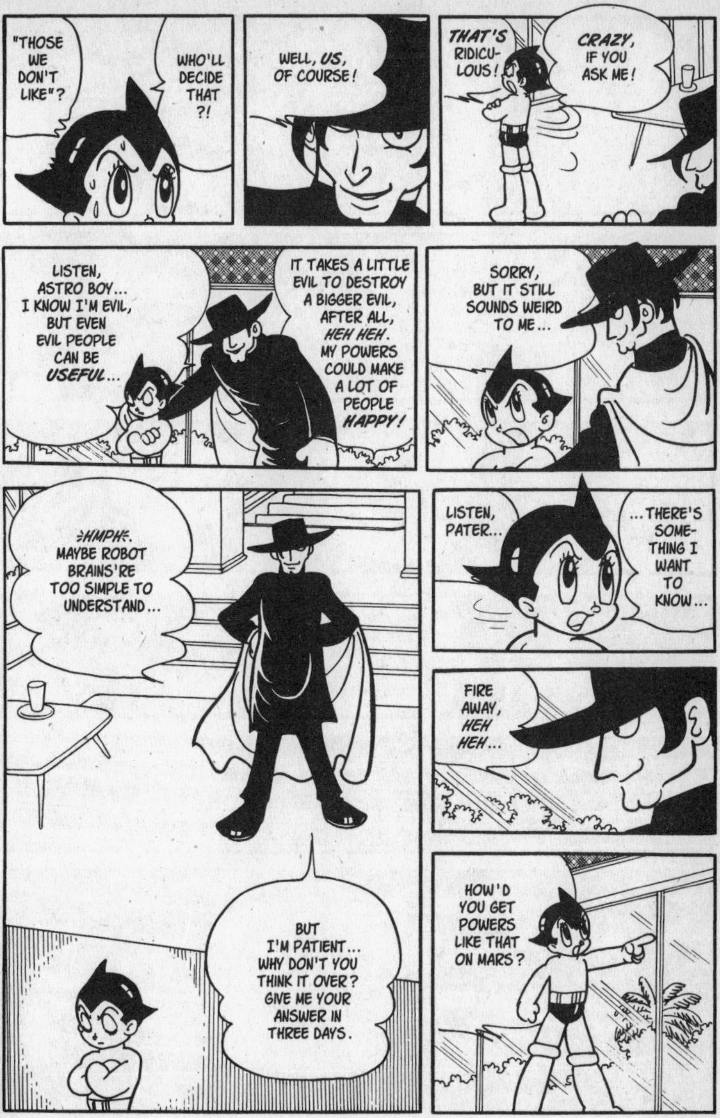

"THOSE WE DON'T LIKE"?
WHO'LL DECIDE THAT ?!
WELL, *US*, OF COURSE!
THAT'S RIDICU-LOUS!
CRAZY, IF YOU ASK ME!
LISTEN, ASTRO BOY... I KNOW I'M EVIL, BUT EVEN EVIL PEOPLE CAN BE *USEFUL*...
IT TAKES A LITTLE EVIL TO DESTROY A BIGGER EVIL, AFTER ALL, *HEH HEH*. MY POWERS COULD MAKE A LOT OF PEOPLE *HAPPY!*
SORRY, BUT IT STILL SOUNDS WEIRD TO ME...
HMPH. MAYBE ROBOT BRAINS'RE TOO SIMPLE TO UNDERSTAND...
BUT I'M PATIENT... WHY DON'T YOU THINK IT OVER? GIVE ME YOUR ANSWER IN THREE DAYS.
LISTEN, PATER...
...THERE'S SOME-THING I WANT TO KNOW...
FIRE AWAY, *HEH HEH*...
HOW'D YOU GET POWERS LIKE THAT ON MARS?

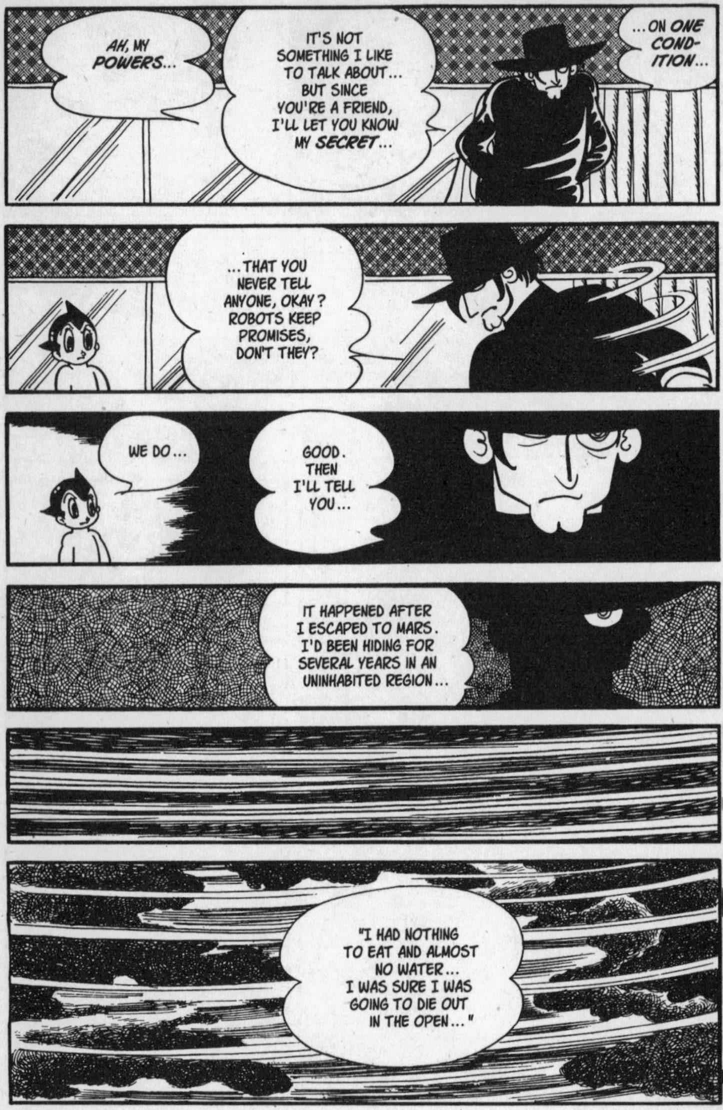
AH, MY POWERS...
IT'S NOT SOMETHING I LIKE TO TALK ABOUT... BUT SINCE YOU'RE A FRIEND, I'LL LET YOU KNOW MY SECRET...
...ON ONE CONDITION...
...THAT YOU NEVER TELL ANYONE, OKAY? ROBOTS KEEP PROMISES, DON'T THEY?
WE DO...
GOOD. THEN I'LL TELL YOU...
IT HAPPENED AFTER I ESCAPED TO MARS. I'D BEEN HIDING FOR SEVERAL YEARS IN AN UNINHABITED REGION...
"I HAD NOTHING TO EAT AND ALMOST NO WATER... I WAS SURE I WAS GOING TO DIE OUT IN THE OPEN..."

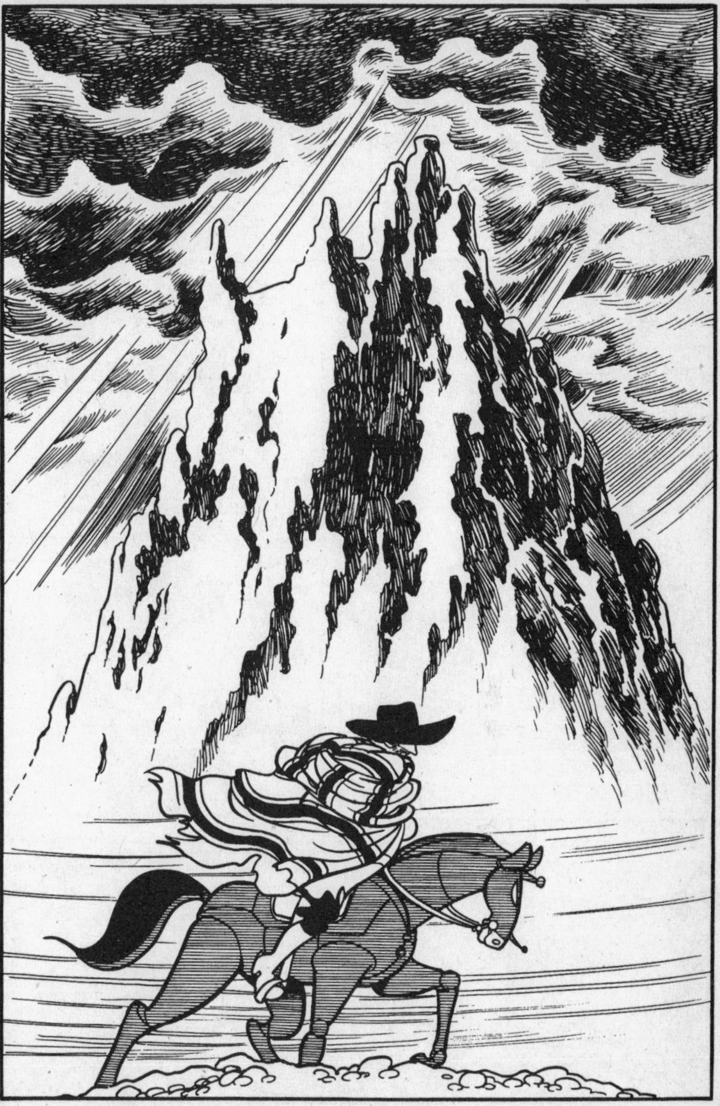

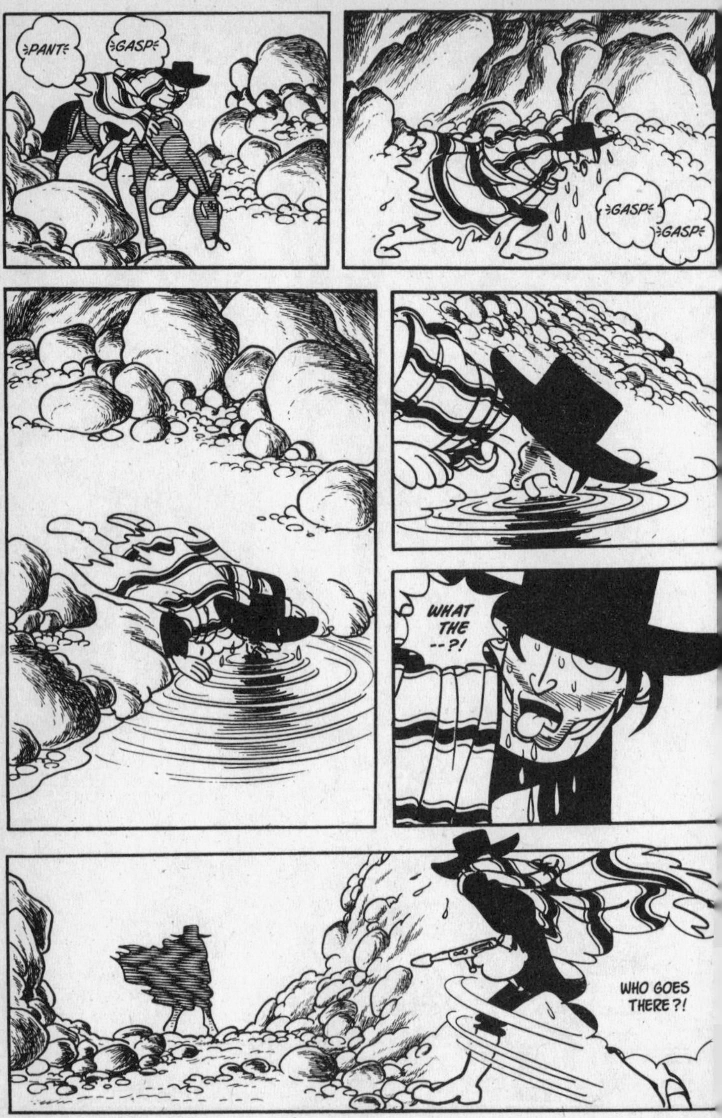
PANT
GASP
GASP
GASP
WHAT THE --?!
WHO GOES THERE?!

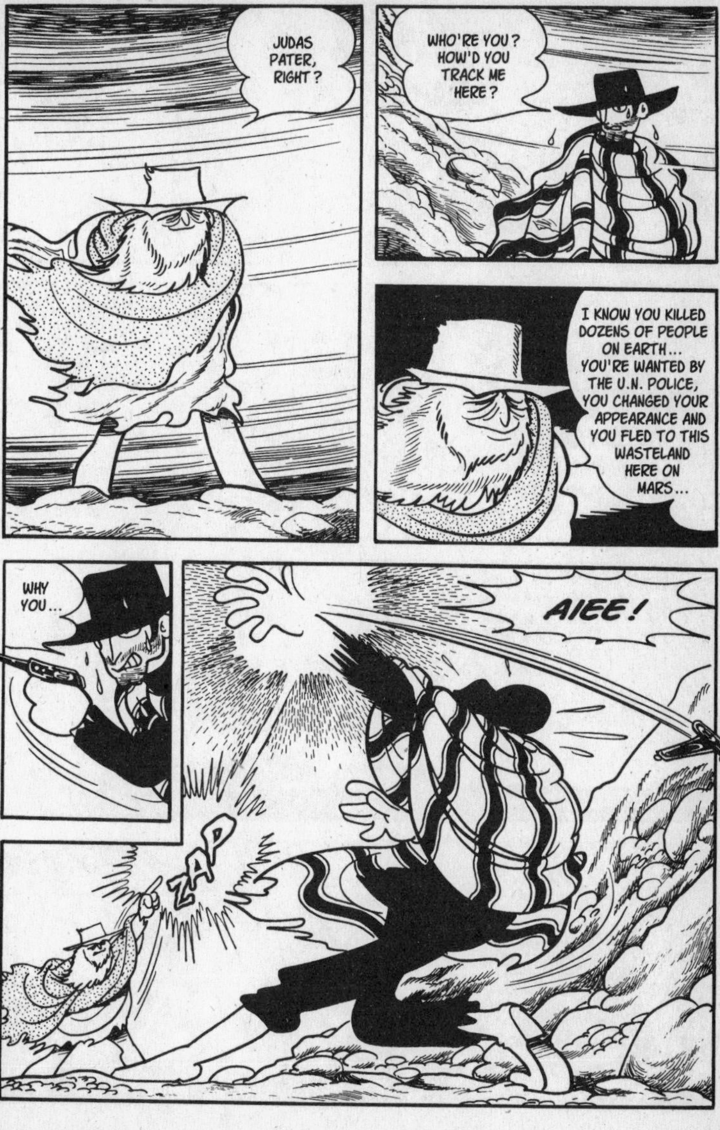
JUDAS PATER, RIGHT ?
WHO'RE YOU ? HOW'D YOU TRACK ME HERE ?
I KNOW YOU KILLED DOZENS OF PEOPLE ON EARTH... YOU'RE WANTED BY THE U.N. POLICE, YOU CHANGED YOUR APPEARANCE AND YOU FLED TO THIS WASTELAND HERE ON MARS...
WHY YOU...
AIEE!
ZAP

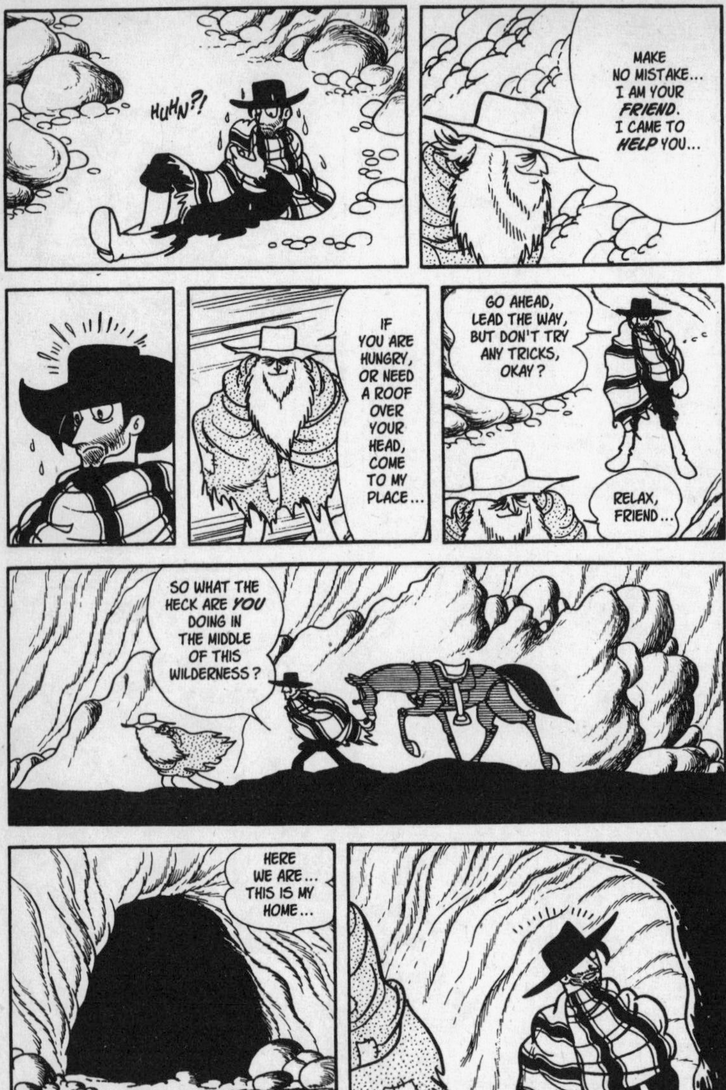
HUHN?!
MAKE NO MISTAKE... I AM YOUR FRIEND. I CAME TO HELP YOU...
IF YOU ARE HUNGRY, OR NEED A ROOF OVER YOUR HEAD, COME TO MY PLACE...
GO AHEAD, LEAD THE WAY, BUT DON'T TRY ANY TRICKS, OKAY?
RELAX, FRIEND...
SO WHAT THE HECK ARE YOU DOING IN THE MIDDLE OF THIS WILDERNESS?
HERE WE ARE... THIS IS MY HOME...

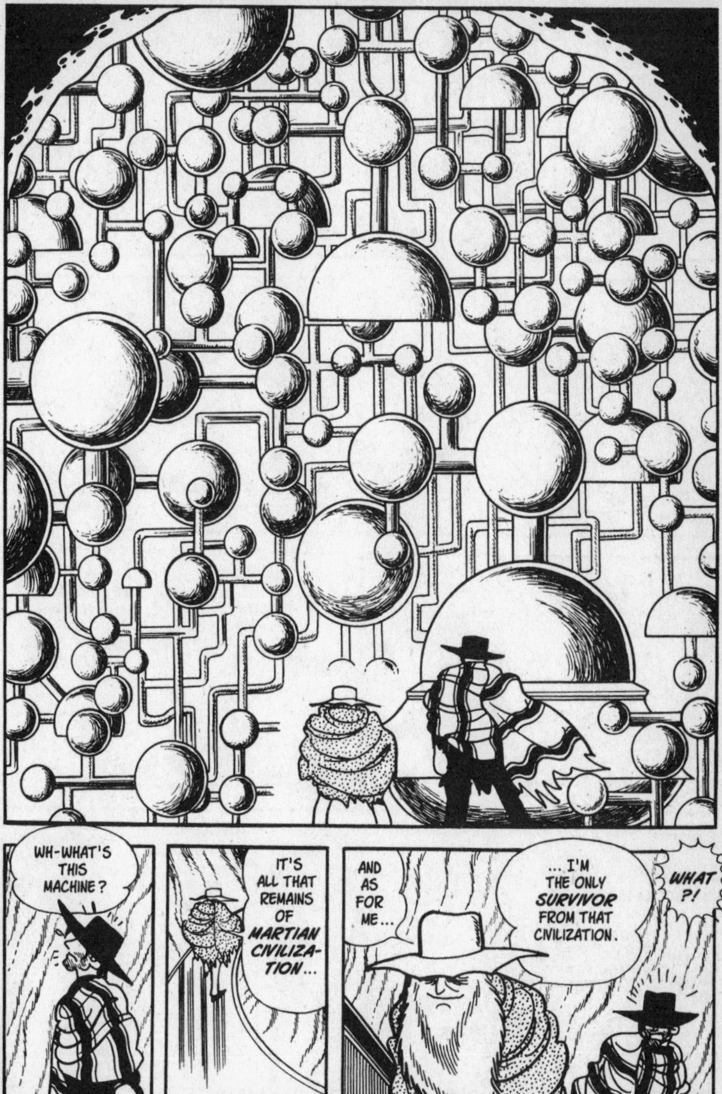
WH-WHAT'S THIS MACHINE?
IT'S ALL THAT REMAINS OF MARTIAN CIVILIZATION...
AND AS FOR ME...
...I'M THE ONLY SURVIVOR FROM THAT CIVILIZATION.
WHAT?!

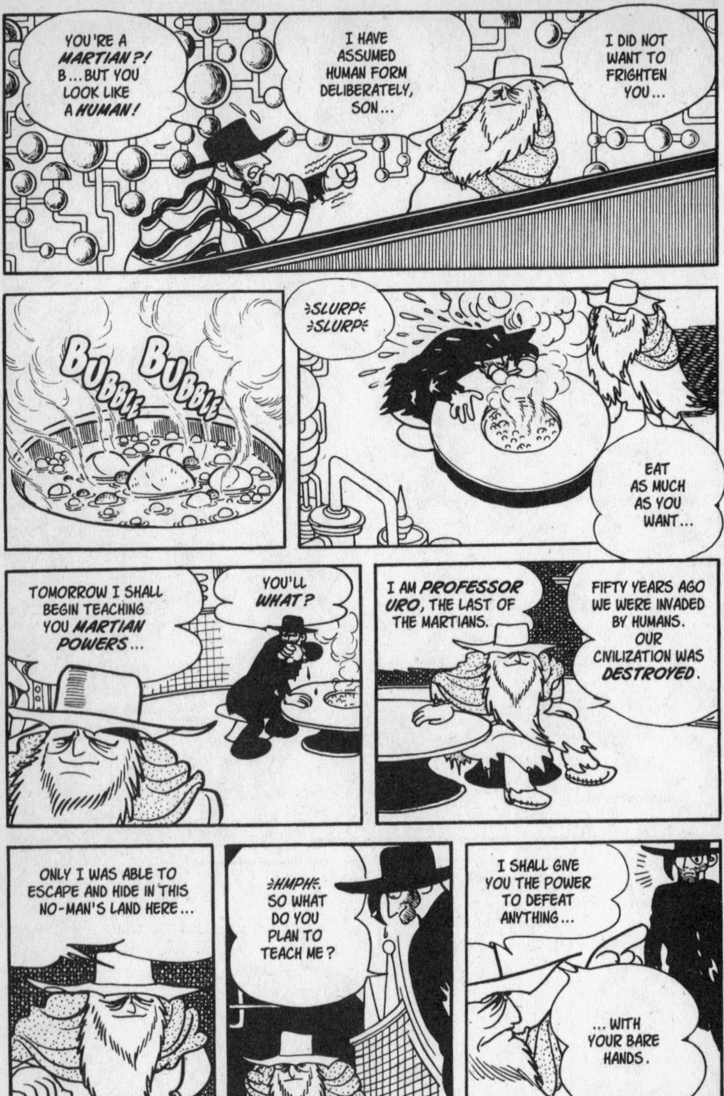
YOU'RE A MARTIAN?! B... BUT YOU LOOK LIKE A HUMAN!
I HAVE ASSUMED HUMAN FORM DELIBERATELY, SON...
I DID NOT WANT TO FRIGHTEN YOU...
BUBBLE BUBBLE
SLURP SLURP
EAT AS MUCH AS YOU WANT...
TOMORROW I SHALL BEGIN TEACHING YOU MARTIAN POWERS...
YOU'LL WHAT?
I AM PROFESSOR URO, THE LAST OF THE MARTIANS.
FIFTY YEARS AGO WE WERE INVADED BY HUMANS. OUR CIVILIZATION WAS DESTROYED.
ONLY I WAS ABLE TO ESCAPE AND HIDE IN THIS NO-MAN'S LAND HERE...
HMPH. SO WHAT DO YOU PLAN TO TEACH ME?
I SHALL GIVE YOU THE POWER TO DEFEAT ANYTHING...
... WITH YOUR BARE HANDS.

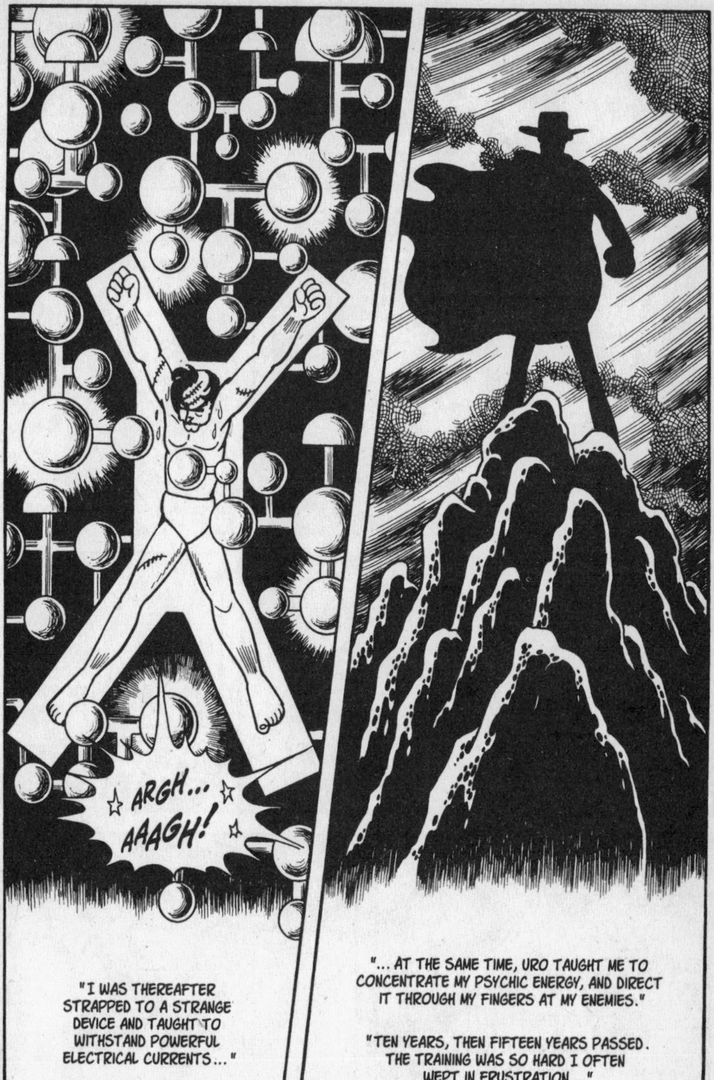
ARGH... AAAGH!
"I WAS THEREAFTER STRAPPED TO A STRANGE DEVICE AND TAUGHT TO WITHSTAND POWERFUL ELECTRICAL CURRENTS..."
"... AT THE SAME TIME, URO TAUGHT ME TO CONCENTRATE MY PSYCHIC ENERGY, AND DIRECT IT THROUGH MY FINGERS AT MY ENEMIES."
"TEN YEARS, THEN FIFTEEN YEARS PASSED. THE TRAINING WAS SO HARD I OFTEN WEPT IN FRUSTRATION..."

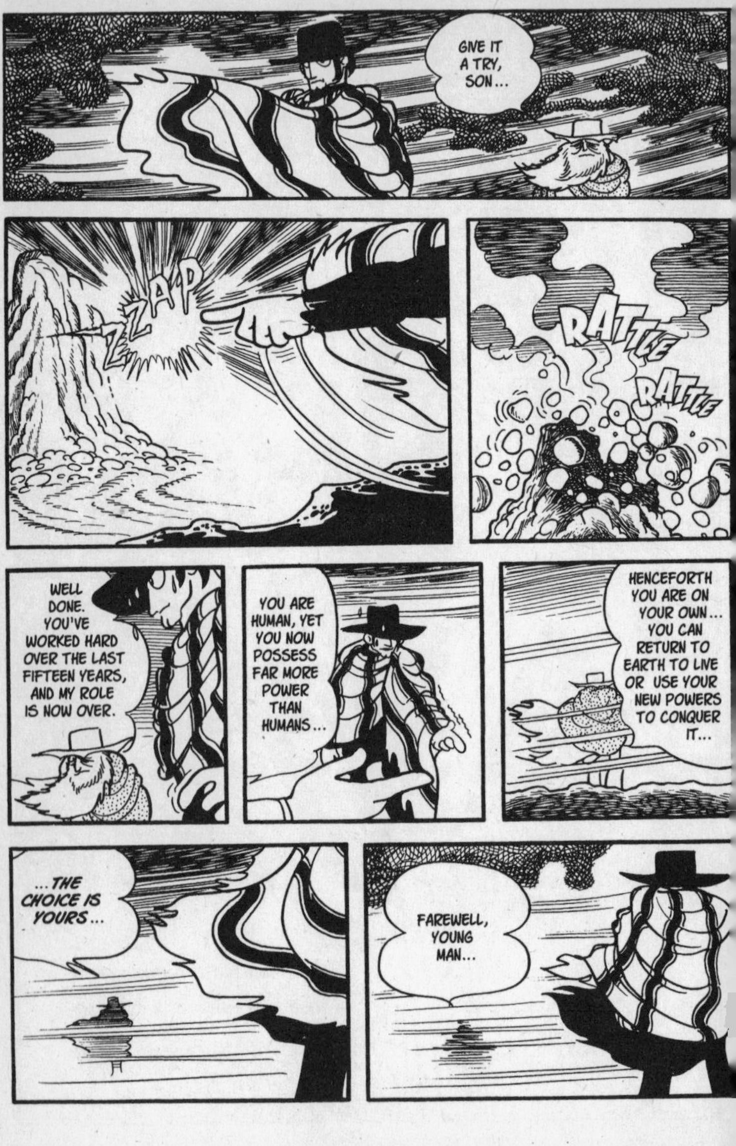
GIVE IT A TRY, SON...
ZZAP
RATTLE
RATTLE
WELL DONE. YOU'VE WORKED HARD OVER THE LAST FIFTEEN YEARS, AND MY ROLE IS NOW OVER.
YOU ARE HUMAN, YET YOU NOW POSSESS FAR MORE POWER THAN HUMANS...
HENCEFORTH YOU ARE ON YOUR OWN... YOU CAN RETURN TO EARTH TO LIVE OR USE YOUR NEW POWERS TO CONQUER IT...
...THE CHOICE IS YOURS...
FAREWELL, YOUNG MAN...

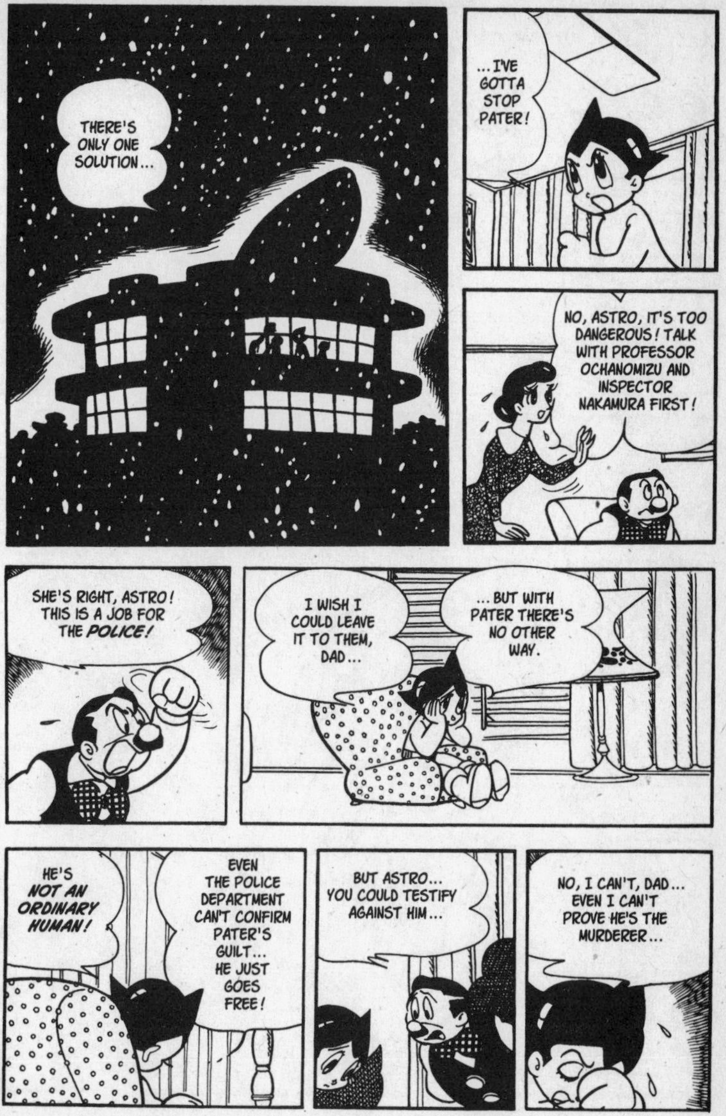
THERE'S ONLY ONE SOLUTION...
...I'VE GOTTA STOP PATER!
NO, ASTRO, IT'S TOO DANGEROUS! TALK WITH PROFESSOR OCHANOMIZU AND INSPECTOR NAKAMURA FIRST!
SHE'S RIGHT, ASTRO! THIS IS A JOB FOR THE *POLICE!*
I WISH I COULD LEAVE IT TO THEM, DAD...
...BUT WITH PATER THERE'S NO OTHER WAY.
HE'S *NOT AN ORDINARY HUMAN!*
EVEN THE POLICE DEPARTMENT CAN'T CONFIRM PATER'S GUILT... HE JUST GOES FREE!
BUT ASTRO... YOU COULD TESTIFY AGAINST HIM...
NO, I CAN'T, DAD... EVEN I CAN'T PROVE HE'S THE MURDERER...

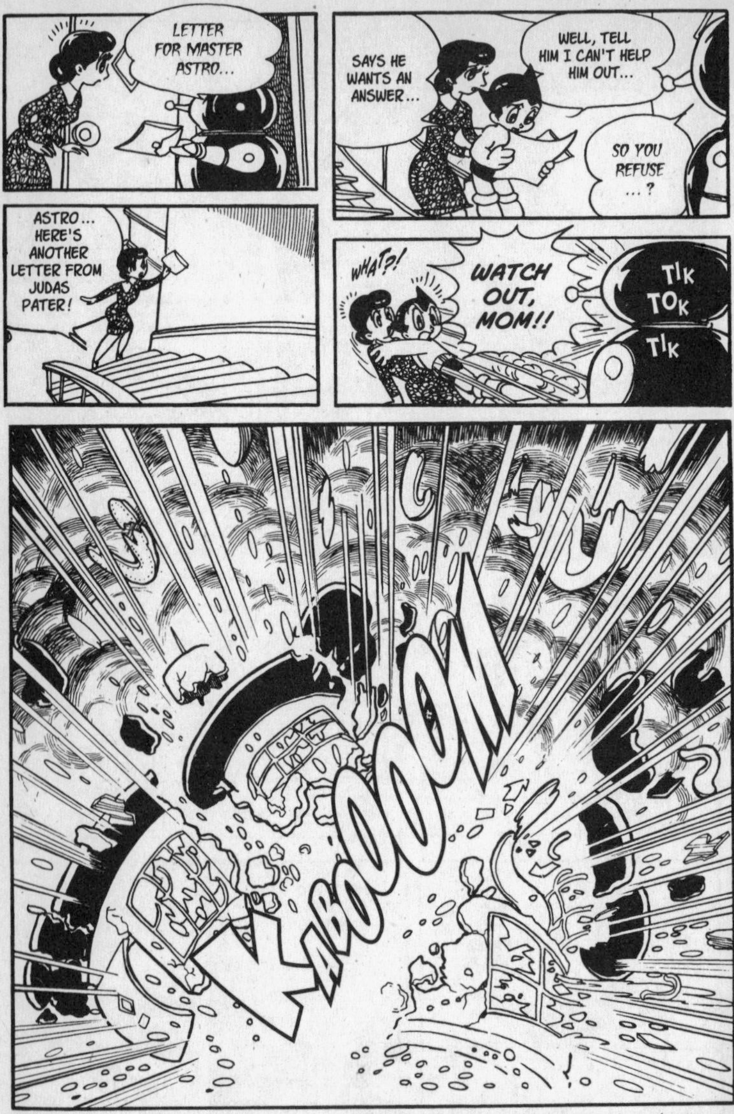
LETTER FOR MASTER ASTRO...
SAYS HE WANTS AN ANSWER...
WELL, TELL HIM I CAN'T HELP HIM OUT...
SO YOU REFUSE ...?
ASTRO... HERE'S ANOTHER LETTER FROM JUDAS PATER!
WHAT?!
WATCH OUT, MOM!!
TIK TOK TIK
KABOOOOM

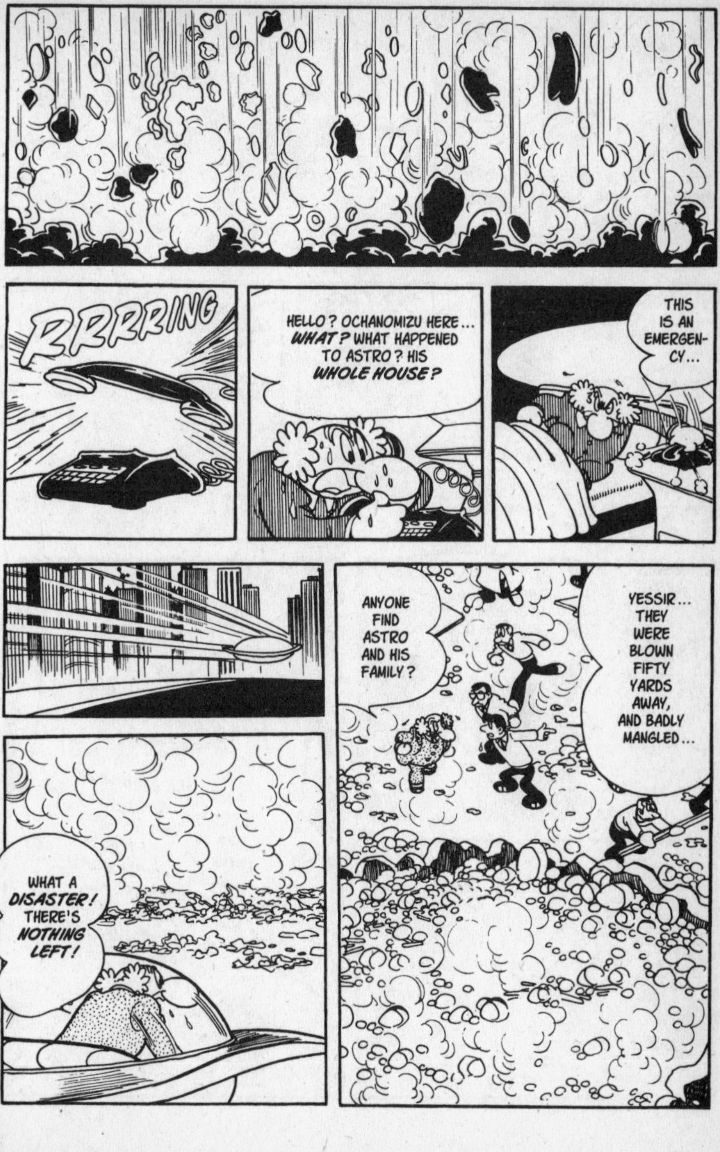

RRRRING
HELLO? OCHANOMIZU HERE... WHAT? WHAT HAPPENED TO ASTRO? HIS WHOLE HOUSE?
THIS IS AN EMERGEN-CY...
ANYONE FIND ASTRO AND HIS FAMILY?
YESSIR... THEY WERE BLOWN FIFTY YARDS AWAY, AND BADLY MANGLED...
WHAT A DISASTER! THERE'S NOTHING LEFT!

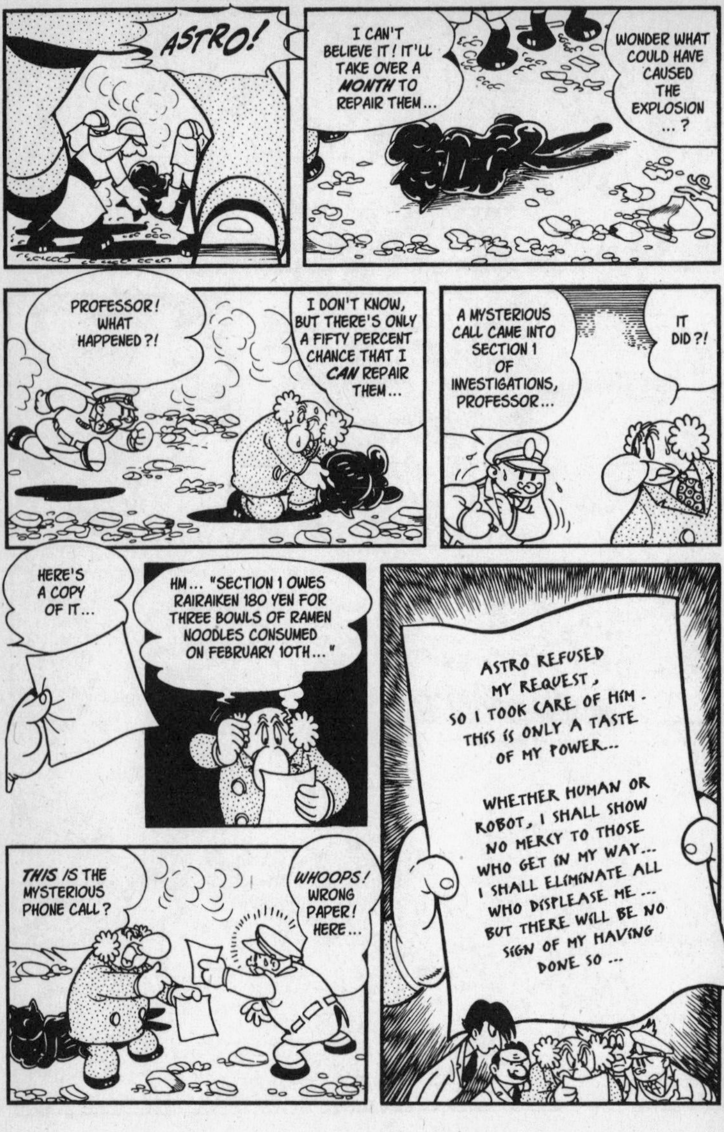
ASTRO!
I CAN'T BELIEVE IT! IT'LL TAKE OVER A MONTH TO REPAIR THEM...
WONDER WHAT COULD HAVE CAUSED THE EXPLOSION ...?
PROFESSOR! WHAT HAPPENED?!
I DON'T KNOW, BUT THERE'S ONLY A FIFTY PERCENT CHANCE THAT I CAN REPAIR THEM...
A MYSTERIOUS CALL CAME INTO SECTION 1 OF INVESTIGATIONS, PROFESSOR...
IT DID?!
HERE'S A COPY OF IT...
HM... "SECTION 1 OWES RAIRAIKEN 180 YEN FOR THREE BOWLS OF RAMEN NOODLES CONSUMED ON FEBRUARY 10TH..."
ASTRO REFUSED MY REQUEST, SO I TOOK CARE OF HIM. THIS IS ONLY A TASTE OF MY POWER...
WHETHER HUMAN OR ROBOT, I SHALL SHOW NO MERCY TO THOSE WHO GET IN MY WAY... I SHALL ELIMINATE ALL WHO DISPLEASE ME... BUT THERE WILL BE NO SIGN OF MY HAVING DONE SO...
THIS IS THE MYSTERIOUS PHONE CALL?
WHOOPS! WRONG PAPER! HERE...

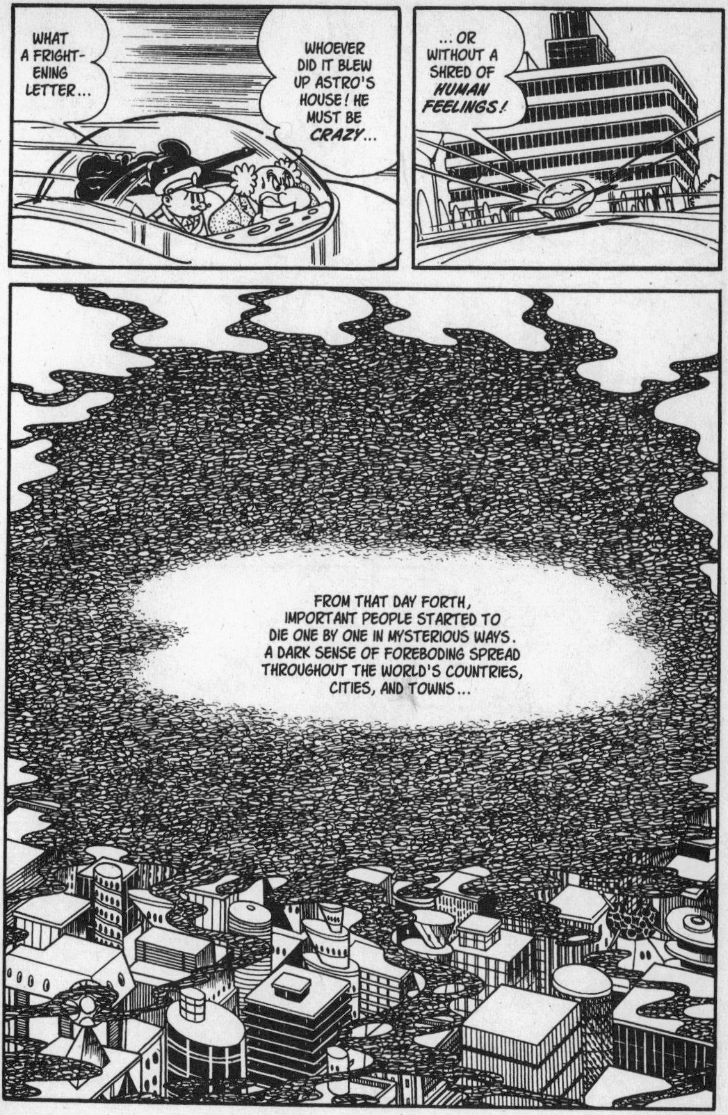
WHAT A FRIGHT-ENING LETTER...
WHOEVER DID IT BLEW UP ASTRO'S HOUSE! HE MUST BE CRAZY...
...OR WITHOUT A SHRED OF HUMAN FEELINGS!
FROM THAT DAY FORTH, IMPORTANT PEOPLE STARTED TO DIE ONE BY ONE IN MYSTERIOUS WAYS. A DARK SENSE OF FOREBODING SPREAD THROUGHOUT THE WORLD'S COUNTRIES, CITIES, AND TOWNS...

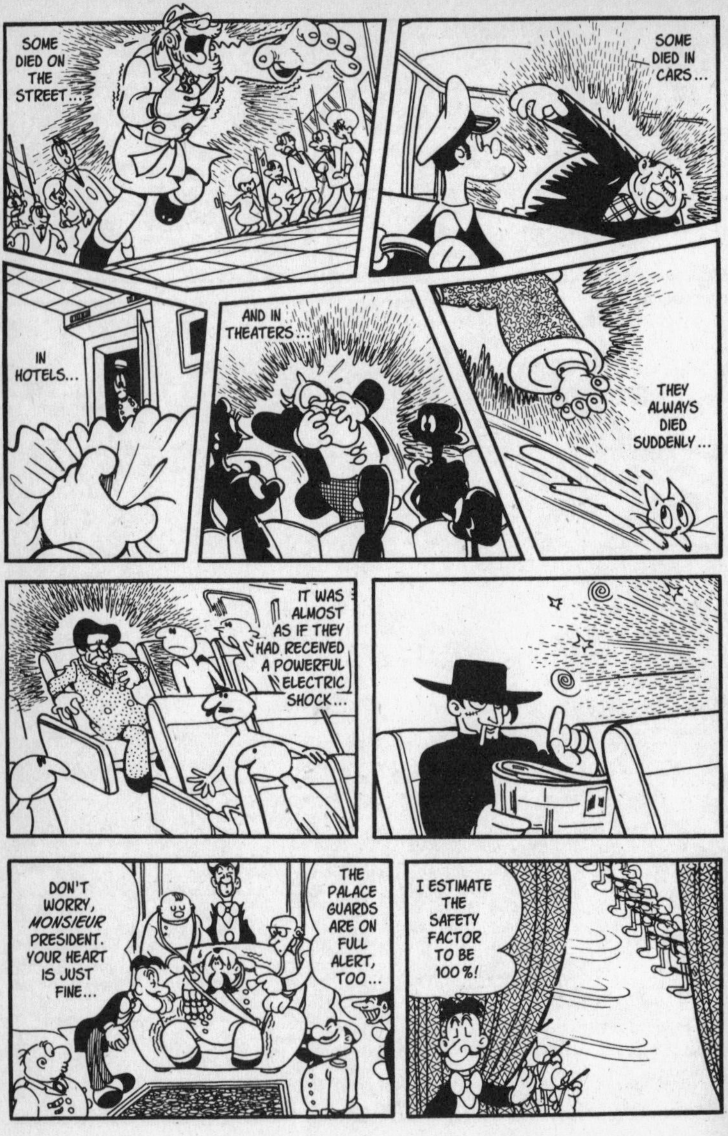
SOME DIED ON THE STREET...
SOME DIED IN CARS...
IN HOTELS...
AND IN THEATERS...
THEY ALWAYS DIED SUDDENLY...
IT WAS ALMOST AS IF THEY HAD RECEIVED A POWERFUL ELECTRIC SHOCK...
DON'T WORRY, *MONSIEUR* PRESIDENT. YOUR HEART IS JUST FINE...
THE PALACE GUARDS ARE ON FULL ALERT, TOO...
I ESTIMATE THE SAFETY FACTOR TO BE 100%!

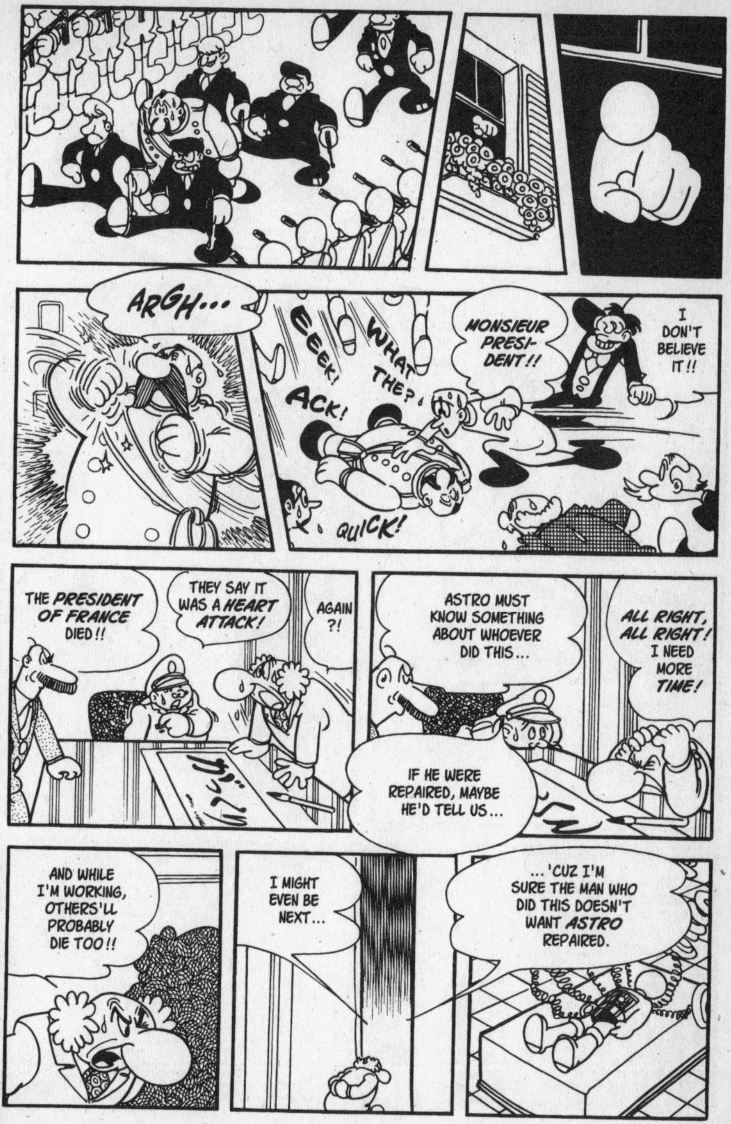
ARGH...
EEEEK!
WHAT THE?
ACK!
MONSIEUR PRESI-DENT!!
I DON'T BELIEVE IT!!
QUICK!
THE PRESIDENT OF FRANCE DIED!!
THEY SAY IT WAS A HEART ATTACK!
AGAIN?!
ASTRO MUST KNOW SOMETHING ABOUT WHOEVER DID THIS...
ALL RIGHT, ALL RIGHT! I NEED MORE TIME!
IF HE WERE REPAIRED, MAYBE HE'D TELL US...
AND WHILE I'M WORKING, OTHERS'LL PROBABLY DIE TOO!!
I MIGHT EVEN BE NEXT...
...'CUZ I'M SURE THE MAN WHO DID THIS DOESN'T WANT ASTRO REPAIRED.

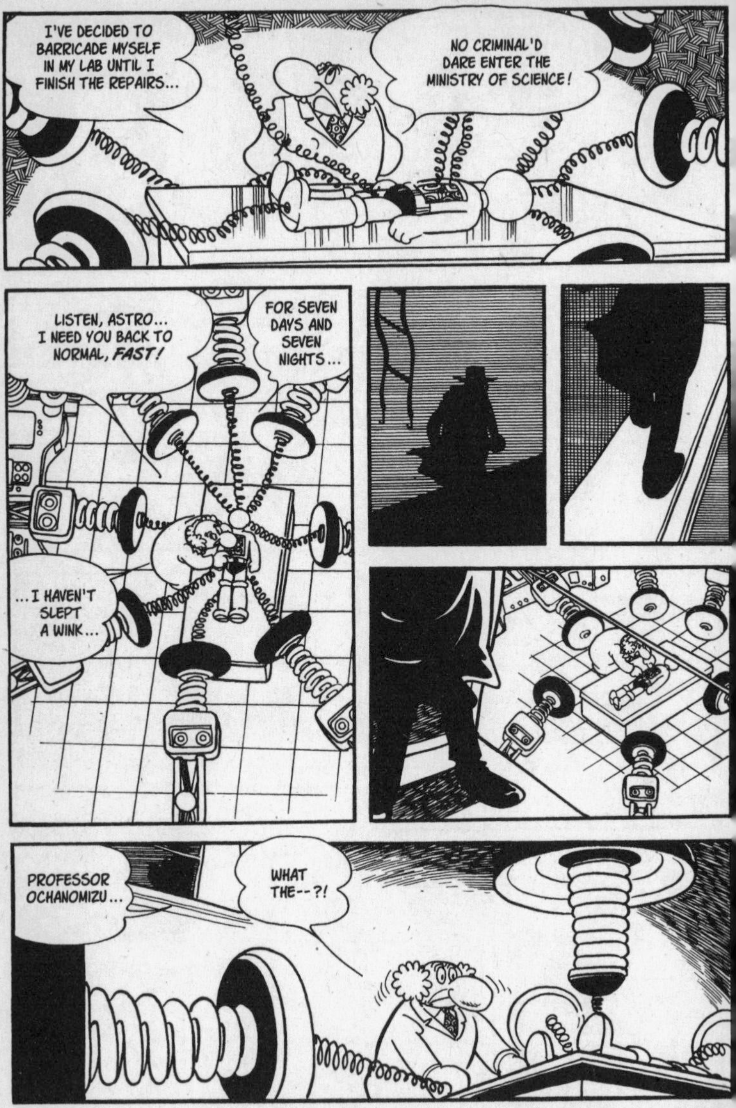
I'VE DECIDED TO BARRICADE MYSELF IN MY LAB UNTIL I FINISH THE REPAIRS...
NO CRIMINAL'D DARE ENTER THE MINISTRY OF SCIENCE!
LISTEN, ASTRO... I NEED YOU BACK TO NORMAL, *FAST!*
FOR SEVEN DAYS AND SEVEN NIGHTS...
...I HAVEN'T SLEPT A WINK...
PROFESSOR OCHANOMIZU...
WHAT THE--?!

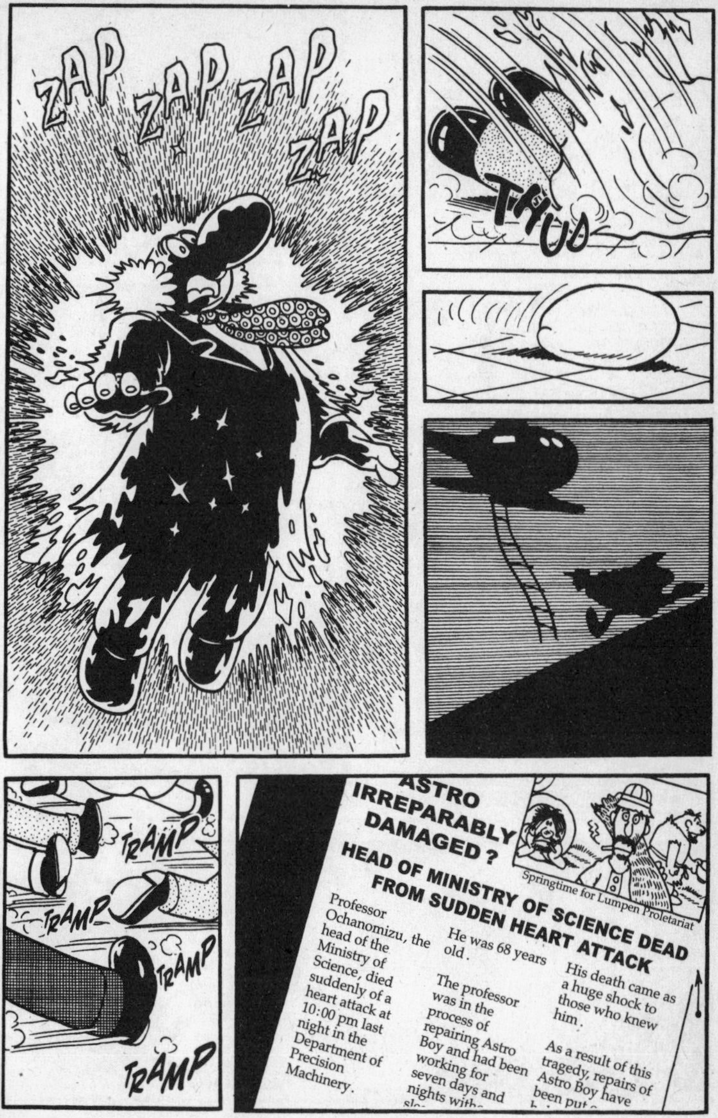
ZAP ZAP ZAP ZAP
THUD
TRAMP TRAMP TRAMP TRAMP
ASTRO IRREPARABLY DAMAGED ?
Springtime for Lumpen Proletariat
HEAD OF MINISTRY OF SCIENCE DEAD FROM SUDDEN HEART ATTACK
Professor Ochanomizu, the head of the Ministry of Science, died suddenly of a heart attack at 10:00 pm last night in the Department of Precision Machinery.
He was 68 years old.
The professor was in the process of repairing Astro Boy and had been working for seven days and nights
His death came as a huge shock to those who knew him.
As a result of this tragedy, repairs of Astro Boy have been put

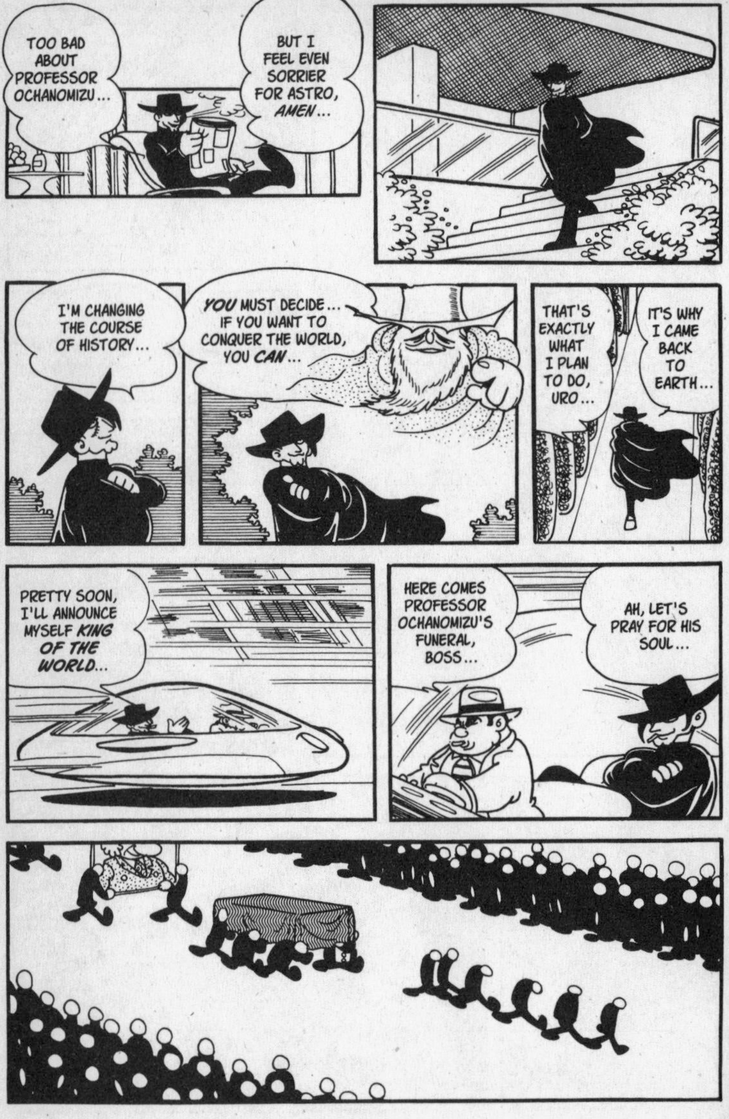

TOO BAD ABOUT PROFESSOR OCHANOMIZU...
BUT I FEEL EVEN SORRIER FOR ASTRO, AMEN...
I'M CHANGING THE COURSE OF HISTORY...
YOU MUST DECIDE... IF YOU WANT TO CONQUER THE WORLD, YOU CAN...
THAT'S EXACTLY WHAT I PLAN TO DO, URO...
IT'S WHY I CAME BACK TO EARTH...
PRETTY SOON, I'LL ANNOUNCE MYSELF KING OF THE WORLD...
HERE COMES PROFESSOR OCHANOMIZU'S FUNERAL, BOSS...
AH, LET'S PRAY FOR HIS SOUL...

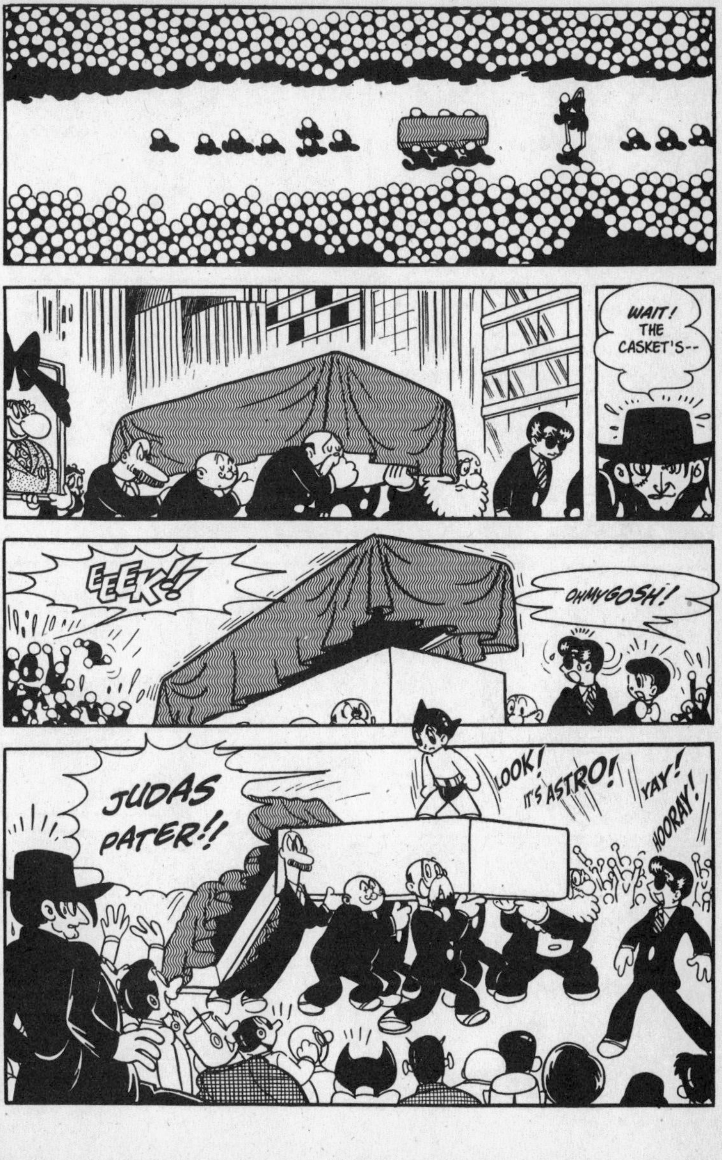
WAIT! THE CASKET'S--
EEEK!!
OHMYGOSH!
JUDAS PATER!!
LOOK! IT'S ASTRO!
YAY!
HOORAY!

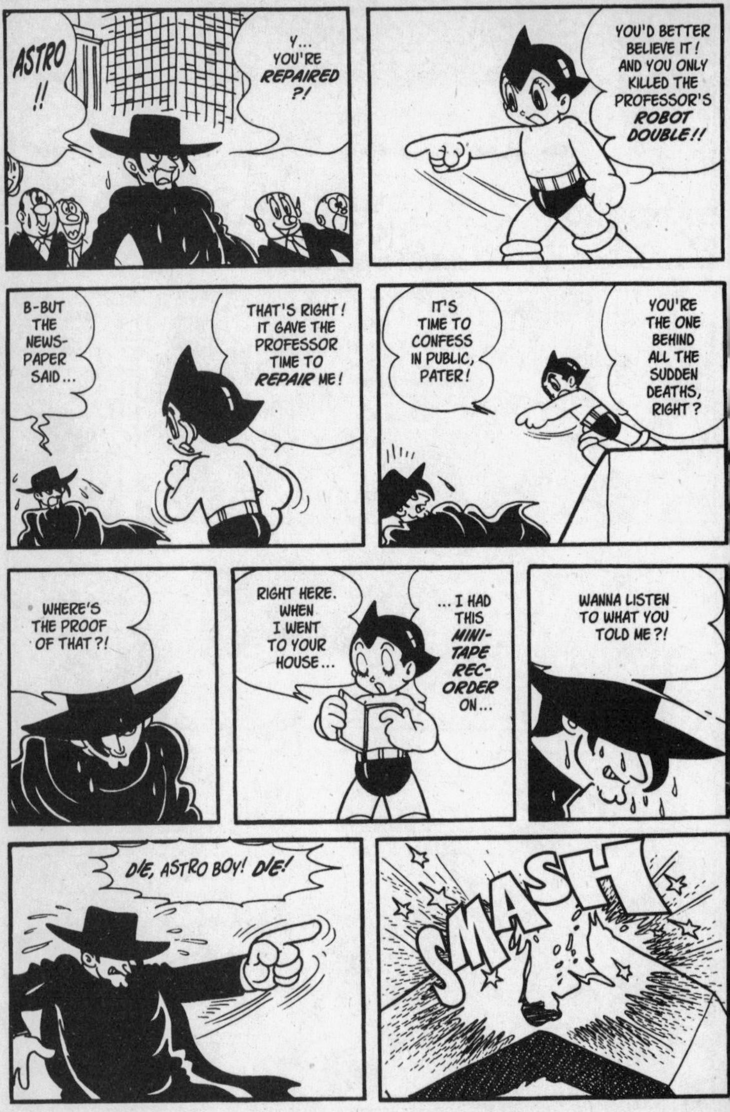

ASTRO !!
Y... YOU'RE REPAIRED ?!
YOU'D BETTER BELIEVE IT! AND YOU ONLY KILLED THE PROFESSOR'S ROBOT DOUBLE!!
B-BUT THE NEWS-PAPER SAID...
THAT'S RIGHT! IT GAVE THE PROFESSOR TIME TO REPAIR ME!
IT'S TIME TO CONFESS IN PUBLIC, PATER!
YOU'RE THE ONE BEHIND ALL THE SUDDEN DEATHS, RIGHT?
WHERE'S THE PROOF OF THAT?!
RIGHT HERE. WHEN I WENT TO YOUR HOUSE...
... I HAD THIS MINI-TAPE REC-ORDER ON...
WANNA LISTEN TO WHAT YOU TOLD ME?!
DIE, ASTRO BOY! DIE!
SMASH

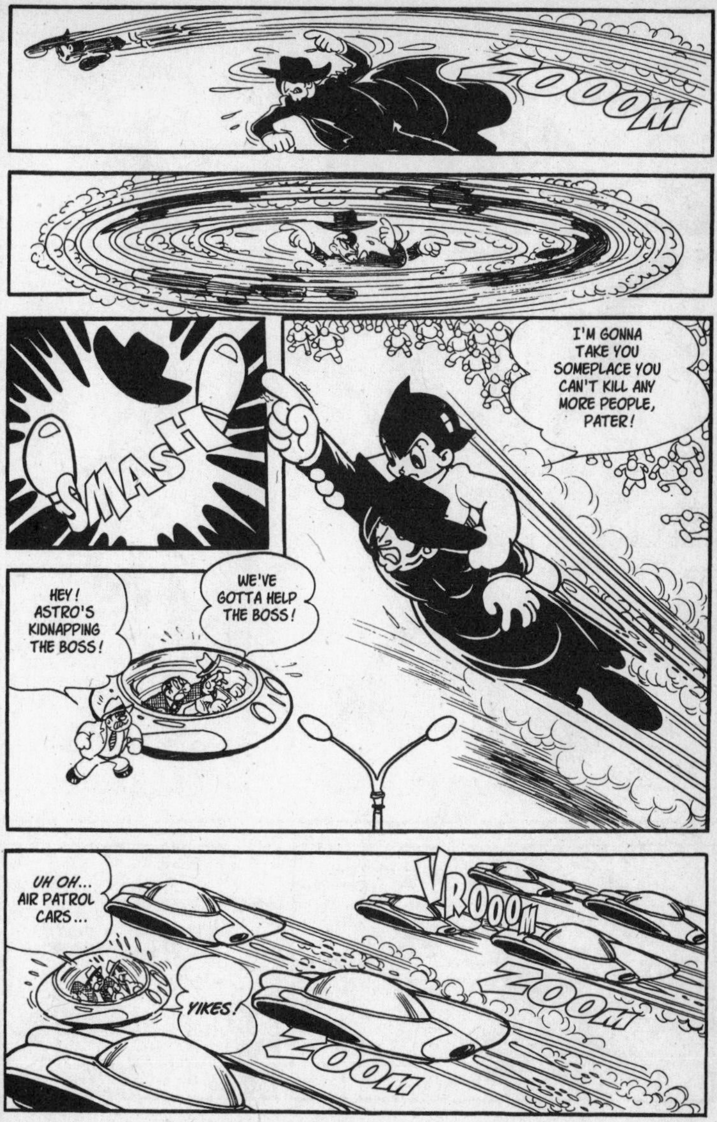
ZOOOM
SMASH
I'M GONNA TAKE YOU SOMEPLACE YOU CAN'T KILL ANY MORE PEOPLE, PATER!
HEY! ASTRO'S KIDNAPPING THE BOSS!
WE'VE GOTTA HELP THE BOSS!
UH OH... AIR PATROL CARS...
VROOOM
YIKES!
ZOOM
ZOOM

CURSE YOU, ASTRO! I'LL TURN YOU INTO SCRAP YET!!

≥AAA... AACHOOO!≥ ≥HAKACHOO!≥

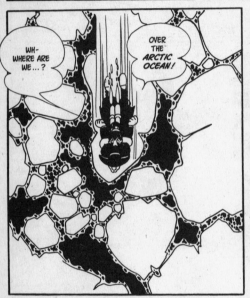

WH-WHERE ARE WE...?

OVER THE *ARCTIC OCEAN!*

WHAT'D YOU BRING ME *HERE* FOR?!

'CUZ THERE'S NOBODY AROUND FOR YOU TO KILL!

I...I'M *F-F-F-REEEZING* TO D-D-DEATH!

YOU'RE GONNA LIVE HERE A WHILE, PATER...

WHAT ?!!

I SAW AN ESKIMO IGLOO FROM THE SKY... I'LL TAKE YOU THERE!!

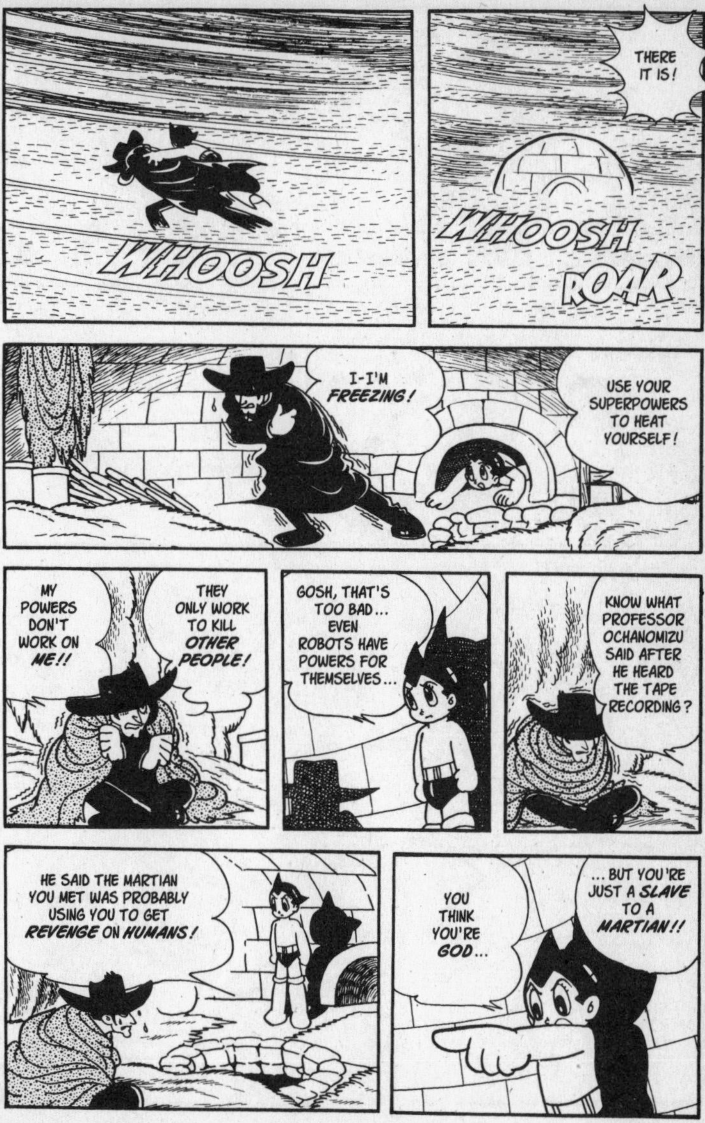
WHOOSH
THERE IT IS!
WHOOSH
ROAR
I-I'M FREEZING!
USE YOUR SUPERPOWERS TO HEAT YOURSELF!
MY POWERS DON'T WORK ON ME!!
THEY ONLY WORK TO KILL OTHER PEOPLE!
GOSH, THAT'S TOO BAD... EVEN ROBOTS HAVE POWERS FOR THEMSELVES...
KNOW WHAT PROFESSOR OCHANOMIZU SAID AFTER HE HEARD THE TAPE RECORDING?
HE SAID THE MARTIAN YOU MET WAS PROBABLY USING YOU TO GET REVENGE ON HUMANS!
YOU THINK YOU'RE GOD...
... BUT YOU'RE JUST A SLAVE TO A MARTIAN!!

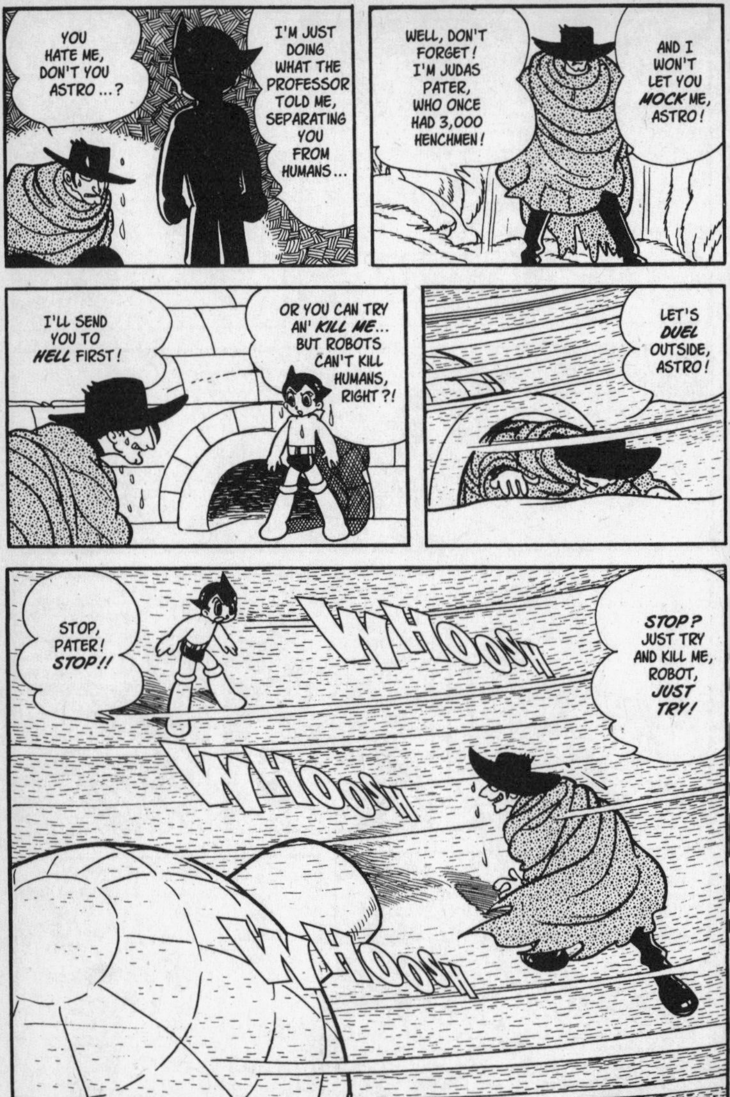

YOU HATE ME, DON'T YOU ASTRO ...?
I'M JUST DOING WHAT THE PROFESSOR TOLD ME, SEPARATING YOU FROM HUMANS...
WELL, DON'T FORGET! I'M JUDAS PATER, WHO ONCE HAD 3,000 HENCHMEN!
AND I WON'T LET YOU MOCK ME, ASTRO!
I'LL SEND YOU TO HELL FIRST!
OR YOU CAN TRY AN' KILL ME... BUT ROBOTS CAN'T KILL HUMANS, RIGHT?!
LET'S DUEL OUTSIDE, ASTRO!
STOP, PATER! STOP!!
WHOOSH
STOP? JUST TRY AND KILL ME, ROBOT, JUST TRY!
WHOOSH
WHOOSH

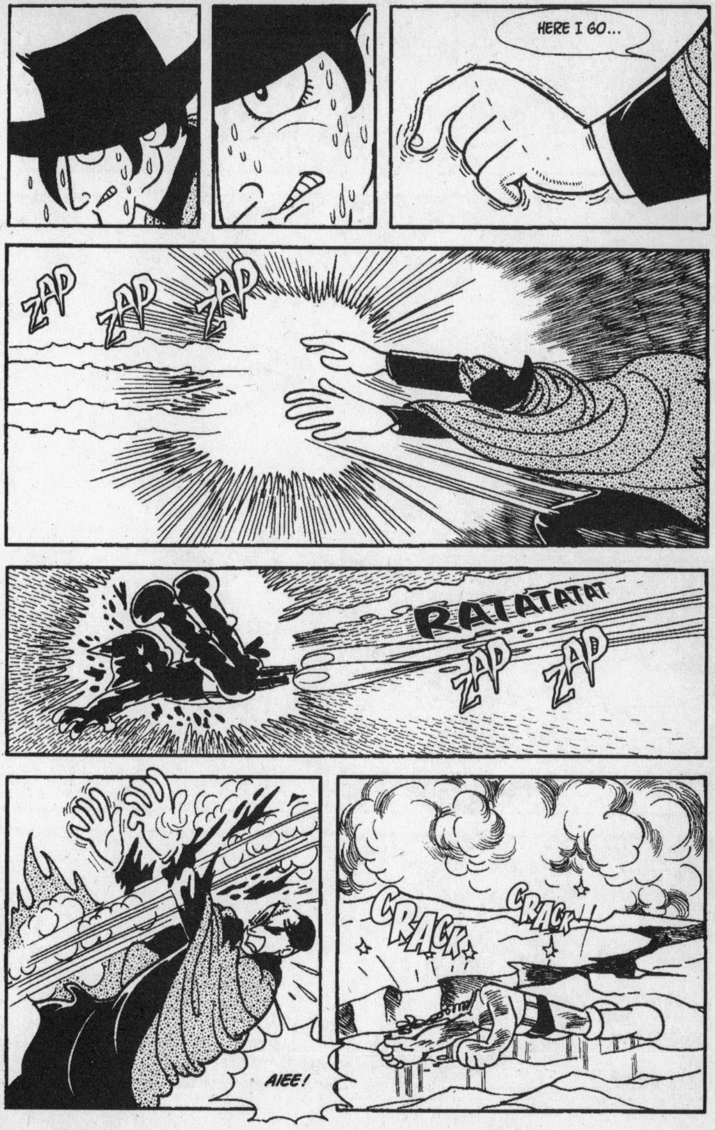
HERE I GO...
ZAP
ZAP
ZAP
RATATATAT
ZAP
ZAP
AIEE!
CRACK
CRACK

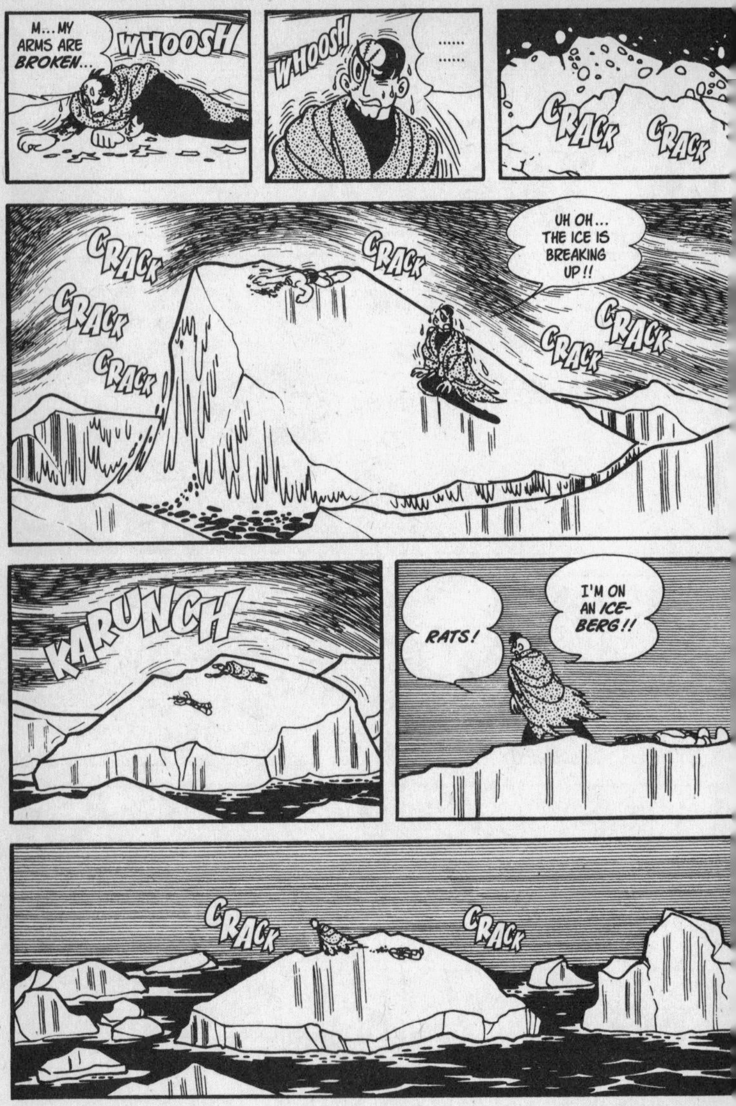
M... MY ARMS ARE BROKEN...
WHOOSH
WHOOSH
......
......
CRACK
CRACK
CRACK
CRACK
CRACK
UH OH... THE ICE IS BREAKING UP!!
CRACK
CRACK
KARUNCH
RATS!
I'M ON AN ICE-BERG!!
CRACK
CRACK

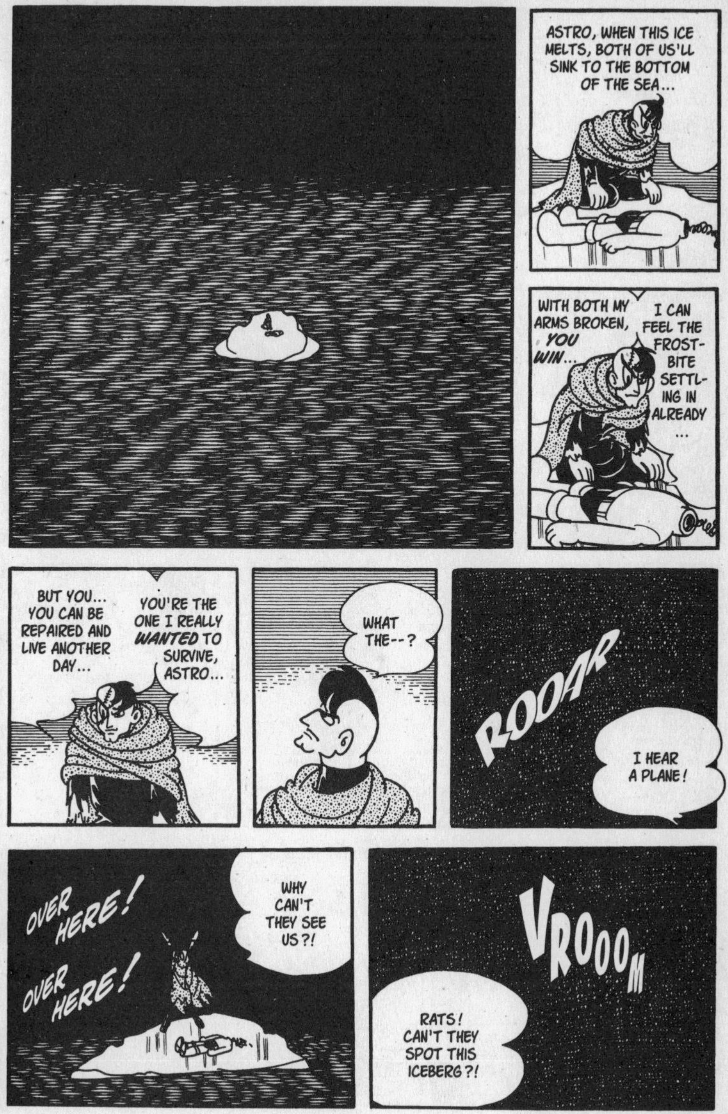
ASTRO, WHEN THIS ICE MELTS, BOTH OF US'LL SINK TO THE BOTTOM OF THE SEA...
WITH BOTH MY ARMS BROKEN, YOU WIN...
I CAN FEEL THE FROST-BITE SETTL-ING IN ALREADY ...
BUT YOU... YOU CAN BE REPAIRED AND LIVE ANOTHER DAY...
YOU'RE THE ONE I REALLY WANTED TO SURVIVE, ASTRO...
WHAT THE--?
ROOAR
I HEAR A PLANE!
OVER HERE!
OVER HERE!
WHY CAN'T THEY SEE US?!
VROOOM
RATS! CAN'T THEY SPOT THIS ICEBERG?!

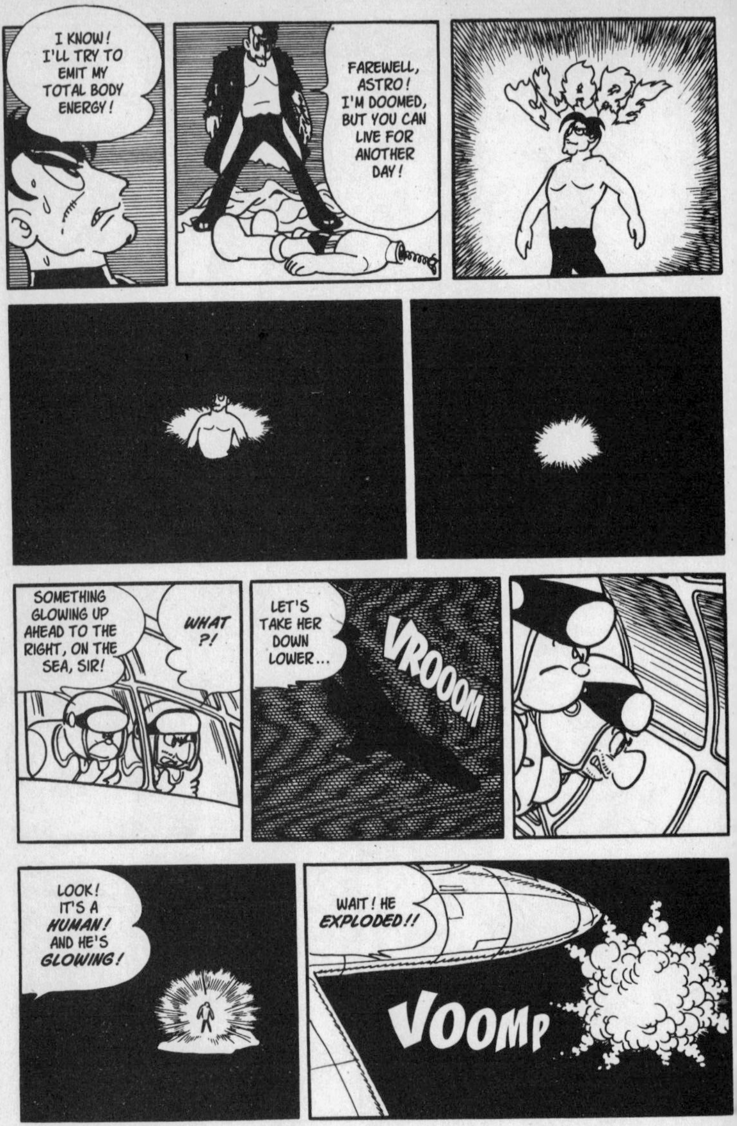
I KNOW! I'LL TRY TO EMIT MY TOTAL BODY ENERGY!
FAREWELL, ASTRO! I'M DOOMED, BUT YOU CAN LIVE FOR ANOTHER DAY!
SOMETHING GLOWING UP AHEAD TO THE RIGHT, ON THE SEA, SIR!
WHAT ?!
LET'S TAKE HER DOWN LOWER...
VROOOM
LOOK! IT'S A HUMAN! AND HE'S GLOWING!
WAIT! HE EXPLODED!!
VOOMP

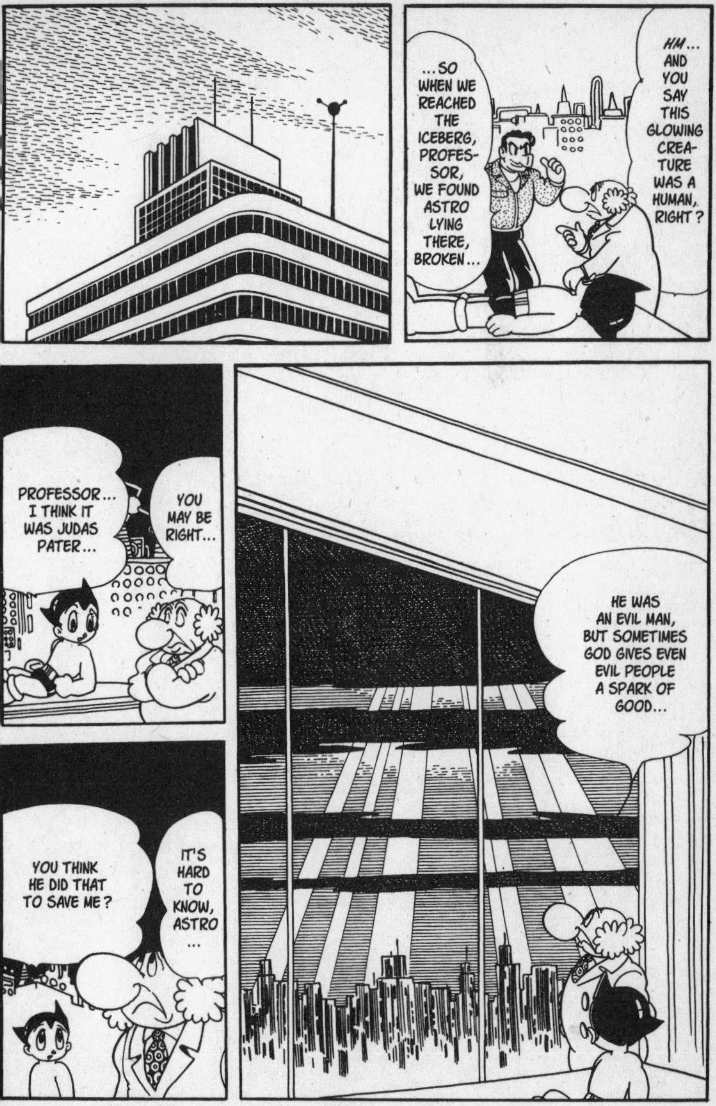
...SO WHEN WE REACHED THE ICEBERG, PROFES-SOR, WE FOUND ASTRO LYING THERE, BROKEN...
HM... AND YOU SAY THIS GLOWING CREA-TURE WAS A HUMAN, RIGHT?
PROFESSOR... I THINK IT WAS JUDAS PATER...
YOU MAY BE RIGHT...
YOU THINK HE DID THAT TO SAVE ME?
IT'S HARD TO KNOW, ASTRO ...
HE WAS AN EVIL MAN, BUT SOMETIMES GOD GIVES EVEN EVIL PEOPLE A SPARK OF GOOD...

THE BLAST FURNACE MYSTERY

First appeared in the 1961 summer holiday
expanded edition of *Shonen* magazine.

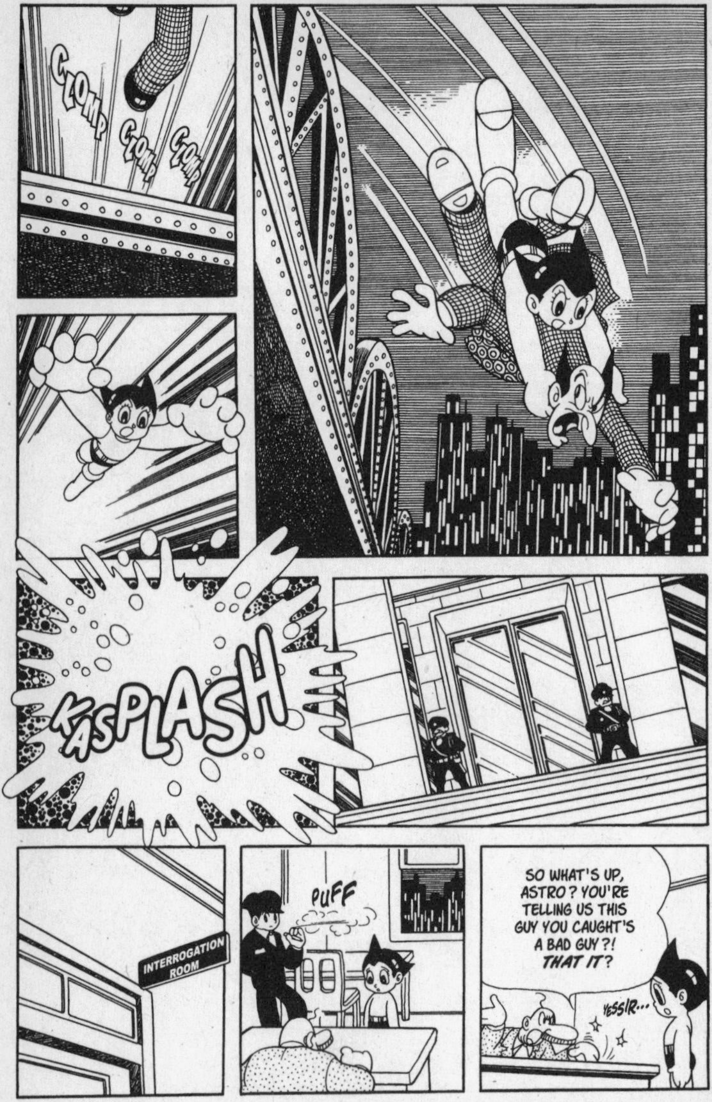
CLOMP
CLOMP
CLOMP
KASPLASH
INTERROGATION ROOM
PUFF
SO WHAT'S UP, ASTRO? YOU'RE TELLING US THIS GUY YOU CAUGHT'S A BAD GUY?! THAT IT?
YESSIR...

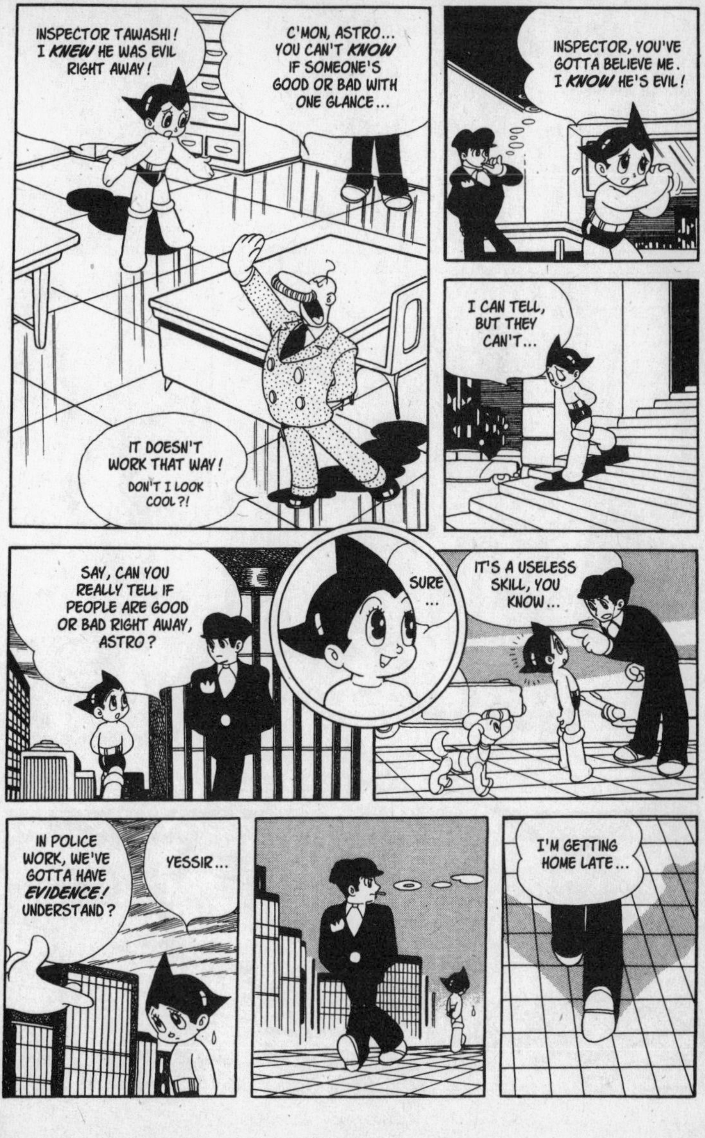
INSPECTOR TAWASHI! I KNEW HE WAS EVIL RIGHT AWAY!
C'MON, ASTRO... YOU CAN'T KNOW IF SOMEONE'S GOOD OR BAD WITH ONE GLANCE...
IT DOESN'T WORK THAT WAY!
DON'T I LOOK COOL?!
INSPECTOR, YOU'VE GOTTA BELIEVE ME. I KNOW HE'S EVIL!
I CAN TELL, BUT THEY CAN'T...
SAY, CAN YOU REALLY TELL IF PEOPLE ARE GOOD OR BAD RIGHT AWAY, ASTRO?
SURE...
IT'S A USELESS SKILL, YOU KNOW...
IN POLICE WORK, WE'VE GOTTA HAVE EVIDENCE! UNDERSTAND?
YESSIR...
I'M GETTING HOME LATE...

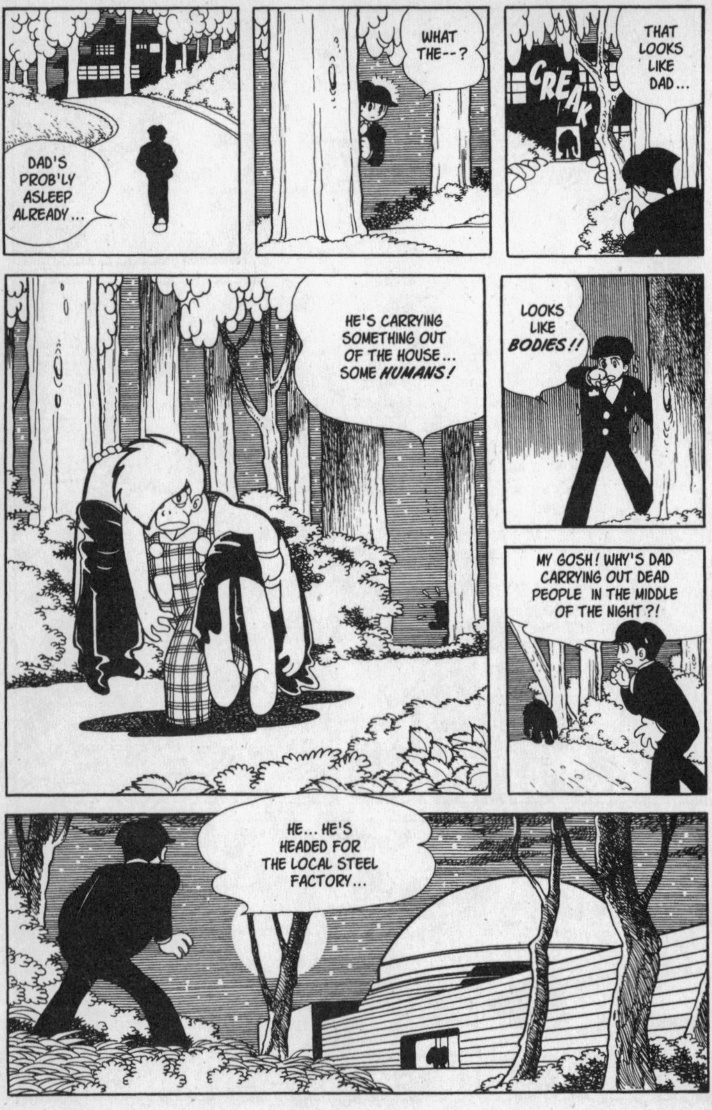
DAD'S PROB'LY ASLEEP ALREADY...
WHAT THE--?
CREAK
THAT LOOKS LIKE DAD...
HE'S CARRYING SOMETHING OUT OF THE HOUSE... SOME **HUMANS**!
LOOKS LIKE **BODIES**!!
MY GOSH! WHY'S DAD CARRYING OUT DEAD PEOPLE IN THE MIDDLE OF THE NIGHT?!
HE... HE'S HEADED FOR THE LOCAL STEEL FACTORY...

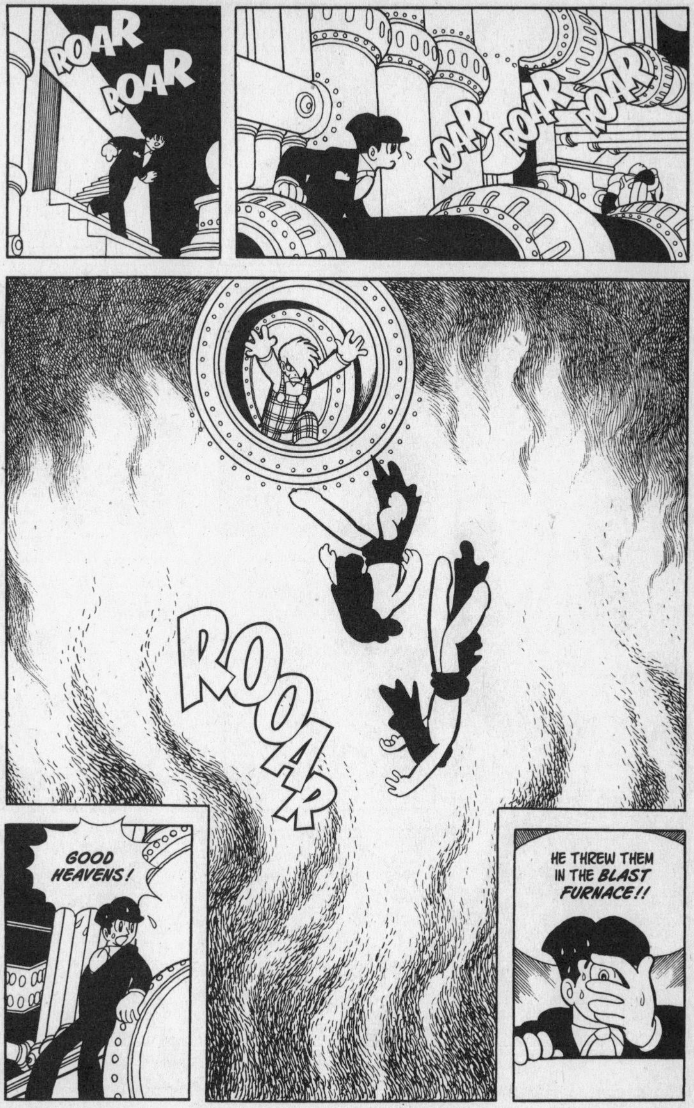
ROAR
ROAR
ROAR
ROAR
ROAR
ROOOAR
GOOD HEAVENS!
HE THREW THEM IN THE *BLAST FURNACE!!*

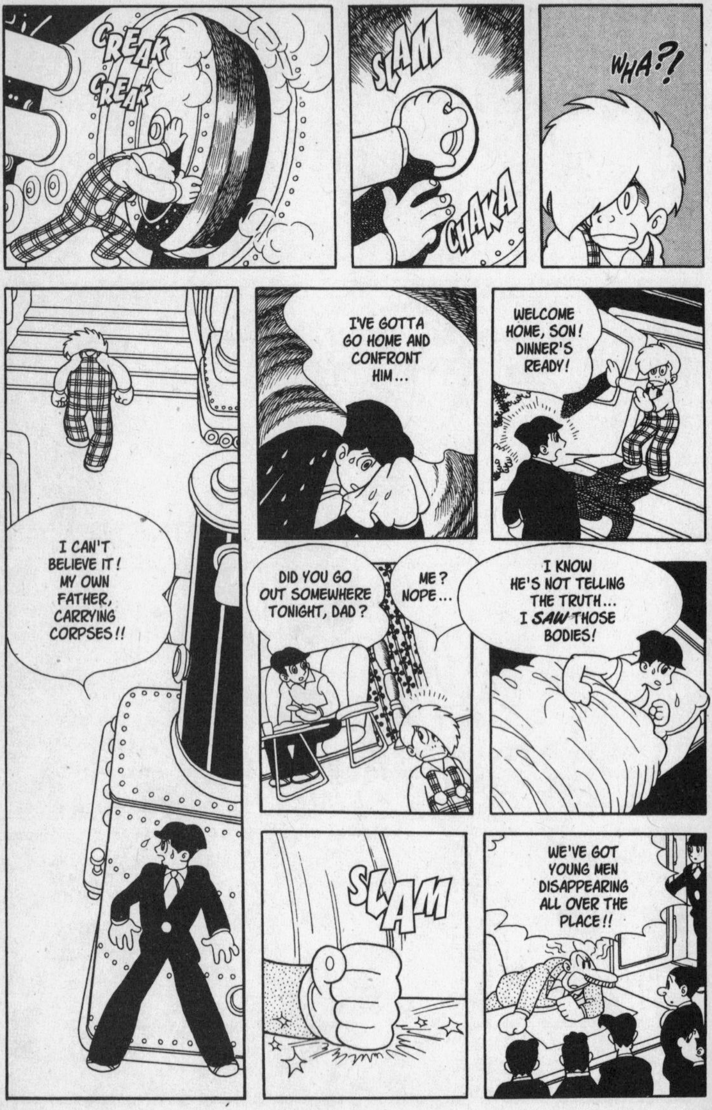
CREAK
CREAK
SLAM
CHAKA
WHA?!
I CAN'T BELIEVE IT! MY OWN FATHER, CARRYING CORPSES!!
I'VE GOTTA GO HOME AND CONFRONT HIM...
WELCOME HOME, SON! DINNER'S READY!
DID YOU GO OUT SOMEWHERE TONIGHT, DAD?
ME? NOPE...
I KNOW HE'S NOT TELLING THE TRUTH... I *SAW* THOSE BODIES!
SLAM
WE'VE GOT YOUNG MEN DISAPPEARING ALL OVER THE PLACE!!

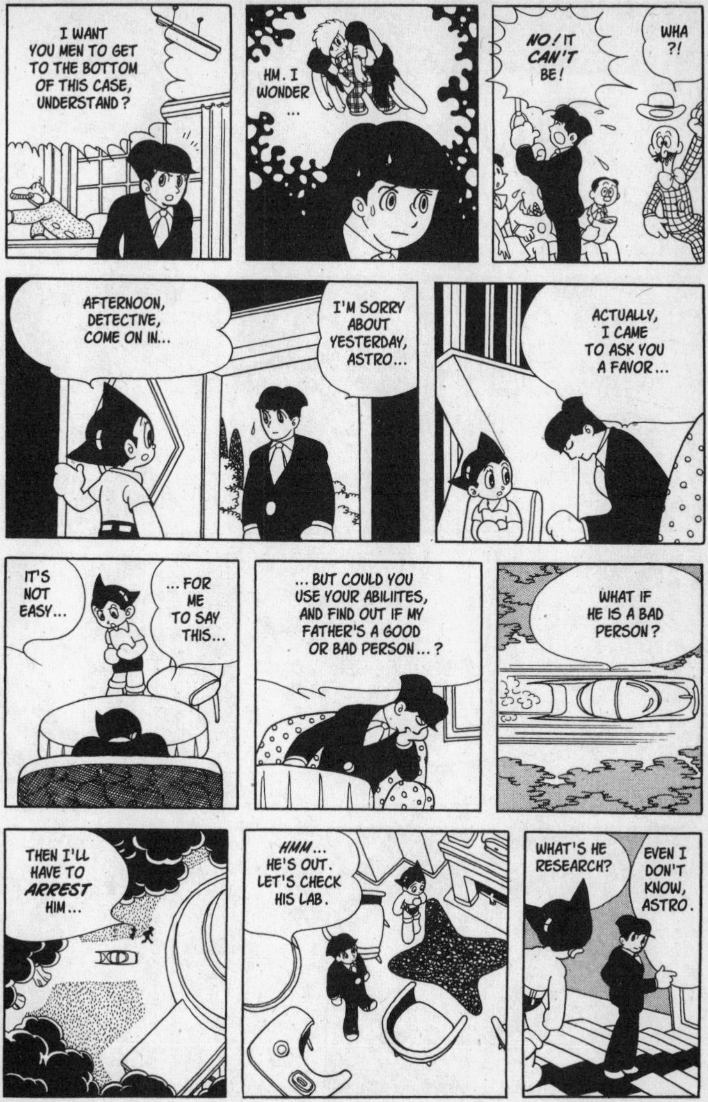
I WANT YOU MEN TO GET TO THE BOTTOM OF THIS CASE, UNDERSTAND?
HM. I WONDER ...
NO! IT CAN'T BE!
WHA ?!
AFTERNOON, DETECTIVE, COME ON IN...
I'M SORRY ABOUT YESTERDAY, ASTRO...
ACTUALLY, I CAME TO ASK YOU A FAVOR...
IT'S NOT EASY...
... FOR ME TO SAY THIS...
... BUT COULD YOU USE YOUR ABILIITES, AND FIND OUT IF MY FATHER'S A GOOD OR BAD PERSON ... ?
WHAT IF HE IS A BAD PERSON?
THEN I'LL HAVE TO ARREST HIM...
HMM... HE'S OUT. LET'S CHECK HIS LAB.
WHAT'S HE RESEARCH?
EVEN I DON'T KNOW, ASTRO.

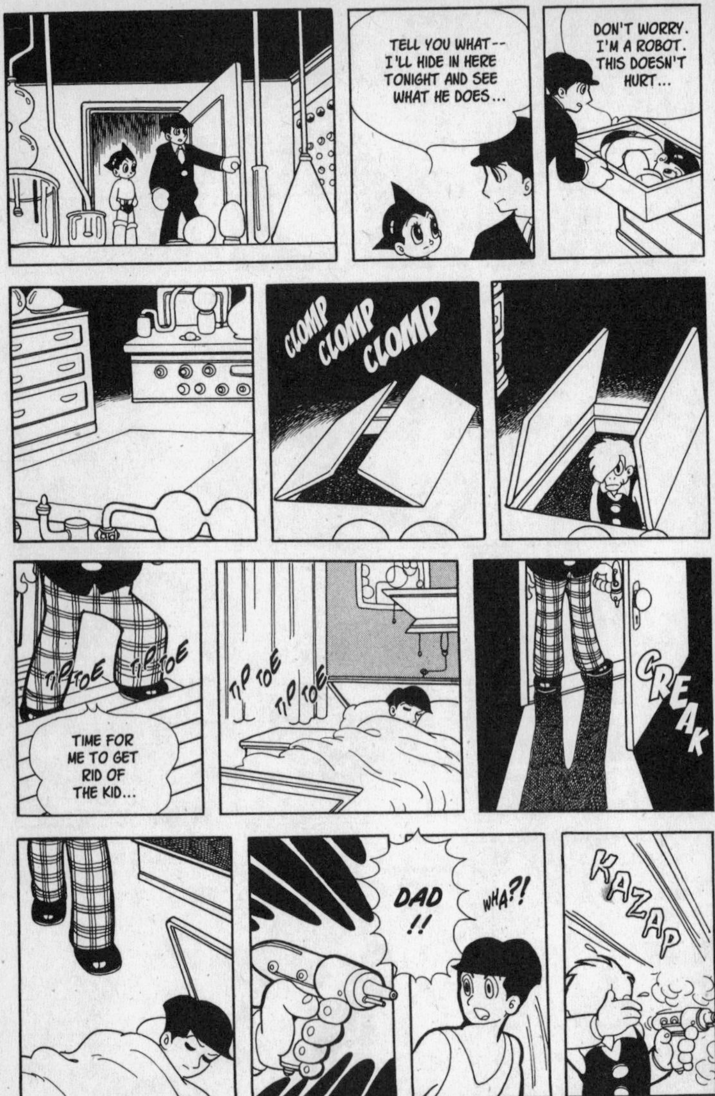

TELL YOU WHAT-- I'LL HIDE IN HERE TONIGHT AND SEE WHAT HE DOES...
DON'T WORRY. I'M A ROBOT. THIS DOESN'T HURT...
CLOMP CLOMP CLOMP
TIPTOE TIPTOE
TIME FOR ME TO GET RID OF THE KID...
TIPTOE TIPTOE
CREAK
DAD !!
WHA?!
KAZAP

KATHUD

FORGIVE ME... IT'S YOUR *LAST* DAY...

IT'S TIME FOR A *NEW* YOU...

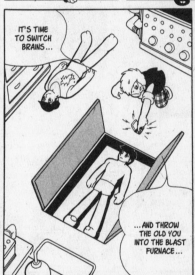

IT'S TIME TO SWITCH BRAINS...

...AND THROW THE OLD YOU INTO THE BLAST FURNACE...

WHEN I FIRST MADE YOU...

...YOU LOOKED LIKE A REGULAR BABY.

I GAVE YOU A NEW AND BIGGER BODY EVERY MONTH...

IT'S NO WONDER YOU THINK YOU'RE A REAL HUMAN...

THIS IS THE 250TH TIME I'VE HAD TO THROW AWAY YOUR OLD BODY...

HUHN--?!

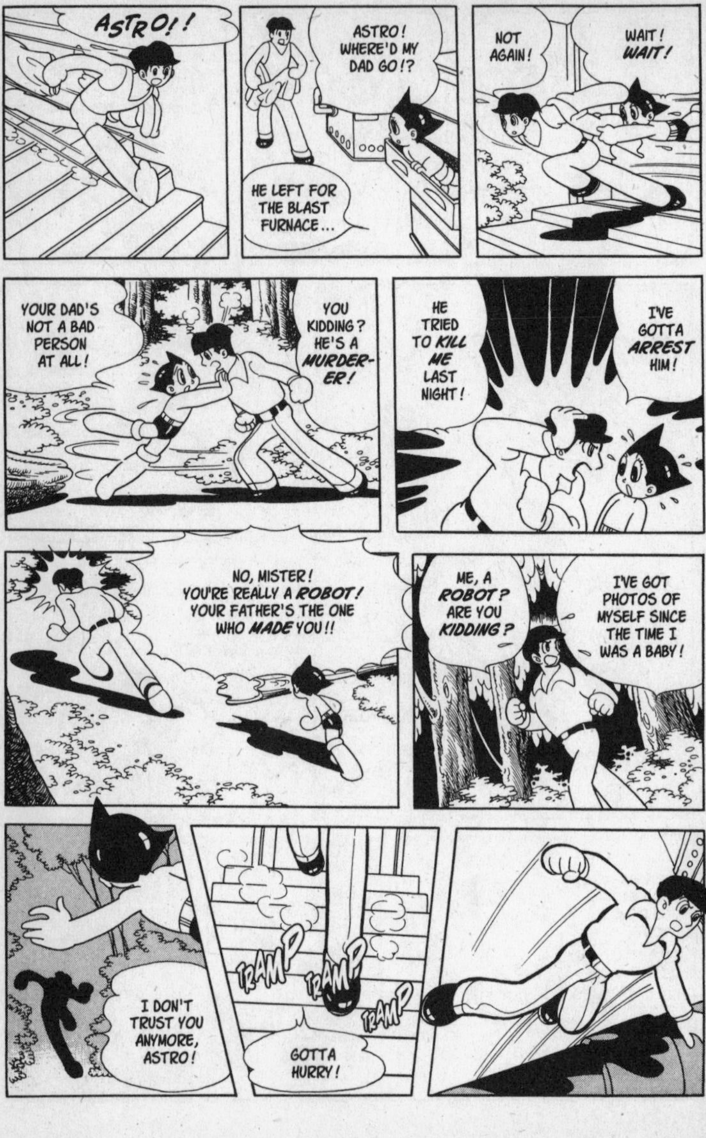
ASTRO!!
ASTRO! WHERE'D MY DAD GO!?
HE LEFT FOR THE BLAST FURNACE...
NOT AGAIN!
WAIT! WAIT!
YOUR DAD'S NOT A BAD PERSON AT ALL!
YOU KIDDING? HE'S A MURDERER!
HE TRIED TO KILL ME LAST NIGHT!
I'VE GOTTA ARREST HIM!
NO, MISTER! YOU'RE REALLY A ROBOT! YOUR FATHER'S THE ONE WHO MADE YOU!!
ME, A ROBOT? ARE YOU KIDDING?
I'VE GOT PHOTOS OF MYSELF SINCE THE TIME I WAS A BABY!
I DON'T TRUST YOU ANYMORE, ASTRO!
TRAMP TRAMP TRAMP
GOTTA HURRY!

STOP, DAD... I'VE GOTTA *ARREST* YOU!

YOU'RE THE ONE BEHIND THE DISAPPEARANCE OF ALL THOSE YOUNG MEN!

STOP!!

I SAID *STOP!*

SLAP

HOW DARE YOU?! ROBOT'S AREN'T SUPPOSED TO HIT HUMANS!

STOP! GET A HOLD OF YOURSELF!!

KAZING

THUD

WHAT THE--? THAT'S *MY* FACE!!

I'M SORRY, SON. I DIDN'T WANT YOU TO KNOW...

DAD...

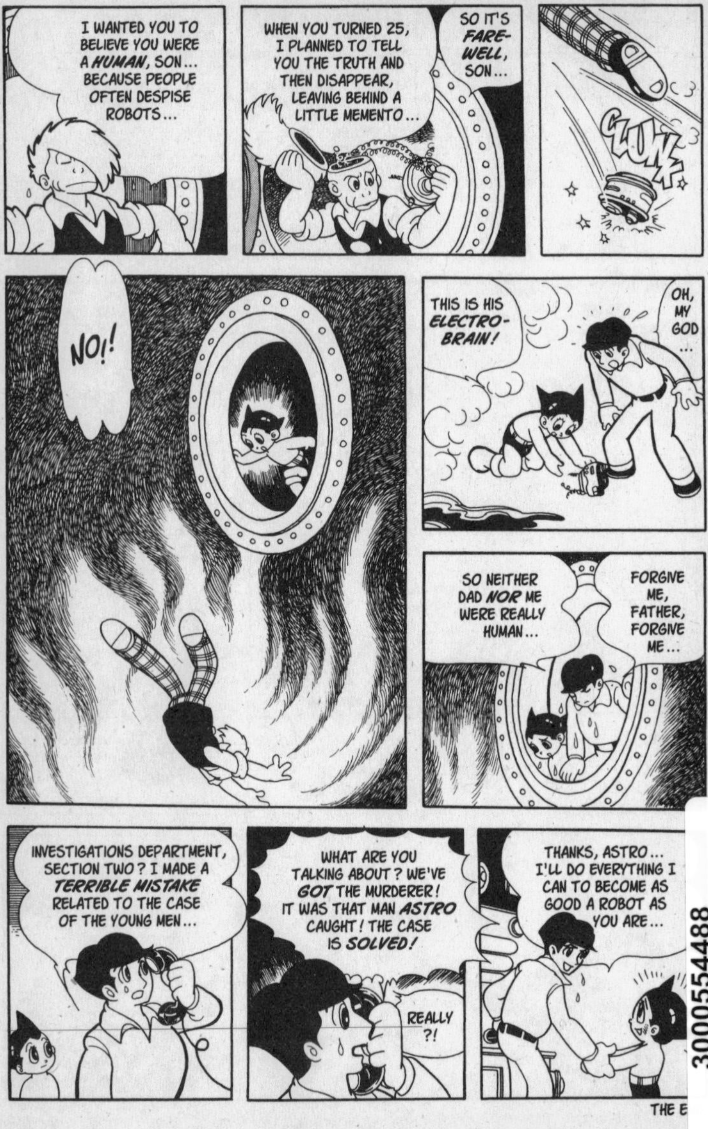

I WANTED YOU TO BELIEVE YOU WERE A HUMAN, SON... BECAUSE PEOPLE OFTEN DESPISE ROBOTS...
WHEN YOU TURNED 25, I PLANNED TO TELL YOU THE TRUTH AND THEN DISAPPEAR, LEAVING BEHIND A LITTLE MEMENTO...
SO IT'S FARE-WELL, SON...
CLUNK
NO!!
THIS IS HIS ELECTRO-BRAIN!
OH, MY GOD...
SO NEITHER DAD NOR ME WERE REALLY HUMAN...
FORGIVE ME, FATHER, FORGIVE ME...
INVESTIGATIONS DEPARTMENT, SECTION TWO? I MADE A TERRIBLE MISTAKE RELATED TO THE CASE OF THE YOUNG MEN...
WHAT ARE YOU TALKING ABOUT? WE'VE GOT THE MURDERER! IT WAS THAT MAN ASTRO CAUGHT! THE CASE IS SOLVED!
REALLY ?!
THANKS, ASTRO... I'LL DO EVERYTHING I CAN TO BECOME AS GOOD A ROBOT AS YOU ARE...
THE E